A NEIGHBORHOOD FINDS ITSELF

A NEIGHBORHOOD

by JULIA ABRAHAMSON

FINDS ITSELF

HARPER & BROTHERS, PUBLISHERS   NEW YORK

TO THE PEOPLE OF HYDE PARK-KENWOOD
WHO ARE LIVING THIS STORY

Contents

CONTENTS

Preface

There is increasing concern throughout the United States over the decline of our cities, the spread of blight, the decay of urban neighborhoods, the flight of middle-class white residents to the suburbs, the rapid in-migration to industrial cities of lower income peoples—Negroes, Puerto Ricans, American Indians, poor southern whites—all attracted by higher wages and better opportunities. On a variety of fronts, public and private agencies have been trying to face these problems. And city neighbors—an increasing number of them—have come together in neighborhood movements that are beginning to spread throughout the nation.

This is the story of the pioneering effort of men and women in a declining Chicago community to fuse the challenges of Negro in-migration and conservation into the excitement of creating a fine interracial community. It is the story of people of all races and creeds who believed in their community and worked together to save it: how they set out to reverse the patterns of blight and flight that threatened to destroy their neighborhood; the difficult problems they faced and their organization of the Hyde Park-Kenwood Community Conference to solve them. It is the story of the hostility, suspicion, and lethargy they met and tried to con-

ix

quer; their involvement with and growing understanding of institutional and power interests; the rumors, fears, panic, and problems of human relationships they dealt with; the methods and techniques they worked out that are of value to other communities; the local, city-wide, and national results of their efforts.

It is a story that has not yet ended. Although city, state, and federal authorities are now sharing with the community in one of the most ambitious urban renewal programs in the United States, it is too soon to judge whether this effort will fully accomplish its purpose and set in motion a process by which the community will continually renew itself. The final outcome of the effort to re-create a fine community on a stable interracial basis will not be known for some years. But so much has already been accomplished and the value of the demonstration to the nation is so great that many people in and out of the community are convinced that it must and will succeed. I share that conviction.

I had the privilege of being part of the Hyde Park-Kenwood story from the beginning: first as co-chairman of the Social Order Committee of the 57th Street Meeting of Friends (Quakers) which played a major role in initiating the movement; then as an officer of the first board of directors of the conference; and later as its executive director for more than six of the nine years covered by this story. Because it is not easy to view individuals, incidents, and problems which are still so close with the proper perspective, I have had this report checked by a number of people whose knowledge is great but whose involvement was not so constant as mine. They attest to the accuracy of the account, though I take full responsibility for the choice of material and the way it is presented.

In writing this book, I have tried to serve two purposes: to report on the history and development of the conference and to provide a possible guide to other communities faced with similar problems.

While every effort was made to achieve objectivity, this report cannot help reflecting the view of a person working in the community from inside a particular organization. Equally accurate accounts with different emphases could be written by executives of the University of Chicago, the South East Chicago Commission, or of other community agencies.

The Emil Schwarzhaupt Foundation, which financed the preparation of this book, gave generous support to the work of the Hyde Park-Kenwood Community Conference beginning in 1954 and thus helped to make possible the expansion of the program and a number of its major achievements.

JULIA ABRAHAMSON

Acknowledgments

Many people helped in the preparation of this book.

I am greatly indebted to all the members of the conference staff, particularly to James V. Cunningham and Wanda Van Goor, who worked with me from the outline stage to the conclusion, providing a constant flow of materials, answering endless questions, and making valuable suggestions throughout; and to Grace Tugwell, Ozzie Badal, Elsie Krueger, Irving Horwitz and Pierre De Visé, for important contributions of fact and feeling to the chapters dealing with the programs they directed.

Those who read the manuscript in whole or in part and offered suggestions and advice deserve special mention. Their cooperation is reflected in almost every page of the book. I gladly acknowledge my indebtedness to Herbert Bain, William Bradbury, Babette Brody, Lucy P. Carner, Marian Despres, William L. Frederick, Maynard C. Krueger, D. E. Mackelmann, Margaret Calbeck Neal, Leslie T. Pennington, Harvey S. Perloff, Bruce Sagan, Herbert A. Thelen, and Ethel M. Vrana.

I owe a large debt of gratitude to Jack Meltzer. In spite of deadlines of his own to meet on Hyde Park-Kenwood's final urban renewal plan, he gave hours of time to helping me with the facts of planning.

ACKNOWLEDGMENTS

For checking parts of the manuscript for accuracy of information and interpretation, I am grateful to Marjorie Andrews, Jean Block, Oscar C. Brown, Sr., Thomas Calero, Leon M. Despres, Elmer W. Donahue, Phil A. Doyle, Miriam Elson, Donald R. Hanson, Philip M. Hauser, Morris Hirsh, Henry W. McGee, Sr., Francis W. McPeek, Ruth Otto, Edwin A. Rothschild, Calvin Sawyier, Ethel Shufro, and Douglass Turner.

My special thanks go to my friend Rachel M. Goetz on whose insight and judgment I have relied most heavily. She helped me to think through the organization of materials and contributed to balance and perspective by her concern that the work of the conference be treated as part rather than all of the Hyde Park-Kenwood story.

The work, experience, and comments of hundreds of people form the base of the book. It is impossible to name them all, but I am grateful to every one. Without them there could have been no Hyde Park-Kenwood Community Conference, and any story about the community itself would have had a most unhappy ending.

It is fitting to close the acknowledgment section with recognition of a debt for which no comment could be adequate. My deepest gratitude is reserved for my husband, Harry Abrahamson, whose constant interest and encouragement sustained me through the writing of this book.

PART **1**

A Proud Neighborhood Begins to Crumble

CHAPTER 1

The Community: Birth, Growth, Decline

A shrewd young man, who was to become known as the "father of Hyde Park," arrived in Chicago in the middle of the nineteenth century. He had ambition, ideas, one suit, $1.50 in cash, and the rest of his capital in cards announcing that he was "Paul Cornell, attorney-at-law."

He found a young, lusty, sprawling city and, to the south beyond its boundaries, miles of woodland, swamp, and thicket stretching west from the shores of Lake Michigan. Following the first settler who had carved his home out of this wilderness in 1836, a scattering of others had come, building as close to the city as they could. But farther south, in all of the community now known as Hyde Park-Kenwood, there were only seven houses by 1855. In that year Paul Cornell bought three hundred acres of land fronting the lake.

It is not clear how he managed to accumulate money enough so quickly, but he began at once to use the land wisely. He gave sixty acres to the Illinois Central Railroad for a right of way with the understanding that the railroad would build a station on the property, name it Hyde Park, and operate daily trains to and from the city. Transportation between Chicago and Hyde Park set off a small real estate boom in Cornell's subdivision. He advertised his property in glowing terms, and soon homes with spacious grounds began to rise. He built the First Presbyterian Church and Hyde Park House, a large frame hotel which attracted fashionable parties from Chicago in spite of the six-mile drive. His bookkeeper became proprietor of the general store which later also housed the postoffice.

In the meantime, a few families had bought homes slightly to the north of Paul Cornell's thriving little settlement. John Kennicott called his estate "Kenwood" after his mother's birthplace in Scotland, a name later taken over by the community. Dr. William B. Egan modeled his "Egandale" after the estates of the landed gentry in Ireland and planned to reproduce around him an area of great manor houses. He failed to realize his dream, but Kenwood did become one of the most beautiful suburbs of Chicago. Some of the city's wealthiest families settled there, building magnificent homes on wooded grounds with wide, sweeping lawns. But in 1861 Kenwood comprised only four or five families and an Illinois Central station.

In the same year, the town of Hyde Park—which included Hyde Park, Kenwood and several other communities—was incorporated, and Paul Cornell elected himself supervisor. His domain was still largely rural. Cows grazed in pastures adjoining some of the best homes. Vendors sold water at ten cents a barrel to those not lucky enough to have wells. On rainy Saturday afternoons men gathered around the wood stove in the general store, debating the issues of the day, chief among them the quarrel over slavery which was soon to explode into civil war. The first public school was not to be built for another two years.

When, a decade later, the town of Hyde Park took on a village government, it was well on its way to becoming the largest village in the world. The Great Chicago Fire had created a demand for homes away from the crowded center of the city and had further stimulated building in Hyde Park. By the time the village was annexed to the city of Chicago in 1889, it had expanded its boundaries, had a population of 85,000, and encompassed in whole or in part what are now eighteen separate communities in addition to Hyde Park and Kenwood.

Before the turn of the century, Hyde Park had established itself as an intellectual and cultural center, even as its Kenwood neighbor was becoming known as a garden spot, a suburb in the city. The two communities had reason to be grateful for their lake-front location and Paul Cornell's foresight. Along the shore, as part of Daniel Burnham's master plan for Chicago, a great park was landscaped; and west from the park the Midway—a wide thoroughfare divided by a sunken parkway.

Here the University of Chicago opened its doors in 1892, the product of John D. Rockefeller's money, Marshall Field's land, and the vision of Professor William Rainey Harper of Yale, its first president, who dreamed of a great center of learning in the heart of the Middle West. The gray, Gothic buildings rose one by one, forming an impressive campus to which Harper invited the leading scientists, thinkers, and creative artists of the time.

A literary society devoted to debates and "elocutionary exercises" and a Lyceum and Philosophical Society had flourished in the Hyde Park-Kenwood area for some time. Now the presence of the university gave impetus to the yearning for culture and self-improvement. Lectures, concerts, dramatic performances drew people from all of Chicago. The opportunities provided by a university community made Hyde Park and Kenwood increasingly attractive to professional people with intellectual interests. Their small homes soon appeared in the blocks near the Midway, mingling with the frame houses of faculty members.

The university was only a year old, however, and most of its campus was still mud and building materials, when the excitement of its founding was overshadowed by a much more spectacular event—the World's Columbian Exposition of 1893. Hyde Park, with its combination of lake front, park, and Illinois Central transportation, was the ideal site. Famous architects and artists came from all over the world to build a temporary city beautiful enough to commemorate the centuries of world progress since the discovery of America.

It was all over in one summer. Most of the buildings came down, but an important legacy remained. It was an artistic atmosphere, the imprint of cosmopolitanism left by the artists and their families who settled in the area and brought to it the customs and cultures of the world. It was the frame buildings—the popcorn and souvenir stands of the exposition—which became the 57th Street Art Colony, housing struggling young artists and writers through the years: Sherwood Anderson, Ben Hecht, Maxwell Bodenheim, Floyd Dell, and a host of others. It was the poets and entertainers who were drawn to this center of art and Bohemianism on Chicago's South Side. It was the elevated trains which came to Hyde Park to help the Illinois Central, the trolleys and the horse-drawn buses handle transportation to the fair. It was an enlarged Jackson Park, the Midway, and Washington Park which all came into being as a result of the fair. It was the tremendous real estate and building boom the exposition set in motion.

This last was not an unmixed blessing. Much of the new building near the exposition was thrown together hurriedly and inexpensively to meet the sudden demand for housing and stores. It was here that the first signs of blight were to appear.

As the years went on, the one-time suburbs of Hyde Park and Kenwood added huge, luxurious apartments. To meet the changing social needs of the 1920's, there were smaller, multi-family apartment buildings and hotels. Later, the demand for housing encouraged the subdivision of many of the large homes and apartments into small units and kitchenettes. Finally came the skyscraper apartments looking down on all alike—the old frame houses, the large family homes, the turn-of-the-century walk-ups.

To serve the growing population, churches and temples were built, and public and private schools, recreation centers, banks, hospitals. Small businessmen set up shop, for the most part in buildings combining stores and apartments which were strung out along the major through streets.

By the end of the 1940's there was little open space left in Hyde Park. Its land had been almost completely covered by buildings crowded close together. In the heart of Kenwood the wide tree-lined streets bordering the still beautiful homes and grounds formed an oasis ringed round by high-density apartment buildings.

The social changes over the years kept pace with the physical changes. The wealthy "aristocrats" of the original fashionable suburbs with their large families and servants were replaced by smaller, more mobile middle-class families, by urbanites with cosmopolitan tastes, by students and single men and women. People of differing nationalities and religions and races, attracted by the advantages of location and atmosphere, followed the original settlers of Scottish and English descent.

In 1949, a community inventory covering the two-square-mile area referred to in this book as Hyde Park-Kenwood, would have shown a wide range of assets: the lake front; a green belt of parks on the eastern, western, and southern boundaries; excellent transportation providing access to the center of Chicago in ten minutes; a number of fine homes and buildings; educational and cultural institutions of outstanding quality—seven colleges, universities, graduate schools, and theological seminaries, including the University of Chicago; fifteen public, private and parochial schools; seven nursery schools; libraries and museums, among them the famed Museum of Science and Industry and the Oriental Institute; religious institutions of many denominations and faiths— eighteen Protestant, two Catholic, nine Jewish, one Buddhist; three recreation centers and youth-serving agencies; adequate health services; a varied and cosmopolitan population.

The largest ethnic group in the community's 72,000 people were Jews of German and Russian stock (approximately 40 per cent of the population). Japanese Americans had come in from the West in 1942 and were well represented. Increasing numbers of Negroes were moving in, joining the few who had lived in the community for many years. Most of the people were in the middle and upper-middle income brackets. They were largely "white collar" workers engaged in insurance, real estate, wholesale and retail trade; an unusual number were in professions (one out of five, four times the proportion for the rest of Chicago); and a small minority earned their living in factories. The educational level was higher than Chicago's average—three and a half years more schooling.

7

It was an articulate, highly organized community, active and effective in civic, educational, political, and social affairs.

The community's liabilities and problems were also great. Like other residential communities in the United States, it was going into a decline as it grew older. The homes intended for large families with servants, the streets designed for horse and buggy transportation, the small shops and other facilities created for an earlier era had outlived their usefulness in a period of new family patterns, mass transportation, big business. Buildings showed unmistakable signs of age, neglect, and misuse.

Serious overcrowding had begun. Two world wars and Chicago's industrial expansion had brought to the city a constantly growing population. There had been little new construction at costs the incoming workers could afford, and they naturally turned to the older residential areas for housing. Their need and the shortage of supply made it profitable to cut up apartments and homes into small kitchenette, share-the-bath units and to convert once fine buildings into rooming houses. Overcrowding began to put pressure on all community facilities and services—schools, recreation, parking; police, fire, and health protection. There were increasing signs of failure in enforcement of building and zoning laws and in municipal housekeeping services.

The crime rate was growing. Taverns—one after another—had begun to establish themselves in vacant stores. Economic downgrading of the area had set in, as lower-income people took the place of residents moving to newer neighborhoods. Having come from different social and cultural backgrounds, the newcomers had little in common with the earlier residents who remained. The fact that so many of the newcomers were Negroes created special difficulties.

There had been tremendous growth in the Negro population of Chicago during the two world wars. In the decade between 1940 and 1950, while the white population remained static, the number of nonwhites had increased by 130,000 or 42 per cent. As the labor supply from Europe was shut off, Chicago industry had turned for workers to the untapped labor markets of the rural South. The result was pressure for living space on the large Negro

8

section directly northwest of Hyde Park-Kenwood. The area was bursting at the seams, and Negroes began to spread out into other sections of the city. The Supreme Court decision of 1948, making restrictive covenants unenforceable, opened up areas formerly closed to Negroes. They still could not compete for housing in the open market by reason of continuing restrictions, unwritten agreements, and occasionally force and terrorism. Housing was consequently in even shorter supply for them than for other Americans, and it cost them more. Their best chance for living space was in the declining apartment house neighborhoods close to the all-Negro sections—Hyde Park-Kenwood and other south and west side communities. Much of the northern section of Kenwood had already become an extension of the Negro ghetto.

White residents began to put their homes up for sale as Negroes moved in. The exodus was encouraged by speculators who made handsome profits by frightening residents into selling, and then reselling to Negroes at exorbitant prices. The first Negro residents had been upper-income people, seeking a better environment for their families and willing to pay high rents to secure it. They were followed by others unable to afford the high rents except by doubling up, taking in roomers, sometimes crowding families into single rooms. Slowly panic grew among the white residents, and it fed on their fears—the fear of falling property values, of crime, of intermingling. Many whites who had not noticed the gradual deterioration of the area, the pockets of blight which had already begun to form, the decline in services, the arrival of lower-income whites, attributed every evidence of decay to their new dark neighbors.

Hyde Park-Kenwood in 1949 was gravely threatened. It was surrounded by blighted and near-blighted sections, and the blight was spreading. There was no comfort in history. Neighborhood after neighborhood throughout the industrial North had gone through the same process: decline, overcrowding, loss of higher-income families, flight of white residents as Negroes moved in, and finally slums leveled by bulldozers and then rebuilt at tremendous expense to the taxpayer.

The threat was not widely recognized. Many went about their

business noticing nothing—indeed, some sections of the community seemed untouched. Others spoke philosophically of trends and fate and prepared to get out when conditions became unbearable. Still others were overcome by apathy, lethargy, or helplessness. The predictions of some of the social scientists and planners were full of doom. "The area will be a slum in ten years," they said.

CHAPTER 2

Facing the Problems

A few people tried to take constructive action. Some were concerned primarily with the physical conservation of the area, others with preventing violence and encouraging good relations between the races. And there were a few who saw the two approaches as necessarily interwoven.

As far back as the 1930's, Louis Wirth, professor of sociology at the University of Chicago, had urged university authorities to buy and improve property in deteriorating sections.

When in 1946 the population began to change from white to Negro along the western border of Hyde Park-Kenwood, Thomas H. Wright, head of the Chicago Commission on Human Relations, tried to stimulate various local groups to face the issues of race relations and conservation. He talked with University of Chicago officials, and later with members of the Hyde Park Planning Association. The association was not a planning agency, despite its name. Its primary concern, according to a former president, was to "keep the area white."

Representatives of the American Veterans Committee approached the Reverend Leslie T. Pennington in his capacity as chairman of the Hyde Park Community Council (an organization of community organizations) about the possibility of setting up a group to work on race relations in Hyde Park. Pennington welcomed the suggestion and, over considerable opposition, such a committee was formed within the council.

Faculty members of the University of Chicago's Committee on Planning urged the university administration to set up a community planning unit to draw up a general neighborhood improvement program.

The flight of white residents from the Kenwood area around K.A.M. Temple led members of its sisterhood to Thomas Wright's office and to a conference with his staff and representatives of Kenwood improvement associations. The K.A.M. sisterhood and their spiritual leader, Rabbi Jacob Weinstein, were committed to the principle of integration and spent some months exploring the possibility of conserving housing for all races by setting up voluntary agreements based on occupancy standards rather than on racial restrictions.

In the spring of 1949, Herbert A. Thelen of the university's Department of Education, searching for a project which would enable his students to "learn something about communities," invited Thomas Wright to visit his seminar and "tell us some hot problems."

"He laid out about five projects in the city," said Thelen, "and we picked the racial thing right here. We decided to begin a study in the fall that would apply the techniques of group dynamics to the solution of problems in a transition neighborhood. My interest was completely academic."

In spite of the concern and the ferment, however, no practical steps had been taken by September 1949. It was then that the Social Order Committee of the 57th Street Meeting of Friends (Quakers), unaware of any of this background, met to consider their next year's program.

They weighed issues and possibilities and finally reached a decision.

"It seems to be the sense of the meeting," said the chairman, "that we want to concern ourselves with the problems right here where we live, in our own community; that the problems of race relations and housing in the Hyde Park area seem most urgent;

that we ask Tom Wright of the Commission on Human Relations what is being done in Hyde Park with which we might usefully associate ourselves, or what is being done anywhere else from which we might learn; and finally that we invite him to our next meeting."

It was a fateful decision. The nine people who made it had no idea that they were about to provide the catalyst the community needed.

Tom Wright met with them a month later. He outlined the dimensions of the problem and the abortive attempts to meet it.

"Nothing constructive is being done," he said unhappily. "Not here in Hyde Park, nor in Chicago nor anywhere in the country that I know of. Lot of talk but no action. So don't count on learning from anybody else. If new patterns are to be developed, they'll have to start here."

He looked at the intent faces before him, and his heavy body began to quiver with enthusiasm. "By God," he shouted, his voice high with excitement, "this is just the group to do it!"

They set to work at once making plans. On the date of the next regular meeting of the Social Order Committee, they would bring together interested individuals from other agencies and institutions to join with them in facing the problems and thinking through the best possible solutions. The various racial and religious groups must be represented in the discussion. The Unitarian Church would be a good meeting place, and Leslie Pennington, its minister, an excellent chairman.

At eight o'clock on November 8, 1949, more than forty people crowded into the parlors of the First Unitarian Church. Members of the Friends' Social Order Committee beamed with gratification. Mrs. Emmanuel Molner and Mrs. Leo Zimmerman, the spark plugs of the K.A.M. Temple Sisterhood had both come. Temple Isaiah Israel was represented by its rabbi, Morton M. Berman, and by Bertram B. Moss, one of its directors, a former alderman of the ward. The ministers of the two Baptist churches were on hand—the Reverend Jitsuo Morikawa of the interracial First Baptist Church, accompanied by William Beaudry, and the Reverend Rolland W. Schloerb of the not-yet-interracial Hyde

Park Baptist Church. The Unitarian group had their minister there and several members of their Race Relations Committee. Some of the most respected of the community's new Negro residents were seated about the room: Earl B. Dickerson, general counsel for the Supreme Liberty Life Insurance Company and president of the Chicago Urban League; Oscar C. Brown, Sr., attorney and former manager of several public housing projects, with Mrs. Brown; Jerome E. Morgan, president of the Midway Television Institute; William Y. Browne, a well-known real estate man; Dr. and Mrs. Walter S. Grant; Mrs. Sydney P. Brown, Mrs. E. W. Beasley, Mrs. Albert Williams. Toward the front, talking to Harvey S. Perloff of the Committee on Planning in the University of Chicago's Division of Social Sciences and William Bradbury of the university's college faculty, was Herbert A. ("Herb") Thelen, flanked by eight of his students. Russell Babcock, director of the Governor's Commission on Human Relations, was there, too, and seated near him, the Reverend David H. Cole from the neighboring Woodlawn community, with the Reverend W. C. Malloy of the Kenwood Community Church. The university's student government had sent Jean Jordan. Observers had come from the Chicago Commission on Human Relations, the Chicago Council Against Racial and Religious Discrimination, and the Morgan Park Council on Human Relations.

The buzz of voices stopped abruptly as a tall, lean man with a mobile face rose.

"I am glad to see so many of you here," he said warmly. "Let's begin by introducing ourselves. I am Leslie Pennington, minister of this church."

Quickly, one after the other, the people in the room rose and gave their names and organizational connections.

"The presence here tonight of so many busy and important people," Pennington said, "shows that we do not intend this to be just another meeting. It was a privilege to be asked by my Quaker friends to chair this gathering, and I am proud that it is being held in my church."

He traced the background of the meeting and spoke easily as to friends and neighbors.

"We have come together tonight to consider a question of great urgency," he continued quietly. "It is—How shall we meet the challenge of the changing population—through conflict or co-operation? Much depends on our answer. Before we begin our discussion, here is Tom Wright of the Commission on Human Relations to give us the facts."

Tom Wright mopped his bald head and plunged in.

"We are here," he began, "because of the changing population in this community and the problems of attitude and action it has engendered. There are four basic facts to bear in mind."

"First, the number of Negroes in Chicago has been increasing rapidly, from 270,000 to over 400,000 in the last ten years.

"Second, they came to Chicago for the same reason as everyone else—jobs—and if Chicago continues to grow as an industrial center, its Negro population will continue to grow.

"Third, Negroes now have millions of dollars in cash and credit. This, together with the Supreme Court decision on restrictive covenants and their desire for more adequate living conditions is bringing about movement from the Negro ghetto.

"Fourth, there is pressure on the periphery of the ghetto because this is natural, because there is less fear of trouble, and because it seems to be the policy of many who sell properties to encourage the expansion of the ghetto rather than dispersal over the city."

He paused to let the facts sink in, and was encouraged by the absorbed faces before him.

"And what is happening as a result?" he continued. "White people have been leaving these peripheral areas in droves, and their place has been taken by Negroes whose need for housing has been encouraging exploitation and changes in the use of property. You know the conditions in your community." He summarized them briefly.

"Hyde Park and Kenwood are faced with four problems that flow from these facts: how to keep from extending the pattern of segregation; how to maintain community standards in housing as well as city services; how to integrate new residents; and how to deal with the general housing need which is a city-wide problem."

Leslie Pennington took over. "Our job tonight is to decide what we intend to do."

There was a long silence. The chairman did not feel impelled to break it. People were obviously overwhelmed by the size of the problem. Their faces showed concern, indecision, frustration, determination, helplessness. They were thinking.

Suddenly hands went up in every section of the room. A man in the front was recognized by the chair.

"Before we consider what if anything we want to do," he said, "shouldn't we know what the alternatives are?"

Herbert Thelen rose.

"I'd like to speak to that," he said. "As I see it, there are three possibilities: We can decide to pack up and leave the community now; we can decide not to do anything, on the grounds that the problems are too big for us; or we can go to work."

"Let's be realistic." The voice came from the back of the room. "I can't for the life of me see what we could possibly do that would make any difference. Exactly the same thing has happened to many neighborhoods in the U.S. Can anyone here name one community—*just one*—that has ever succeeded in reversing a trend of this kind?"

The sudden hush was broken by a dignified looking Negro in the front row.

"I don't believe any community has ever really tried," Oscar Brown said quietly.

Earl Dickerson interrupted. "Some of us get mighty tired of hearing what a menace we are," he said sharply, "and of having people talk of slums and Negroes as if they were tied together by edict. Every one of the Negroes in this room moved here, as I did, to get away from a slum. We've spent thousands of dollars on our properties, and they look a lot better today than when we bought them from the white people who left. We have an even greater stake than white neighbors in keeping the area from deteriorating."

A timid voice came next. It belonged to a white woman who seemed determined but embarrassed. "Suppose we do decide to go to work. There are many whites who would like to stay; yet I am told that Negroes *want* to concentrate block by block, and that this concentration is encouraged by power politicians who profit by an expansion of the ghetto."

She twisted her handerchief nervously. "How do we know the Negroes *want* to be integrated? This is their problem as much as ours."

Several Negroes tried to get the floor at once, but it was Oscar Brown who spoke again. The tension could be felt as everyone leaned forward to catch his words.

"Of course it is our problem, too," he agreed, "and we are willing to go at least halfway in helping to solve it. The answer to the Negro ghetto is interracial communities, and it is clear that there can't be such communities unless both races work at it."

He paused, seemed undecided about going on, and then made up his mind.

"Some of us are sensitive, perhaps too much so," he said, and he was obviously choosing his words with care, "to the constant references to 'the Negro problem.' We would like to see more recognition that the difficulties we face are a white problem as well, caused by attitudes that white people themselves have to do something about. If white people would just stay put when a Negro family moves into a block, there wouldn't be any panic and Negroes couldn't take over all the buildings. No one forces white people to sell."

Pennington held up his hand to stop the applause led by a stout white woman in a feathered hat who kept repeating in an audible whisper, "Good for him! Good for him!"

The chairman recognized Mrs. Molner of the K.A.M. Temple Sisterhood.

"That needed to be said," she began in a clear voice. "All of us have a job to do. A number of members of our temple are leaving the community, but the congregation as a whole intend to stay. Our new community house is still being built. Quite aside from our stake in this community, however, we share Rabbi Weinstein's conviction that the extension of segregated communities is morally and ethically indefensible. We are willing to go to work."

There was a buzz of approval.

Rabbi Morton Berman said that his temple had just completed its new building and spoke of his faith in the community and its people. "We are more than willing to do our share."

"It is not just a question of willingness." A man in a brown suit was on his feet. "I like this community. I want to keep on living here. But I don't see what we can *do*. White people might stay if they weren't being offered double the value of their property and weren't being persuaded that they'd better take it while the taking is good. There wouldn't be so much overcrowding if prices to Negroes weren't so inflated. But absentee landlords don't care about conserving the community. They're out to make a fast buck. How can *we* deal with the problem?"

"It isn't just housing." A man in the back had risen. "I'm not sure it's possible to restore confidence. People are full of apathy and pessimism. A lot of them are convinced nothing can be done. Just look at the increase in taverns. The people next door to me are moving because the wife is afraid to go out at night. What about police enforcement? And look at the condition of some of our streets and alleys. How can a handful of people move the city government to the kind of action that is needed?"

"We don't know yet," the chairman answered. "We must decide first whether we want to try."

He pointed next to one of the Quakers who had been trying to attract his attention.

"Our group has come here out of a religious concern for putting the preachments about the brotherhood of man into practice," he said. "We would welcome the opportunity to work for a fine interracial community. It is true that the problems stagger the imagination—but so do the possibilities. If we succeed, we will have created a demonstration that might set a pattern for other communities throughout the country. We will have given the world an example of democracy at work."

He smiled at his own earnestness. "If we fail," he shrugged . . . "at least we will have tried."

"The time has come for a show of hands," Pennington said. "How many of you are in favor of going to work?"

Every hand went up.

He beamed on the assembly. "That's settled. Now, how do we organize to do it?"

"Before we consider any form of organization," said Jitsuo Morikawa, the Nisei pastor, "I'd like to know whether there is any organization now in existence that could expand its functions to take this on."

Pennington turned to Bertram Moss. "Bert, you're the new chairman of the Hyde Park Community Council . . . how about that organization taking it on? It is, after all, an organization of almost all the organizations in the area. I know there was a lot of opposition within the council several years ago to any suggestion of a race relations operation, but a lot of water has flowed over the dam since then."

Moss shook his head. "It couldn't be done. The forces which opposed the idea in 1946 are still present in the council. We would either split the council or defeat the project. As you know, the council cannot take action on controversial issues without referring them to the member organizations. These are business groups and the improvement association as well as PTA's and churches, and all have such different approaches that any program of effective action would be blocked."

William Bradbury agreed that there was no group in existence capable of doing the job. He wasn't sure, however, that it was wise to organize immediately—organization brings on inhibitions, he said, and consolidates the opposition.

A long discussion followed. It ranged over the pros and cons of organization, the problems of overcrowding, deterioration, interracial living, flight to the suburbs, schools, crime, maintenance of services, possible next steps. Perhaps the thing to do was to continue the discussion another time, bringing in a much larger group of people. Real estate men and others in positions of power and influence ought to be included.

"No," Tom Wright said firmly, "I've talked with those people and I tell you you won't get anywhere with them. They'll kill any constructive effort you try to start. You'd be better off waiting until you're strong enough to buck the opposition."

The group finally agreed to steer clear of members of antagonistic power groups, at least for a while and to concentrate instead on securing the cooperation of people "who believe as we do."

"How do we plan to get cooperation?" the chairman asked.

A slight, young looking man with prematurely gray hair, signaled.

"It's getting very late," Russell Babcock said, "and a group as large as this can't work out all of the details. I move that we authorize Leslie Pennington and Tom Wright to name a temporary steering committee, and that we give the committee responsibility for enlarging the scope of this meeting, for suggesting ways to educate our own groups, and for considering how we might move toward organization."

The motion was seconded.

"Any discussion?"

There was none.

"All those in favor signify by saying Aye."

The room reverberated with Ayes.

"Opposed?"

There was a loud silence.

"It is so voted." Leslie Pennington's eyes were bright as he said solemnly, "This was a good night's work, I think. Who knows what might come of it?"

People did not want to go home when the meeting adjourned. They stood around talking in small groups. When the lights in the Unitarian parlors went out, they continued on the church steps, on the sidewalk, over coffee in a nearby restaurant.

A few miles away, on Peoria Street, another kind of action was being taken. An angry mob had formed in protest over the presence of Negro guests in a white home. It was to take the police four nights to restore order.

Fingers in the Dike

CHAPTER 3

Preliminaries to Action

Leslie Pennington and Tom Wright lost no time. They appointed a steering committee which promptly met, decided to plan for a public meeting the following month, and divided themselves up into three committees to get the work done: one on invitations, another to frame a policy statement, and the third to plan the program for the meeting.

Every institution and organization in the area believed to be sympathetic was invited to send two interested representatives who would participate as individuals rather than as official delegates.

"We hope very much," they were told, "that out of the forthcoming meeting will emerge a program designed to maintain high community standards, to persuade white residents to remain, and to welcome Negro newcomers into all community activities."

On the night of December 12, long before the scheduled hour, people began to arrive at the new community house of Temple Isaiah Israel. They kept coming. More and more chairs were brought in. When Leslie Pennington called the meeting to order at 8:15, the room was packed. Three hundred people had come. The signed cards indicated representation by fifty organizations. The churches and temples were all represented, some by several people, as well as the PTA's and the recreation centers. Faculty members of the University of Chicago and George Williams College were there. Those who had come to the first meeting had brought friends and neighbors. There were dark faces and a few Oriental ones among the white, all looking at the chairman with solemn expectancy.

Leslie Pennington spoke briefly about the reason for the meeting. Tom Wright followed with an analysis of population movements in Chicago. Herb Thelen's students were inconspicuously noting reactions as the program proceeded.

"We are now going to show you some of the problems that arise from these population movements."

Thelen had taken on the narrator's job. He moved from the center of the platform to make way for the first socio-drama.

"Mrs. Smith is cleaning the house when the doorbell rings," he said.

The spotlight picked up a woman in an apron opening the door to an excited friend.

"Mabel," the friend burst out, "do you know that Negroes have bought the house down the street and the Gordons are moving? Can't say I blame them. You know what happens when Negroes move in!"

"No, what happens?" Mabel asked.

"Why the neighborhood turns into a slum. Everybody knows that! We won't be safe on the streets at night."

The spotlight dimmed. When the lights went on the white faces looked embarrassed; the dark ones showed shock and anger.

"Mrs. Smith is confused and uncertain. She is discussing the situation with friends," said Thelen, as the next drama showed Mabel talking earnestly to a group in the grocery store. Rumors were flying. The neighborhood was definitely on the skids. Look what happened to Prairie Avenue years ago. The new Negro family was going to start a rooming house. That was the beginning of the end.

"Now let's look in on the Morgans," the narrator announced. "They are the Negro couple who are preparing to move into the

Hyde Park area the next day. Their friends, Mr. and Mrs. Jones, have come to call."

"You don't understand," John Morgan was saying. "We just want to live in a better neighborhood. Our children aren't going to be brought up in a slum."

"But John," his friend said, "it's the children I'm thinking of. You don't know what kind of reception you'll get. There may be violence. Even if there isn't, what will it do to their spirits if they are ostracized or ridiculed at school? Who will they play with?"

"We've thought it all out," Mrs. Morgan said wearily. "We *have* to take the chance. Surely there must be *some* white people who think of us as human beings, wanting the same things for our children as they do for theirs!"

In the fourth scene, the Reverend Thomas Cate and Mrs. Cate are discussing the Negro family who had just moved in.

"I don't know what I ought to do," he said in a troubled voice. "They might be embarrassed if I called on them. They probably already have a church affiliation and won't want to join our church. But if they do want to it might be even worse—can you imagine how some of the members of our congregation would react? I can just see them withdrawing their support."

Mrs. Cate put a comforting hand on his shoulder. "You'll do what you think right, Tom. You always have."

Audience interest was at its highest peak as the fifth scene opened on the Negro family the first evening in their new home.

The doorbell rang. A frightened look passed between husband and wife.

"Children, go into the bedroom and shut the door please," John Morgan directed calmly. And then to his wife, "Do you suppose it's starting already?"

He opened the door cautiously, and the white couple entered, Mrs. Cate carrying a pie.

"Sorry to intrude," the man said heartily. "I am Thomas Cate, minister of the church around the corner, and this is Mrs. Cate. We thought we might be helpful as you got settled in, so we came to get acquainted."

The Negro put out his hand. "I can't tell you how welcome you are," he said, and his voice shook.

A deep quiet followed. Women dabbed at wet eyes. A man blew his nose loudly. The shock had disappeared from the Negro faces. Suddenly the room rocked with applause.

A panel of experts pointed up some of the questions raised in the socio-dramas. They spoke of the advantages of the community, and of the problems of deterioration and their causes, stressing the fact that these bore no relation to race. They touched on some possible areas of action.

"The time has come for general discussion on problems and suggested action," Thelen said. "So that everyone may participate, we'll divide this crowd up into small discussion groups. Introduce yourselves to one another and appoint a member of your group to report back to the full meeting after twenty minutes the ideas brought out in your discussion."

Chairs were pushed into position quickly. The buzz of voices grew louder. The panel experts and students moved from group to group—listening, observing, putting in a word here and there to guide and encourage the timid and floundering.

"All right now," Thelen said. "One group at a time. Let's have your ideas."

They came pouring out and were written on a blackboard.

"We should get more police protection and better street lighting in borderline neighborhoods."

"More recreation facilities. Wider use of school plants."

"Let's get Kenwood re-zoned. Those large homes are white elephants."

"The residents themselves should improve neighborhood habits and morale in community housekeeping of walks, lawns, etc. Let's set up a block system of good neighbors."

"Visit responsible leaders of various communities and discuss the coming of Negroes."

"Educate the people against the idea that the coming of Negroes leads to deterioration of property."

People could be seen nodding or shaking their heads as ideas were greeted with approval or disapproval.

"To prevent the cutting up of large rental units, groups could buy buildings together."

"Plant flowers everywhere to make the district the most beautiful in the world."

"Overcome the bugbear of interracial marriage fear. That's not the issue."

"Study rumors and how to handle them."

"Study the relationship of these issues in our community to opening up the city as a whole to Negro occupancy."

After every group had spoken, Pennington resumed the chairmanship.

"I am encouraged by the wealth of ideas here," he said approvingly. "Before we decide how to implement them, however, we ought to have a policy to guide our actions. A committee has been at work for the past month framing a tentative statement for your consideration. It is quite long. Shall I summarize it?"

They wanted it read in full.

He began slowly, his voice clear and resonant.

"We stand for basic human rights, taught in common by our religious faith, by ethics and by the Constitution of the United States, among them the rights of all persons, irrespective of race, creed, or national origin, peacefully and lawfully to bargain for, rent, buy and occupy living space, to entertain guests in their homes, and to travel in our community unmolested.

"Population pressures of intense overcrowding of Negro districts are leading Negroes to seek living space in other parts of the city, including our own community. We believe this to be inevitable and essential to the welfare of the city as a whole. We believe that this population movement can and should be used creatively by the cooperation of Negroes and whites to build up the standards, morale, and character both of our community and of the city."

The statement pointed out that the chief obstacle to such a

program was fear based on misinformation and prejudice; that the real concern must be to prevent urban decay, which is caused by overcrowding, exploitation, and overuse of property. It suggested areas of activity: "Dispel fear by education"—"Maintain and advance occupancy standards against overcrowding"—"Set up standards of occupancy, and develop creative programs of planning and improvement"—"A constructive program for youth"—"Community integration." The relationship of the community's problems to those of the city as a whole was recognized, and the necessity to work with city agencies on a city-wide basis for "a more adequate program of slum clearance, of both private and public housing, and of city planning, to serve the welfare of all citizens without discrimination."

The statement was unanimously approved.

The meeting went on to discuss the question of organization. Possibilities in existing organizations were explored. The Hyde Park Community Council had already indicated that it would not be willing or able to take on these new responsibilities. The recently reorganized Oakland-Kenwood Planning Association, a property owners' group covering the area from 39th Street to 51st Street, did not take in Hyde Park and, even if it had, its earlier support of restrictive covenants caused the Negroes present to view it with suspicion. The history of the Hyde Park Planning Association and its present policies were widely known to be anti-Negro.

Eleven o'clock struck. A woman moved that the temporary committee be authorized to suggest a structure for a permanent organization and begin to plan an action program based on the evening's discussion.

It was so voted.

As the group moved slowly out into the chilly night, one of the students whispered to another: "Am I dreaming or does every one of those people really support that policy statement?"

"Of course not," was the reply. "Notice the expressions. Some of them are bewildered and confused. They aren't convinced even yet. But how brave can you be? Would *you* have nerve enough to stand up in a crowd like this and say you don't agree?"

He shook his head. "Exciting though, isn't it?"

They walked on.

For the next six weeks there were meetings almost every night. The Steering Committee met as a group; they broke down into committees which met separately; the committee chairmen got together on their own. In between meetings they sought the best advice they could get.

What kind of organization could work most effectively to maintain standards, keep abreast of the facts of community change, plan for the future? How could thousands of citizens be reached under conditions that would lead to intelligent decisions?

The Steering Committee decided that there should be four working committees, interracial in membership and, where possible, in co-chairmanship.

A committee on block organization would "consider ways and means of helping individual citizens, with their neighbors, to diagnose their neighborhood problems and to take action; to build a greater sense of community throughout the neighborhood." Herbert Thelen was the obvious chairman, and Russell Babcock agreed to serve with him.

Harvey Perloff, of the Committee on Planning of the University of Chicago, took general responsibility for a committee on planning, zoning, and reconversion. Its job was "to develop a coordinated approach to problems of community planning; to maintain contacts with various planning agencies, both local and city-wide; to help establish and enforce appropriate zoning provisions within the area; to help prevent undesirable conversions through the enforcement of building, health, and other city-wide regulations." Two subcommittees would help him—one on planning, headed by Martin Meyerson, an able planner who had recently joined the university faculty; and another on enforcement, under Truman K. Gibson, Jr., a well-known lawyer.

To get the facts, St. Clair Drake and Everett C. Hughes, sociologists, undertook to head a community survey committee. Their committee would "study the types of property in the community, their use, changes going on, the attitudes of citizens toward these changes, as a service to the entire program."

A committee on community organizations was set up "to gather information concerning the policy and practices of recreational centers, schools (through PTA's), restaurants, hotels, places of business, civic and religious organizations; to study ways and develop a program of harmonious intercultural adjustment in changing neighborhoods." Lucy P. Carner, a member of the Quaker Social Order Committee, who was also head of the Division of Education and Recreation of the Welfare Council of Metropolitan Chicago, became chairman; and Jerome E. Morgan, president of the Midway Television Institute, co-chairman. William Bradbury volunteered to help.

The chairmen of all the working committees would serve on the Steering Committee.

What geographical area would the new organization cover? Hyde Park and Kenwood had different problems. Part of Kenwood was already far along the road to blight. Besides, the Oakland-Kenwood Planning Association covered the entire Kenwood area, and it would be unwise to overlap organizationally. Logic was on the side of restricting activity to the Hyde Park community. But the K.A.M. Temple was in Kenwood; its representatives had played an active part in beginning the new organization; they had no faith in the ability of the Oakland-Kenwood group to deal with the problems Kenwood faced. The professional planners agreed that part of the Kenwood area might well be included in the new organization, since the section between 47th Street (in the center of Kenwood) and 59th Street (the Midway and the southern boundary of Hyde Park) made a more desirable planning entity than Hyde Park alone.

The Steering Committee had already suggested that the new organization take in all of Hyde Park and part of Kenwood, covering the two square miles between 47th Street and the Midway, Cottage Grove Avenue and the lake. They were now prepared to make this recommendation to the community. They thought the agency that was to be created should be called the Hyde Park-Kenwood Community Conference and should be an organization of individuals rather than of organizations. While each individual would represent himself alone, he would be expected at the same time to provide a channel of communication to his group.

What was the best way to put the organization to work? How could the best advantage be taken of the interest already aroused?

Another public meeting, carefully planned, was held on February 1, 1950, for the double purpose of reporting back to the community and starting action.

It opened in the large assembly room of Temple Isaiah Israel's community house. Several hundred people came, including specialists in the fields of proposed action who had been persuaded to help with the work sessions following the general meeting.

Leslie Pennington reviewed developments to date and summarized the recommendations of the Steering Committee, which were quickly approved. The continuation of the Steering Committee was authorized.

To help with the cost of paper and postage, hats were passed, and $127.25 was collected—the first funds of the newly organized Hyde Park-Kenwood Community Conference. Then the audience broke up into four planning-working groups.

Owners and operators of large properties who had special zoning and housing problems were invited to join resource people in the section on planning, zoning and reconversion. Anyone who wanted to do so was encouraged to join the block organization session. Those interested in and having time for surveys were asked to share in the community survey group. People informed about community organizations and concerned about their policies and practices were urged to work in the community organization section.

Each group was asked to (1) formulate working plans; (2) decide what help was needed from and could be given to the other groups; (3) make plans for the continuation of the group, including the method by which there would be communication with its members; and (4) select two or three representatives for service on the central Steering Committee.

Thelen's block organization people remained behind in the assembly hall while those who chose the specialized groups filed upstairs to three smaller rooms reserved for them.

Thelen began at once.

"Let's try to do several things tonight," he said. "First, let's look at the kinds of problems block groups might solve. Second, let's listen to the experiences of a few who have already started action on their own blocks to see what is involved. Third, let's look at how we can coordinate all of our activities so that if one block, for example, starts to tackle a problem that is too big for it, it can mobilize other resources to help out and so that we can have the kind of communication that will prevent one block from repeating another's mistakes. Fourth, let's break up into manageable units. Russ Babcock, co-chairman of the block program, has divided Hyde Park-Kenwood into twenty zones of equal population. Go to that section of the room designated as the zone in which you live and there talk with your neighbors about the major problems in your area and what might be done about them, trying to seek out at the same time people who would be willing to work at pushing the program along. And finally, let's come together again and tell each other what the various neighborhoods have decided."

They became so interested in the detailing of problems, possibilities, and experiences that it was a long time before they were ready to follow the street boundary signs—51st to 53rd, Woodlawn to Dorchester; 47th to 51st, Cottage Grove to Ellis—directing them to their neighborhood discussion groups.

In the meantime, the groups on the second floor were also hard at work.

The two sections of Harvey Perloff's committee were meeting separately. Martin Meyerson's planning section agreed that it should compile, analyze, and present to the conference any public or private proposals that would affect the Hyde Park-Kenwood area; eventually prepare an over-all sketch plan specifically oriented to the achievement of the goals of the conference; prepare recommendations for zoning, standards of occupancy, and other devices for effectuating such a plan; provide zoning information to conference members. Truman Gibson's enforcement section decided that it should provide information to conference members on regulations covering buildings, occupancy and health standards, and what constitutes violations of these regulations; obtain information on illegal conversions and other violations; bring pressure on city officials for the enforcement of regulations. They would seek the cooperation of real estate men and block groups.

The community survey group thought its work would be done best in cooperation with the block organization, since people on the blocks were in an ideal position to collect information. St. Clair Drake, Everett Hughes, and their small committee discussed the major survey needs and techniques for getting the necessary data.

The community organizations section decided early in its meeting that subcommittees would have to deal with different types of organizations, and agreed that separate groups should work with parents and teachers in the public schools, with private schools, with employer and employment groups, with restaurants, and with recreation agencies. The religious institutions could be left to the Council of Hyde Park and Kenwood Churches and Synagogues.

The janitor, looking patient and long-suffering, appeared at each door. It was long past closing time. "When are they going to go home?" he asked in a loud whisper.

There was so much yet to do. The sections and subsections summarized their decisions and made arrangements to meet again with the least possible delay.

Next on the agenda: ACTION!

CHAPTER 4

The Program Gets Under Way

Even before the public gathering on February 1, 1950, Herb Thelen had decided to try to hold an experimental block meeting. The opportunity came in his own block, a quiet street on which there was a row of sixteen modest homes all occupied by their owners.

A panic was in the making. Rumors had spread up and down the block that a speculator was planning to sell one of the houses on the street to Negroes who would then crowd a family into every room. Four people had already put their homes up for sale. Most of the others were anxious and worried and not sure what to do.

A group of four worked out plans for a meeting of the residents. Each arranged to invite his own friends and acquaintances on the block.

"Some of us thought it would be a good idea if we all got together to see what ought to be done about the situation," they said, as they called on their neighbors. "Will you join us?"

They would indeed.

They met in Thelen's home. As he moved among his guests before the meeting came to order, Thelen overheard snatches of conversation.

"I wonder what we should do to keep the Negroes out," one said.

A woman spoke earnestly about Christianity and brotherly love.

From another corner a man was insisting that "White people have rights, too!"

A very old man climbed up on the stair landing and took it upon himself to open the meeting.

"All right," he said, "what do you want me to tell you about those damn niggers?"

There was a startled silence. Thelen stepped smoothly into it, in his role as chairman.

"Before tonight's meeting began," he said, "I learned from the conversations that we all have different attitudes about Negroes. We might as well accept that as a fact about ourselves that is not going to change no matter how much we debate it.

"I suggest that we go on then to consider our situation. Negroes have bought the building across the street," he went on matter-of-factly, "and looking at this development objectively, three courses of action are possible:

"We could form a mob to try to drive the Negroes out.

"We could ignore them.

"We could visit them and ask them to join us in preventing deterioration and keeping the block a pleasant place to live in."

The group made its decision quickly. The idea of mob action was shocking. Ignoring the Negroes seemed no solution either. They appointed a committee of three to call on the new neighbors.

"Now what are some of the concrete things we ought to be doing something about—like improving the appearance of the block? Every time I walk to the corner, for example, I keep noticing that . . ." Thelen was directing the discussion toward positive action on definite problems.

Other signs of deterioration had been noticed. They were soon deep in a review of conditions and were deciding what to do about them. Everyone agreed that another meeting should be called as soon as possible to have reports on the action taken, and to go on from there.

The committee of three called on the Negroes without delay.

Fortunately, the newcomers were sensitive people who recognized at once the committee's embarrassment and helped them to talk about block problems. They appreciated the visit, thought a block organization was a fine idea, would be happy to cooperate.

Anxiety was relieved. The four homes were taken off the market. The block group continued its meetings, working successively on a variety of projects: an eyesore of a building, a threatened illegal conversion, the development of a playground.

Slowly other blocks organized and went to work.

Meanwhile, the Enforcement Subcommittee had decided to concentrate its first efforts on the violations in a beautiful building on Drexel and Hyde Park boulevards which had recently changed ownership.

The building contained six luxurious apartments of seven and eight spacious rooms plus two and three bathrooms, butler's pantry, and sun parlor, each apartment occupied by an individual family with children and, usually, domestic help. The rent was $145 per month.

Now a "kitchenette operator" was in possession. When the first vacancy occurred, she had crowded Negro families into single rooms of the apartment and was charging them $90 per month per room. The neighbors were appalled. The white families in the building were threatening to leave—an idea encouraged by the new owner. The upper-class, professional Negroes who had just bought property in the block and invested heavily in improvements, saw in this overcrowding operation the beginning of the slums from which they had fled. It was believed that the woman who claimed to be the sole owner was fronting for a group of investors. Calls on her had no effect. Negro and white neighbors alike reported to the Building Department that the property was being converted illegally. The violations continued.

It was at this point that the enforcement group, led by Truman K. Gibson, Jr., and Frank Kenney, lawyers, together with Alderman Abraham Cohen of the Fourth Ward and neighbors of both races, called on the city building commissioner.

"I don't want to discourage you folks," the commissioner said, "but there isn't too much we can do. Our office now has a back-log of two thousand cases ready for trial, and the one judge hearing these cases disposes of only about forty a week.

"We'll inspect the premises," he went on. "We'll probably find violations and issue a police stop order to prevent further conversion. We'll notify the owner that plans for a legal conversion must be submitted and approved and construction made to conform with them or court action will be initiated."

He shrugged. "But having done that, where are we? As I pointed out, court action is slow. We have no authority to secure injunctions. We are limited to proceedings for the assessment of fines, and these fines are so low that 'sneak' conversions make a pretty good business proposition. Look at the money that woman is making!"

The committee pointed out that the harassment and expense of a series of court cases in which fines were assessed might be a deterrent to other violators, that a convincing example made of one case might lighten the Building Department's burden. They pressed for special proceedings to ensure speedy court action. The commissioner agreed.

This was the beginning of a stubborn and tenacious fight. The Enforcement Committee, the block group, and the Conference Steering Committee became involved in it, and the Metropolitan Housing and Planning Council, and a good part of the city's Building Department and Department of Law. A succession of different lawyers appeared before a series of different judges on behalf of the alleged owner. A warrant was issued for her arrest when she failed to respond to a summons. She was fined $200 and costs, subjected to weekly building inspections, haled into both housing and building courts again and again.

Matters only grew worse. As the months passed, the alleged owner not only continued to flout authorities on the original violations, but converted each of the remaining five apartments into overcrowded kitchenettes and sleeping rooms. A careful count by building inspectors revealed as many as three adults and five children in one room.

The community refused to give up. Neighbors and volunteer

lawyers appeared at every hearing prepared to testify. If the judge allowed a continuance, as he frequently did, community representatives were annoyed and angered, but they turned up again at the next court session.

Some months later the breakthrough came. The alleged owner, on the advice of her lawyer, agreed to evict all the tenants preparatory to a legal conversion which would make two apartments of four and five rooms each out of the larger units. At the request of the conference and the corporation counsel's representative, the office of the housing and redevelopment coordinator promised to provide relocation services.

The reason for the victory? It seemed to have no relation to the fines—which were minor compared to the owner's profits—nor to the harassment of constant building inspections—to which she grew accustomed—nor to the good opinion of neighbors, since she did not live in the area. The fact was that she suffered from fear of riding in elevators. The courtroom was on the eleventh floor and she had had to walk up and down eleven flights of stairs every time there was a hearing on her case. She was just plain tuckered out!

Finally the last family was moved and the building stood empty. Plans for remodeling were approved by the Building Department.

Two and a half years had gone by.

During that time, the Enforcement Committee, the block groups and interested individuals took on scores of other cases. Some they lost; others they won. The story of their struggle over enforcement of building codes is part of a later chapter.

The Planning, Zoning and Reconversion Committee, following its organization, went to work on several other projects.

To help members of block groups and others recognize and report building and zoning violations, they made available information from the Municipal Code on residential conversions, minimum housing standards, and the zoning regulations for the Hyde Park-Kenwood area.

This was only a beginning. Reports of residents could not get at all the violations. They might help to stop the further spread of deterioration, but conservation of the area called for much more drastic action. If the Building Department could be persuaded to set up certain zones as "conservation areas" . . .

Harvey Perloff talked with Alderman Robert E. Merriam who, as chairman of the City Council's housing committee as well as Hyde Park's representative, had given a great deal of thought to problems of deteriorating areas. The alderman arranged a conference with the building commissioner.

"Why not use Hyde Park as a testing laboratory?" urged Alderman Merriam. "Select certain blocks for special treatment and begin with a house-to-house inspection?"

The commissioner would not commit himself. "What about areas of the city that need it more?" he demanded. "I'd have a dozen other aldermen on my neck. But I'll think about it and let you know."

Later, Perloff said: "We have to realize that there are very strong pressures against strict enforcement of building codes. There just isn't enough housing available to accommodate all of our people under decent standards. Instead of facing up to this problem on a city-wide basis and providing the necessary housing, some city officials seem to believe the only thing to do is to let certain areas—like the South Side—deteriorate in order to provide inadequate housing for Negroes, and to maintain tough enforcement in other sections, thereby keeping them white. We're going to have to work on every front—for adequate enforcement, for more housing throughout the city, and for open occupancy as well."

A few weeks later, the building commissioner, acting on the recommendation of the city's newly formed Interim Commission on Neighborhood Conservation, decided to undertake house-to-house inspections in five areas of the city, including Hyde Park-Kenwood.

As a result of the South Side inspection, notices of violation went to more than one thousand property owners. They were given the opportunity to get further information from officials through evening sessions (Compliance Board hearings) in the neighborhood. These were arranged cooperatively by the conference and Ray Grahn, assistant commissioner of the Building Department, who, with five of his men, gave time outside of office hours to listening to building problems and complaints.

It was late in 1952 before reinspection of the properties was completed and the Building Department reported to the conference: the Hyde Park-Kenwood area showed an unusually high proportion of compliance; 925 of the 1,000 property owners had complied with the law; the others would be brought to court.

The report seemed too good to be true even to some of those who wanted to believe it. The skeptics asked, "How many inspectors were bribed?"

In the early days considerable effort also went into a community conservation agreement drafted by Martin Meyerson's subcommittee. Various forms of the document made the rounds. There were conferences with the Commission on Human Relations, the Metropolitan Housing and Planning Council, and representatives of the Oakland-Kenwood Planning Association, which was circulating its own form of covenant in the Kenwood single-family area. The agreement was tested on property owners, studied and debated by block groups, the Steering Committee, lawyers.

Nothing came of it for several reasons. Property owners feared their buildings would be less salable if possible future purchasers felt themselves bound to abide by higher standards than those officially in force; people could not agree on whether or not conversion should be permitted, and if so under what conditions; there was concern about responsibility for payment of legal fees.

After a year of effort, the agreement was abandoned. A much more exciting idea was soon to take its place—the redevelopment and conservation of the South Side area from 31st Street to the Midway.

In the meantime, the Community Survey Committee, led by St. Clair Drake, with the advice of Everett Hughes, was concentrating on "dispelling fear by education"—the first need pointed out in the conference policy statement. Where to begin? Rumors were rife: "Crime in Hyde Park is increasing rapidly"; "Ninety per cent of the buildings in west Hyde Park have changed hands in the past two years"; "The property taken over by Negroes has deteriorated." There were others—many of them—but the committee decided to begin on these.

With a group of volunteer researchers from his committee, Drake set out to get the facts. He called on the officer-in-charge of the local police station who opened the police records to the researchers. A careful check of crime statistics showed how the rumor had arisen. There had been an increase in the crime rate for the Hyde Park police district, which included several communities—Oakland, Kenwood, Hyde Park—but this was not true of that part of the area covered by the conference. The rate in Hyde Park itself remained about the same.

The research team next checked property ownership in the area of greatest turnover. They found that not 90 per cent but less than 10 per cent had changed hands in two years.

The committee's investigation of deterioration in the area of greatest turnover showed that deterioration had set in before Negroes began to arrive and that they had in fact made a considerable investment in improvements.

All of this information was promptly relayed to block groups through their leaders as well as to the general conference mailing list through a periodic report to the membership. Those who received the information were urged to pass it on.

The Community Organizations Committee and its subcommittees were also covering the community on different missions.

The most serious problems facing the Public Schools Subcommittee were the racial attitudes of white parents and teachers and the integration of Negroes into the schools and PTA's. Mrs. Martin M. Cohn, the subcommittee chairman, called on the superintendent of schools and got his approval of an interracial council to be formed within the Hyde Park-Kenwood schools. The PTA's were persuaded to have general programs on interracial matters, to welcome new Negro members, and to add Negroes to boards and committees.

At the same time, another subcommittee, led by Mrs. Lucien Isenberg, Mr. Warren C. Seyfert, and Mrs. William F. Morgenstern, called on the heads of private, parochial, and nursery schools. They discussed with their educators the aims of the conference and the admission policies of the schools, invited formal cooperation by those whose policies were nondiscriminatory, tried to encourage a change in policy by the more timid who feared the loss of students.

Virginia Kenney sparked the team on the Restaurant Subcommittee. Under her leadership small interracial groups visited every restaurant in the community. Ostensibly they were there to order a meal; their real purpose was to discover the restaurant's policy. This was done very quietly. If the proprietor refused to serve them, they left without making a scene.

Only one restaurant was found to discriminate. The conference did not act directly against that one. Instead, it sent a letter to all of the restaurants, reporting the results of the survey and stating its gratification that only one had refused to serve Negroes. Nothing further needed to be done. Those with a good policy were reinforced by knowing they were not alone in it, and the one guilty of discrimination, feeling alone, promptly changed its unpopular stand. The subcommittee disbanded, its purpose accomplished.

John G. Guinessy's subcommittee on recreation, which involved people from the recreation agencies in the community and interested individuals, found out that most of the agencies opened their facilities to all groups. In the case of the one or two exceptions, the subcommittee tried to work out ways of influencing a change in policy.

Probably the experience of the Employment Subcommittee, headed by Mrs. Adele Erenberg, was the most frustrating. Its members tirelessly went about calling on chain store managers and others, urging employment on merit irrespective of race or national background. They engaged the entire conference organization in getting statements from residents indicating that, as patrons of these stores, they wanted a policy of nondiscrimination in both employment and service. In a very few instances, fair employment practices were followed. The subcommittee spent weeks arranging a workshop to explore with other community groups methods of opening up job opportunities in Hyde Park-

Kenwood on a nondiscriminatory basis. It was an excellent session, but no action resulted.

For the most part, the subcommittee was defeated. Local chain stores insisted that employment policies were made in the central office. The central office felt local circumstances should be the guiding factor. In the end the subcommittee felt the answer lay in the top policy-forming groups outside the community, and the conference abandoned the employment effort.

A subcommittee on hotels, chaired by Mrs. Oscar C. Brown, Sr. and Emil G. Hirsch, had a much briefer life. It was born a year after the other subcommittees and died following its first visit to a hotel owner.

The hotels in the community, with one exception, had been finding ways to circumvent the Illinois law prohibiting discrimination in public places. It was true, of course, that to avoid embarrassment Negroes did not generally try to stay at these places or patronize their restaurants. If they did, it was easy enough for the manager to claim there were no vacancies or that all the tables were reserved. One hotel owner, however, was known to have entertained mixed conventions and to have served Negro guests.

The subcommittee decided to call on him to enlist his advice and help. He dealt with them courteously but firmly. While he felt it was his duty to obey the law and would continue to do so, he could not interfere in the policies of other hotels. He could suggest no approach to them. Nor was he willing to publicize his own policy. This would encourage more and more Negroes to patronize his hotel and he would lose his white clientele.

He ushered his visitors out. Word of the call and its purpose promptly went to the other hotel owners. No further interviews were possible.

Work with the churches was going forward at the same time, outside the conference structure but directed by conference leaders. Leslie Pennington, chairman of the conference board of directors, was also president of the Council of Hyde Park and Kenwood Churches and Synagogues. He, Rabbi Jacob J. Weinstein of K.A.M. Temple, the Reverend Jitsuo Morikawa of the First Baptist Church, Rabbi Morton M. Berman of Temple Isaiah

Israel, Rabbi Bernard Wechsberg of Congregation Habonim Jewish Center, and the Reverend Walter R. Van Hoek, assistant pastor of the Hyde Park Baptist Church, tried to get the united churches to spearhead the work of the conference.

The church council voted to give the conference general support. It appointed a brotherhood committee, with Van Hoek, a member of the Conference Steering Committee, as chairman. This group tried to encourage each religious institution to set up its own brotherhood committee responsible for working out a policy of open membership. A few churches did. Less liberal congregations almost split on the issue. Some churchmen did not introduce the idea at all. The brotherhood enterprise failed—at least for the time.

"Although we did not try to force it on any church at any time," said Leslie Pennington recently, "it took longer to move them than we anticipated."

Everything was to take longer than anticipated.

CHAPTER 5

The First Year

The new organization was not hailed with universal rejoicing. In spite of all the activity, most of the people in the community were not aware of its existence. Among those who were, reactions varied widely.

A relatively small group of enthusiasts worked zealously "preaching the gospel." A number of others watched with approval and wished them well but were not sufficiently concerned to take active part. Some accepted the conference principles but did not believe they could be put into practice, "human nature being what it is." There were those who disapproved of one aspect of the program and dismissed the whole movement: "Good Heavens! Meetings with neighbors! My social life is more than adequate, thank you." Others were tolerant, amused, pessimistic, apathetic, skeptical, cynical, or defeated.

Most threatening to the success of the new organization were the attitudes of those in positions of influence and power—the business, real estate, and large institutional interests. The majority of these were indifferent, suspicious, or actively hostile.

From the beginning it had been obvious to the founders of the conference that the University of Chicago, as the major institution and the largest property owner in the area, would have tremendous influence for good or ill on the future of the community, depending on how its influence and resources were used. The university's past support of restrictive covenants was no secret. Rumor had it that the university still followed the policy of excluding Negroes from the immediate university area. This, it was said, was now accomplished through the real estate practices of the university business office whose representative was accused of having referred to the university and its policy publicly in terms of "a white island in a black sea."

The approach to be made to the University of Chicago administration was discussed in several conference sessions. On March 17, 1950, a committee of three met with top university officials. The meeting was distinguished chiefly for its brevity. After listening to a quick review of the program and work of the conference, Chancellor Robert Maynard Hutchins announced that he was going to have to do what he was frequently forced to do because of his busy schedule—make a statement of his own position and then leave for another appointment.

"He made an excellent declaration of principle on the race issue and began putting on his hat and coat," said one of the committee members later. "But before he left, the vice-president in charge of business affairs did everything he could to discredit the work of the conference and attribute all gains in conserving the community to the work of his office. There was no chance to carry the conversation further. And there proved to be no later opportunity for a conference with the chancellor. It seemed to me that he was not deeply enough interested to reckon with the policy of his own business office." (Although a number of faculty members had been involved in the conference from the beginning, the university began to take active leadership in community improvement through the South East Chicago Commission only after a change of administration.)

The failure to secure university support was an even deeper blow than was recognized at the time. A representative of the university's business office sat on the boards of several community organizations: the Hyde Park Community Council, the 55th Street Businessmen's Association, the Hyde Park Planning Association, and Woodlawn, Inc. (an organization of business and property interests in the community south of Hyde Park). Both of the latter organizations had supported restrictive covenants in the past and were continuing to receive financial contributions from the university. The staff representative of the Hyde Park Planning Association was also active in several of the local community agencies. Since there was no direct contact between the conference and these community organizations, their members naturally accepted the opinions of the conference held by the representatives of the University of Chicago and the Hyde Park Planning Association, which were uniformly unfavorable.

They were not alone in spreading distrust of the conference. The seeds of disapproval had been sown several years before when a race relations committee had been appointed in the Hyde Park Community Council over the opposition of certain of the delegates. Leslie Pennington had led that fight and incurred the enmity of some of the community's businessmen. They, together with university and Planning Association representatives, were convinced that Pennington's purpose was to "invite Negroes into the community," that this would deflate property values, cause white people to leave the area, and destroy Hyde Park.

The feeling against Pennington was transferred to the new organization he headed, which was sometimes disparagingly referred to as "Pennington's Gang." The opposition was thoroughly persuaded that the conference, not population trends and other social factors, was responsible for the in-migration of Negroes. There was also a strong feeling that the conference was an extreme left-wing organization and that "Communists are behind the whole thing." These rumors spread through the business community.

Unfortunately, conference representatives sometimes harmed rather than helped their cause. Full of zeal, eager to make converts to the new "religion," they did not always approach difficult situations with the delicacy they demanded. Since they were all volunteers, frequently self-appointed rather than chosen for specific tasks, it is not surprising that some were lacking in tact and sensitivity. Instead of talking with the unconvinced on the basis of facts—the facts of deterioration, of community change, of population trends, and the need to deal constructively with these problems—instead of trying to understand the fears and problems of the "unconverted," which were very real, they occasionally took an offensively moral tone, pointing out the meaning of democracy, Christianity, and the brotherhood of man.

People who already had unconscious feelings of guilt were made defensive and more antagonistic by this approach. Others regarded it as another evidence of the naïveté and impracticality of the entire conference group.

Some of the businessmen were infuriated by visits from members of the Employment Committee. Through misunderstanding of the nature of certain business concerns, the committee had called on several family enterprises having only a few employees, all of whom had been with the firm many years. To suggest a change in employment policy on the basis of merit obviously had no bearing in these instances.

One such call was made on the owner of a fine clothing store, a former president of the Businessmen's Association who continued to be influential in its affairs. In reporting on the visit several years later, he was still livid with rage. "The nerve of them —coming into *my store* and telling me how to run my business! I ordered them out!" His account of the experience was soon known to other businessmen.

Real estate operators had conflicting views on the conference. Many believed that it wished to put Negroes into every building in the community. Speculators who tried to panic white residents into selling their property regarded the intrusion of the conference as unwarranted interference with their rights. Some of the reputable real estate men resented the frequent references to "unscrupulous real estate operators" and the tendency to put so much of the blame on their calling. Requests for information on the sale of buildings were politely rejected. Telephone calls were not answered. Appointments were difficult to arrange. With both real estate people and conference representatives guarded and distrustful, the infrequent interviews, far from promoting cooperation, ended with an increase in suspicion and antagonism.

Conference leaders were so convinced further conversations would be fruitless that they did not even try to see most of the real estate men.

There was difficulty in other quarters as well. The Oakland-Kenwood Planning Association resented action by the conference on building and zoning cases in Kenwood, which was their domain. In an annual address, published in the *Hyde Park Herald*, the president of the Hyde Park Planning Association stated that the conference was not acting "in the best interests of the community." A trustee of the University of Chicago told a conference representative that he was sharing in "a dangerous experiment."

Conference leaders, for the most part, reacted to criticism the way human beings generally do. They placed the blame for these difficulties on the recalcitrance of their opponents, not on their own failures. It did not occur to some of them that words spoken thoughtlessly and critically of the university, the business community, or a rival organization were reported back and were likely to cause a further breakdown in already strained relations. They did not see that some of the misunderstanding was the natural result of failure in communication. They did not examine too closely the attitudes with which they approached others or the basis on which understanding might be achieved.

A few conference members recognized that some of the problems lay within their own leadership, as well as in other overzealous volunteers. Herb Thelen kept urging that groups and individuals be approached with concrete proposals for cooperation on the basis of their own interests. This was enthusiastically seconded by another leader: "We must assume that the motives of other organizations are good, try to understand their point of view, and seek their cooperation in ways in which this is possible. We must not concern ourselves with how badly other groups behave, but do our own job so well that it will speak for us and win us friends."

This was the view that eventually prevailed. But it took several years to overcome the deep resentment left by early mistakes.

So much was going on that first year and there was so much to do that little time could be given to evaluation of program or methods. In spite of blunders and errors in judgment, for the most part conference people worked thoughtfully and well.

To give direction to the many program activities, the Steering Committee sometimes met twice a month—its members usually crowded into the Unitarian Church parlors. The full committee, now numbering thirty-three, included four ministers, two lawyers, three office workers, five housewives, a social worker, six university professors (from the fields of planning, sociology, political science, education, the humanities), a race relations specialist, a school administrator, a recreation leader, a doctor, three businessmen, an editor, a salesman, two members of the labor movement, and a student. There were six Negroes and two Nisei; two Catholics and seven Jews in a predominantly Protestant list. Their homes were spread out over Hyde Park and part of Kenwood. (The three businessmen were all Negroes. It was taken for granted that the white business community and white real estate men would not cooperate.)

An executive committee coordinated the work of the conference and acted in the interim between Steering Committee meetings when decisions had to be made quickly. Program chairmen spent countless additional hours with their committees.

Conference leaders tried to set up channels of communication within the organization and the community. They recruited and trained block leaders. They buttonholed their friends, rang doorbells, made public speeches, used their membership in other organizations to spread the story of the conference.

Slowly interest grew.

On June 6, 1950, when the conference called its first public meeting "to report to the community," 750 people came.

Several months before, the Steering Committee had recognized the need for a central office and at least one paid staff member, but had delayed action because of lack of funds. It was clear, however, that the office files could not continue to be carried around in dozens of heads. With an increase in activities, coordination of the various efforts had become more and more difficult, sometimes impossible. The burgeoning movement could not continue to grow without central direction and a place to which people could go for information.

On June 12, 1950, the Steering Committee expressed itself in favor of "employing Julia Abrahamson as executive director on a half-time basis for July, August, and September," *if* funds could be obtained. (The committee believed my previous experience in race relations and administration at the Julius Rosenwald Fund would be useful; I knew the conference well, since I had been involved in its organization and had served as secretary of the board from the beginning; and, probably most important, I was available and sufficiently concerned to be willing to take a chance on not getting paid at all.)

It was estimated that approximately $1,000 would be needed to meet salary and office expenses for the summer months. A group was hurriedly called together to consider ways and means of financing the conference. Under the leadership of Martin M. Cohn, the first finance chairman, they acted at once. Nine individuals made loans of $100 each, with the understanding that these would be repaid from the returns of a financial drive to be undertaken in the fall. A letter was sent to every church and temple in the area asking for generous contributions. The Unitarian Church offered space rent free for the summer. Henry L. Kohn and Samuel W. Block, lawyers, volunteered to work on articles of incorporation and an application for tax exemption.

On July 1, 1950, the office opened in the basement of the Unitarian Church. The two desks, a table and four chairs—donated by Sinai Temple or on loan from the Unitarian Church—seemed lost in the large, bare room. The number of the newly installed telephone had been distributed to all committee members. Friends of the conference had been notified that the gift or loan of file and storage cabinets would be gratefully accepted. Very little money had been spent—$75.42 for a rebuilt typewriter and a small stock of stationery, office supplies, and postage.

The lack of tangible assets was more than balanced by an overabundance of enthusiasm. Having an office which the group had brought into being and for which it was responsible, encouraged and heartened them all. It gave the conference more reality and stability. Its leaders threw themselves into the work with renewed energy.

A letter was sent to the entire mailing list announcing the

opening of the office. The *Hyde Park Herald* printed the news. The telephone began to ring at an increasingly accelerated rate; there were calls from the general community on rumors, crime, illegal conversions; from committee members with reports and suggestions for action; from potential volunteers; and requests for information.

To complete the articles of incorporation and bylaws, formal action was taken on the election of officers, the definition of membership, the quorum for membership meetings. The Steering Committee felt that the rules by which the organization governed itself should be carefully worked out. Recognizing, however, the immediate need for formal documents in business dealings and in applying for tax exemption, the committee agreed to a temporary set of bylaws with the understanding that these would be revised or amended at the first opportunity.

The first bylaws provided, among other things, that the membership for voting purposes should consist of members of the Steering Committee, the zone coordinators for the block program, and the chairmen of any committees to be appointed; that twenty should be the quorum for a membership meeting; that a board of thirty-six directors should be elected each year for one-year terms. "Let's have a period of shakedown before we put any limitation on the term of service," the Steering Committee decided. Two years later the bylaws were amended to give the vote to every dues-paying member, and service on the board was increased to a three-year term.

The first elected officers were Leslie T. Pennington, chairman; Henry L. Kohn, treasurer; Julia Abrahamson, secretary; Russell Babcock and Lucy P. Carner, vice-chairmen.

A system for handling building and zoning violations was organized. Witnesses were in and out of court on the Drexel Boulevard building, and action on a number of new violations was begun.

The conservation agreement made the rounds, and there were periodic contacts with Alderman Merriam and city authorities on the house-to-house inspection.

The zone coordinators responsible for the block program met every two weeks, and individual block activities continued.

The Restaurant and Employment subcommittees proceeded with their visits.

Get-acquainted calls were made and friendly relations were established with civic leaders and public officials in and out of the community.

The churches and temples began to send in contributions, with K.A.M. Temple and Temple Isaiah Israel heading the list. Five of them agreed to have at least one meeting on the conference in the fall and to print information about it in their publications.

Pressure to extend the conference boundaries to take in neighboring communities was firmly resisted because the problems and resources of adjoining areas differed too greatly and the conference was already in danger of spreading itself too thin to be effective.

The Planning, Zoning, and Reconversion Committee was officially divided into two separate committees: Planning, headed by Martin Meyerson and Oscar C. Brown, Sr., and Enforcement, with Frank Kenney and Truman K. Gibson, Jr., as co-chairmen. Harvey Perloff, who had sparked the planning work and made invaluable contributions to general policy and program, was away on a year's field-work mission.

A public relations committee headed by Marjorie Andrews was appointed and mapped out a series of five articles which the editor of the *Herald* agreed to print. The conference participated in two radio programs and was asked to share in several forums and discussions.

One hundred and fifty names were added to the conference mailing list during the summer, bringing the total to 880. Each new individual received a personal letter and information about the conference, and his name was promptly turned over to the zone coordinator or block leader with a request that he be invited to the next meeting.

Individuals of all races came to the office to help. There was Irene Kantner, who had read about the conference in the *Herald* and who came in regularly with her small baby, took dictation, carried the work home to do in the evening, returned it the next day when she was out walking the baby, and collected more. Laura Swabey, employed in a downtown office, frequently stopped in after her workday to pick up typing. Randall Pittman, a student at the theological seminary, dropped in and offered to cut stencils and do the mimeographing. Numbers of others volunteered their services.

Many who were just curious came to find out what the conference did, and passed on this information or remained to help. Individuals from other sections of Chicago and other cities, interested in starting similar movements, asked for information and advice.

During that first summer the Finance and Steering committees planned for the future. The temporary office space would have to be given up October 1, since the Unitarian Church had need for it. Experience had shown the importance of office operations, and conference leaders believed these should now be undertaken on a full-time basis. Somehow the money would be found.

A special budget committee decided that $11,500 would be needed for the fiscal year beginning October 1, 1950. The Finance Committee worked out plans to get it: through a series of special parlor meetings to which people of means would be invited; an approach to foundations; an appeal to community organizations; perhaps through the zone coordinators and block leaders as well.

William J. Andrews, a persuasive, distinguished looking man, was appointed a committee of one to find office space. He had to cope with an exceedingly limited budget, a tiny and rapidly dwindling bank account, and no credit rating. Ironically, it was a realtor who took a chance on the fledgling organization. John Connelly, head of the Charles Fox Realty Company, after a hurried visit to Alderman Merriam who vouched for the conference, agreed to sublease three hundred square feet at the southern end of the Fox offices. It was an ideal location. The space—in a storefront building entered from the street level—was just off the corner of two widely used business streets—Harper Avenue and 55th Street in Hyde Park. Partitions and a private entrance separated it from the real estate operation. For a rental of $70 per month, Mr. Connelly included light, heat, janitor service, and office furniture. The signing of a lease was never suggested.

Moving was simple. The typewriter, files, and office supplies were gathered up, driven six blocks from the church to the new office, a telephone was installed, and the conference was again ready for business. The executive director was employed on a full-time basis at $5,000 a year with the understanding that this would be a month-to-month arrangement for two or three months until additional funds were in sight.

"HYDE PARK-KENWOOD CONFERENCE OPENS OFFICE; EXPANDS COMMUNITY BETTERMENT PLANS" announced the *Hyde Park Herald* on October 4, as it began its series on the conference program.

"This move is part of a success story that is hard to match," wrote Rachel Goetz. "It is the story of a neighborhood trying to pull itself up by the bootstraps—and producing results." She listed them: illegal conversions reported, inspected, and acted on; rumors tracked down and neighbors given the facts; neighborhood cooperation stepped up; alleys cleaned, playgrounds organized, parties held; parking violations corrected; premises cleaned up. "The movement is growing," she reported. "It is now attracting nation-wide attention."

Most of the interest centered around concrete activities and results. But those who were closest to the movement noted that other—perhaps more significant—changes were taking place, intangibles impossible to measure. Something important was happening to the attitudes of the people the conference touched. A feeling of optimism was beginning to replace the defeatist assumption that nothing could be done. An increasing number of people were thinking of community problems as *their* problems. The big-city atmosphere of isolation and indifference was slowly giving ground to the re-creation of "a neighborhood." Individuals of differing racial groups and national backgrounds were beginning to behave like neighbors, forgetting their differences in work on common projects.

The first busy year came to an end. By the fall of 1950 the conference had a corporate seal, a program involving a thousand people, a growing number of volunteers, a reservoir of friendship and good will, some powerful enemies, a small office, one staff member, $72 worth of equipment, a bank balance of $19.01, a $900 debt, and unshakable faith and determination.

CHAPTER 6

First Steps in Planning: The Community Appraisal Study

One of the most serious of the many problems facing the conference was the urgency of developing and implementing plans to conserve and rehabilitate the area. The programs of its several committees might slow down the process of deterioration and keep residents in the area awhile longer. The inevitable decline could not be stopped, however, short of removing the blight-producing factors, rebuilding, modernizing, providing the facilities and the atmosphere essential to a desirable community.

The problems and possibilities were analyzed and investigated in and out of meetings of the Planning, Steering, and Executive committees. The production of an over-all sketch plan would be a monumental task. Technically able people served on the Planning Committee, but these volunteers could not give the time and effort that were needed.

Perhaps, Martin Meyerson suggested, some planning work might be done through the facilities of the university's Committee on Planning, under the direction of the Conference Planning Committee.

How would any plans that were drawn up be effectuated? Somehow, the University of Chicago, as the wealthiest and most powerful institution in the area, must be persuaded to invest in planning, in new housing, and in rehabilitation of the old. In August 1950, the Executive Committee suggested that Martin Meyerson plan an approach to the university administration on this basis.

The support of public agencies would have to be obtained as well. Meyerson's committee had already been working closely with Alderman Merriam and the Chicago Land Clearance Commission to determine whether it was possible to have "portions of the area declared suitable for redevelopment."

In the fall of 1950, before these possibilities could be thoroughly explored, an unexpected development brought new hope to conference leaders.

A number of public agencies and citizens' groups had begun to plan a study of the two-and-a-half square mile area north of the conference for a pilot project in redevelopment and conservation. The initiator of the study, who was to be the leading spirit in its direction, was Reginald R. Isaacs, head of the Michael Reese Hospital planning staff, a brilliantly able man, widely respected in his field. Under Meyerson's urging and the pledge of the Steering Committee to give full cooperation, Isaacs and his group agreed to extend the project to include the additional two square miles covered by the conference.

Never before had agencies and individuals of such variety and caliber joined together for a common purpose. They included, in addition to the conference and the Michael Reese Hospital planning staff, the South Side Planning Board headed by Morris Hirsh; classes of the University of Chicago, the Illinois Institute of Technology, and Harvard University Graduate School of Design; the Metropolitan Housing and Planning Council; Pace Associates, architects; Draper & Kramer, Inc., a large real estate and mortgage firm; and such public agencies and officials as the Chicago Land Clearance Commission, the Chicago Housing Authority, the mayor's housing and redevelopment coordinator, Alderman Robert E. Merriam, the Chicago Plan Commission, the Chicago Dwellings Association, the Chicago Park District. These groups, through the collaborative project which became known as the Community Appraisal Study, hoped to develop ideas that would lead to the improvement of the four-and-a-half square mile area from 31st Street to the Midway and from the Rock Island Railroad tracks to Lake Michigan on Chicago's South Side.

After a careful survey of conditions and needs, plans would be prepared for the redevelopment of the slum sections and the conservation of the Kenwood and Hyde Park regions.

The primary responsibility of the conference would be to supply information on the community through the efforts of volunteer interviewers and to handle the organization and supervision of the interviewing group, while the other agencies worked on planning and technical matters.

The small office of the conference soon became the headquarters for the housing and social survey. Scores of workers were needed. A call went out for volunteers and the response was immediate and enthusiastic. Volunteers kept the single phone tied up; a new line had to be installed. They came to the office in such numbers and with so many questions that a coordinator for the survey had to be employed. A graduate student in planning at the University of Chicago, D. Reid Ross, took on the job. His salary, as well as a good part of the cost of the total study, was provided largely by the Michael Reese planning budget. Another desk, chairs, and a table were donated, and the three staff members—Reid Ross, the executive director and the newly acquired office secretary—rearranged the furniture and themselves in their tight quarters to make space for visiting volunteers.

Conference people from the Division of Social Sciences of the university—Louis Wirth, Martin Meyerson, Herbert Thelen—joined with staff members of public agencies and private research groups to draft the survey questionnaire.

The purpose of the questionnaire and interviews was to produce as complete information as possible on the people of the area: who they were, where they came from, the size of their families, what they did, where they lived, under what conditions, the organizations they belonged to, their participation in community affairs, how they felt about living and working in the area. Among the hundred or more questions were a number directed toward determining the adequacy of existing community facilities: transportation, shopping, schools, playgrounds, parks.

Philip M. Hauser, internationally known census expert, and his assistants at the Chicago Community Inventory, together with staff members of the National Opinion Research Center (all of the University of Chicago), worked out the statistical techniques for the survey—a 4½ per cent sampling of the area—and planned the field work.

In December of 1950 planners explained the total project to volunteers, and the following month survey experts and the coordinator conducted two training sessions for them.

On a cold week end in January, the volunteers, instructions in hand, fanned out over the 4½ square miles to get addresses and descriptions of the structures in the area and the number of dwelling units in each. On the basis of their information, the sampling procedure was applied and interview assignments were made. Until the survey was completed, the conference office remained open most evenings and week ends. The coordinator, the staff, or volunteers trained in sampling and interviewing techniques, were on hand to answer questions, assign additional interviews, or put new volunteers to work.

Four months later, the first phase of the survey ended. A sample consisting of 1,600 families had been interviewed.

New training sessions began at once. Volunteers were taught to translate the information from the questionnaire into code numbers which were later to be entered on punch cards for tabulation. Leopold J. Shapiro, the new chairman of the Conference Survey Committee, who helped both to train the coders and to analyze their findings, reported to the Steering Committee that the conference could claim the distinction of another pioneering effort: it had developed the first "cottage industry" in coding. Volunteers crowded into the small office for coding lessons—only eleven at a time could fit in—did a batch of questionnaires under the watchful eyes of the trainers, and then were allowed to take work home. A few were taught to punch the code numbers into cards for tabulation of the statistics by IBM machines.

Two hundred community residents gave 25,000 hours of time

to the survey. They were housewives with previous experience in teaching, social service, and research; men in professions and offices with odd evenings to spare; young unattached men and women who considered the opportunity a great challenge. Scores of others volunteered as baby sitters to allow their friends to work more directly for the community. Students from the Illinois Institute of Technology, Roosevelt College, and Wright Junior College shared in the interviewing.

The results of their work appeared in a "Report on Housing and Social Survey" of the Community Appraisal Study, published jointly by the conference and the South Side Planning Board in the autumn of 1952. The survey findings showed that:

Eight per cent of the dwelling units in Hyde Park-Kenwood west of the Illinois Central tracks were in structures requiring replacement.

Nine and a half per cent were overcrowded; 10 per cent did not have private sanitary facilities.

The highest proportion of conversions were in two Hyde Park census tracts which ranked low in nonwhite population.

The total nonwhite population in Hyde Park-Kenwood (1951) was about 8 per cent.

Thirty-six per cent of those living in the area had moved there within the past three years, many of them lower-income whites. Even so, the median income was close to $5,000—considerably higher than the city's average.

Much of the population turnover was occuring in converted or inferior housing units.

A larger number of dwelling units than average for the city were tenant-occupied.

The proportion of family heads in professional and semiprofessional work was four times that of the rest of Chicago, although migration in and out of the community was causing a downward shift in family occupational status.

There had been a downward trend in number of persons per household, showing a decrease in family size.

The survey pointed up the liabilities and assets in the total study area. In every respect, the Hyde Park-Kenwood community was in far better condition than the more rapidly deteriorating sectors north of 47th Street. However, "the entire area is threatened by creeping blight as the result of a high rate of conversion, overuse of already aged buildings, absence of normal maintenance and repair, and failure to observe minimum occupancy standards . . ." Families seem "most disturbed by increasing physical deterioration and by the poor quality of public services and facilities."

On the positive side were a low vacancy rate, a desirable location, the high income and high occupational status of some of the recent newcomers, some physical rehabilitation and new building, absence of racial tension, the fact that seven out of ten people wanted to remain in the area, and the impressive number who had joined in efforts to improve it.

The positive factors would diminish in importance, the survey warned, "unless the present trend toward deterioration is arrested." To show how this might be done most effectively was the purpose of the total Community Appraisal Study.

Other sections of the study were being carried forward simultaneously with the survey.

Three university groups devoted a full term to the preparation of a series of alternative plans covering traffic and transit, new housing, more open space, increased community facilities, and other provisions considered desirable. Graduate students in planning at the University of Chicago, under the direction of Martin Meyerson (as chairman of the Conference Planning Committee) worked on the Hyde Park-Kenwood community itself. Plans for the total study area were developed by Professor Ludwig K. Hilberseimer and his associates at the Illinois Institute of Technology and by students and faculty of Harvard University's Graduate School of Design, under the direction of Reginald Isaacs.

For information on conditions the planners relied heavily on the preliminary findings of the survey, which were made available to them week by week, and on a physical appraisal of every structure in the area conducted by teams of real estate appraisers, architects, and engineers. The city's Building Department cooperated by extending its house-to-house inspection, originally planned for selected blocks, to the entire Hyde Park-Kenwood community.

Meyerson's students were the first of the three planning groups to complete their assignment. Their results—described in hundreds of pages of manuscript, maps, drawings, and charts—were translated by the conference into "A Report to the Community."

The production and distribution of this report were again made possible by the cooperation and devotion of volunteers. A special committee analyzed, debated, reviewed, and edited the materials. An expert typist cut the stencils. Another volunteer mimeographed them. A crew of workers stood by to assemble the pages and attach the covers. For less than $150—the cost of the paper, reproduction of maps, wrapping and postage—the first published report of the Community Appraisal Study was ready for distribution.

A letter introducing the report indicated that it was intended to stimulate thought and discussion about the future of Hyde Park-Kenwood, pointed out the importance of getting agreement by planners and the community on some kind of over-all plan to guide its development, and urged the community to reverse the pattern that had in the past led to the creation of slums by "going to work now."

A chapter covering "The Threat of Creeping Blight" investigated the facilities, services, and conditions requiring attention, including the structures in need of replacement. It warned:

At present Lake Park Avenue, parts of Harper Avenue, Cottage Grove Avenue and 47th Street form a band around our area from which blight may spread inward. Pockets of deterioration dot the area, particularly in Hyde Park, and 55th Street shows the effects of overcrowding and inadequate maintenance. A number of conversions into rooming houses and cramped light-housekeeping quarters, together with the encroachment of small factories, are taking place (here).

There is also evidence of an inward movement of near-blight along certain parts of Drexel, Ingleside, and Maryland, the streets closest to Cottage Grove, and along Blackstone and Dorchester, adjacent to Lake Park and Harper. Here a number of large apartments and single family homes have been converted into small, overcrowded kitchenette and share-bath units. Because of the excessive wear and tear now put on them, these will be our tenements of 10 or 20 years hence.

The report listed the community facilities and made tentative suggestions for improvement. Proposals included the creation, location and, where possible, the method of providing additional thoroughfares and street widenings to handle the flow of traffic; the closing off of residential streets; off-street parking; improved transportation facilities; elimination of blighted structures; constructive uses for the cleared land; a concentrated shopping center with local neighborhood convenience stores; schools, tot-lots and playgrounds.

"The approach to community conservation," the report concluded, "will have to be four-pronged":

(1) Widespread education concerning the needs of the community and the alternatives that lie before it.

(2) Community-wide organization of individuals and groups to accomplish agreed-upon goals.

(3) Encouragement of private investment.

(4) Cooperation of government at all levels.

The neighborhood's leading institutions will have extra responsibility for community leadership, just as they will have the most to gain through neighborhood conservation . . . Hyde Park and Kenwood are rich in schools, churches, and energetic business groups. Their cooperation could bring the necessary community support to a conservation program.

On June 30, 1951, copies of "A Report to the Community," together with a letter asking for reactions and advice, went out to the agencies involved in the study, to block captains, area leaders, and committee members of the conference, and to the head of every civic, religious, educational, and business organization in Hyde Park-Kenwood.

In general, the reaction to the report was positive. But the most powerful local groups—the University of Chicago administration, the Hyde Park Planning Association, the real estate men, the businessmen's organizations—remained silent.

The proposals of Meyerson's students for the Hyde Park-Kenwood community, as well as the plans for the larger area produced by classes of the Illinois Institute of Technology and the Harvard University Graduate School of Design (the latter illustrated by a twenty-foot model) were analyzed at a special showing for the agencies participating in the study. The South Side Planning Board, which housed the plans and acted as general coordinator of the study activity, thereafter received a steady stream of interested groups of citizens who viewed the alternative proposals, asked for briefings, and raised questions.

Reaction to the plans varied widely. Each proposal had a fair share of enthusiasts and critics. The proposals of the University of Chicago students in planning, less detailed and more conservative than the others, produced the least antagonism. The Illinois Tech plan, which suggested separation of residential, working, and recreational sections and an eventual reduction of the area's population by two thirds, was considered even by some of its admirers to be much too drastic. A number of the features of the Harvard plan were widely approved, but many thought that it, too, suggested changes too far-reaching and costly to be possible of achievement.

Since all the plans were, at best, tentative proposals, a continuing planning effort was essential. Reg Isaacs, who stepped into the temporary chairmanship of the Conference Planning Committee during Meyerson's absence from the country in the summer of 1951, pressed for immediate action.

"Effective planning cannot be done for small individual areas. It must take in the South Side as a whole," he urged. "This means joint action of all groups or their amalgamation, and a planning budget for the South Side of about $60,000 a year."

The idea of a federation of organizations for the redevelopment and conservation of the South Side had been mentioned in "A Report to the Community" and had the support of conference leaders, Morris Hirsh of the South Side Planning Board, and Isaacs' Michael Reese group. Much more was needed: assurance of adequate financing and the cooperation of all the leading organizations and institutions on the South Side, particularly the

University of Chicago administration. These were not forthcoming.

How could the planning program be carried forward? Conference leaders were discouraged at the failure of the Community Appraisal Study to produce the hoped-for support. They had put many months of work and faith into the study. They had counted on the power of facts and the prestige of the cooperating agencies to influence a change in attitude on the part of those local groups whose participation in the struggle for community improvement would make all the difference between success and failure. Nothing tangible had come of it.

Nevertheless, the study had important and far-reaching results. It set a precedent for a collaborative effort by public and private agencies and institutions unequaled in Chicago's history. It brought them understanding of the problems to be met and new approaches to their solution. It produced a tremendous body of information and proposals which were to provide the base for future planning. It involved people—several hundred of them—in working for their community, and the working and learning released undreamed-of potential for constructive action. It spread the story of the conference through the community, as survey interviewers called on residents. It brought new volunteers to the conference, some of whom were to become its leaders. It struck a blow against apathy by touching the imagination of many community residents and bringing them confidence and hope.

The Community Appraisal Study proved in the end to be a significant chapter in a planning story that was soon to capture the interest of the nation.

CHAPTER 7

Grass-Roots Organization and the Grass Roots *

Meanwhile, block groups had been organizing in different parts of the community. Encouraged by conference leaders, neighbors had begun to get together to work on the problems of their blocks.

The people in one block, concerned over both the appearance of a debris-littered lot and the need of their children for a place to play, disposed of the two problems by cleaning the lot and converting it into a playground.

In another block people were afraid to go out at night because of the dimness of the street lights and the frequent failure of power which plunged their street into total darkness. A new street-lighting system by the city was indicated, but this seemed unlikely in the near future. Keeping porch lights on after dark and putting fluorescent lamps in front of window shades provided a temporary solution at a cost of two cents per night. Alley lights were purchased and installed through an agreement between building owners and tenants to share the cost of equipment and electricity.

* The block organization program is described in considerable detail in "Neighbors in Action," a manual by Herbert A. Thelen and Bettie Belk Sarchet, published by the Human Dynamics Laboratory, Department of Education, University of Chicago, 1954.

The desire to beautify their immediate neighborhood, in spite of slum buildings in their midst, led neighbors in a third block in unexpected directions. Finding that grass did not thrive in their area, they were encouraged to approach a botanist for advice. The residents then banded together, bought the recommended seed and fertilizer, and the grass grew green and strong. But they could not keep it beautiful. What was the use of growing grass, they asked, when children from the overcrowded slum buildings kept trampling it down? The suggestion that an effort be made to reach the children plunged the block group into enthusiastic activity. Neighbors decided to give a party for the children. They obtained the use of a small college auditorium, a movie projector, and an operator from reluctant officials who were fearful of possible damage to the institution; they persuaded local women to bake cookies, neighborhood merchants to supply other refreshments at cost, and the conference office to obtain films; and they sent out flyers to all the block's youngsters announcing "A PARTY JUST FOR YOU—EVERYTHING FREE, MOVIES AND EATS!" Over one hundred delighted children turned up. During intermissions between movies, while the young guests munched on refreshments, they were complimented on their fine behavior and told something about the purposes of the block group and the problem of growing grass. To the amazement of college officials, the children carefully collected candy wrappers and paper cups and deposited them in trash containers, and one was heard to say as he left the building, "Gee, we didn't know about not trampling down grass; there's no fence around it."

Thereafter the lawns were no problem. The slum buildings, however, were. Some time later, members of the block organization worked with the conference in a direct attack on this problem by keeping the office fully informed of conditions and by showing up in force when cases against the slum owners came to court.

The people in a fourth block—all property owners, Negro and white—were concerned over the maintenance of high standards and jointly decided on steps to protect their interests. They agreed to consult with their neighbors if it ever became necessary to dispose of their property, shared with local real estate agents their views on the desirable use of property, and visited prospective buyers to tell them of the block's standards and invite their participation. One purchaser, rumored to be a kitchenette operator, relieved her future neighbors of anxiety when she responded to their approach by expressing enthusiasm for their program and offering to share with them her architect's plans for structural changes.

Block groups worked on a long list of additional projects:

The rehabilitation and maintenance of buildings and grounds; paint-up and fix-up campaigns; landscaping; sidewalk repair; getting the city to enforce building and zoning laws, remove abandoned cars, stop illegal parking, install traffic signs, provide crossing guards, plant trees, and improve police protection, garbage collection, and street and alley cleaning.

They worked on social as well as physical conditions:

Local option to prevent the spread of taverns; developing programs for youth; assembling facts to dispel rumors; dealing with fear and anxiety about newcomers by bringing neighbors together to get acquainted.

They set up standards governing truck deliveries, trash disposal, and the control of disturbing noise as well as property use. They held meetings to educate themselves on such assorted questions as the care of grounds, the prevention of illegal conversions, the incidence of crime, the status of law enforcement, new developments in the community.

Not all groups were equally successful. Sometimes failures could be traced to incompetent leadership, but more often they were caused by factors outside the control of individual blocks. One peculiarly difficult problem, for example, on which very few could operate successfully, was overcrowded and substandard housing. Even though many worked diligently at it, the means at their disposal were too limited to have any significant effect. Experience showed that a coordinated approach directed by the central organization was essential here and that it was unrealistic to expect success on the basis of block efforts alone. (See Chapter 11, "The Effort To Stop Blight.")

Unfortunately, when groups did not accomplish their objectives, instead of accepting the fact that their expectations had been too high, they sometimes reacted with a sense of failure so strong as to end block activity. The central organization, therefore, constantly encouraged newly organized blocks to begin on projects simple enough to promise success. As residents tackled one problem after another and learned that it was possible to solve them by working together, their confidence grew, and with it their ability to overcome the inevitable frustrations.

Pride of accomplishment produced less desirable results as well, particularly in the early stages of a block group's development: jealousy of its own autonomy; complete involvement with the affairs of the block; little or no identification with the wider community. This changed as block organizations grew in experience and training. Just as residents learned that they could accomplish more by working with their neighbors to improve their own blocks, so block groups gradually learned that by joining with neighboring blocks they could achieve results that none could manage alone. Moreover, they came to realize the extent of their interdependence. What good was it to clean up their own street if winds blew the next block's litter into it? Why have adequate lighting only on their own blocks when they had to walk across neighboring dark streets to reach home?

The beginning of collaboration by block groups on neighborhood and community-wide projects was a welcome sign of increasing maturity.

The first such effort came in the fall of 1950 as the result of concern over purse snatchings and burglaries. Several blocks joined together, secured six hundred signatures to petitions asking for increased police protection and, through the conference office, presented them to the mayor and the new police commissioner. Three teams of plain-clothesmen were promptly assigned to the area.

The fear of crime was responsible also for the development of a more far-reaching collaborative program along different lines. A series of rumors, begun by one unbalanced resident, created the impression that a crime wave was rampant in the block. Residents talked of asking the University of Chicago to provide a private police force, of raising money to hire a private watchman, of marching en masse to the police station to demand more protection. Exploration of the rumors revealed that the crime stories were imaginary. A report of a shotgun-brandishing neighbor rushing out into the night to disperse "a gang of young vandals" had no foundation in fact. An attempted burglary turned out to be a panhandler appealing for food. "Molestation" of an eight-year-old girl was resolved into a push by an eight-year-old boy. The block group promptly gave up the idea of seeking extraordinary police measures. There was, however, cause for concern over a teen-age gang which used the corner drugstore for a hangout, and a neighboring block group was invited to join in a discussion of the problem. Deciding that "kids have problems, too," the two block organizations turned from the idea of hiring a night watchman to a plan for the employment of a recreational worker to serve the needs of the entire area—if other block groups could be interested. They were. The Hyde Park Neighborhood Club agreed to supervise a recreation leader who would go out to work with the teen-agers on their own ground. The money to employ him was raised by a "street jamboree" sponsored jointly by the block groups, the conference, the Neighborhood Club, and the Hyde Park Youth Project.

Two other areas in Hyde Park-Kenwood developed similar "on-street" recreation programs. This demonstration of cooperation between area residents and youth-serving agencies in going out to young people not reached by activities centered in institutions is under study by the Welfare Council of Metropolitan Chicago as a technique for possible use by other agencies in areas throughout the city.

Other blocks joined in such area-wide activities as neighborhood clean-up projects, working with the city to make possible the mechanized sweeping of streets, the creation of joint community play lots, help to special conference committees in obtaining new and improved facilities and services.

Experience and the growth of the conference staff combined to produce more efficient ways of dealing with constantly recurring problems. Activities begun by block groups and repeated over and over again at an enormous cost in time and energy were taken over by professionals in city departments and the conference office. A few examples illustrate the increased effectiveness and the new role of block groups resulting from this change.

Because of heavy parking, most of the street cleaning in Hyde Park-Kenwood had been done by hand sweepers. Even so, parked cars had prevented the sweepers from getting at the accumulated litter along curbs and gutters. Nor could hand sweeping be done as frequently as necessary since the city lacked personnel and funds. Through the conference office, block groups solved the problem by proposing to ward superintendents and police a collaborative effort that would clear the way for mechanical sweeping. Thereafter, for many months, in one section of the community after another, the same process was repeated again and again. Block groups distributed flyers asking that cars be removed on a particular day and, as reminders, tucked notices under windshields the night before the clean-up; police blocked the streets to traffic; on the morning of the clean-up, block members routed out the owners of the remaining cars, and the mechanical sweepers came in. This seemed a needlessly laborious process, and the conference, Leon M. Despres (who succeeded Alderman Merriam in 1955) and Harry Seeberger, the ward superintendent, pressed the city to improve street-cleaning services by taking full responsibility for regular mechanical sweeping. As a result, signs posted by the city now announce the clean-up days, cars which are not removed are ticketed by the police, and their owners are fined $10; the streets are cleaner, and block groups have gratefully relinquished responsibility for a burdensome task.

The processing of housing violations similarly passed out of the hands of block members and a volunteer enforcement committee as it became evident that effectiveness demanded expert direction and a close daily working relationship with the enforcement agencies.

A number of groups had also tried, with frustrating ineffectiveness, to get property owners on their blocks to repair cracked and broken sidewalks. While residents of the block occasionally did so, it was impossible to make any impression on absentee owners. Block groups had repeatedly reported sidewalk conditions to the conference; they and the staff had notified the city's Department of Streets and Sanitation which had made an inspection and sent a notice to the owner; and there the matter had usually ended. Repairs were not made because no penalty was attached to allowing the condition to exist, and traditional procedures required aldermen to follow a cumbersome procedure: they had to ask the city individually *in each separate case* to ask the Department of Streets and Sanitation to repair the walk and assess the owner. Finally a conference staff member approached Hyde Park-Kenwood's aldermen, Leon M. Despres and Claude W. B. Holman, with a suggestion: the conference would survey the entire area for broken sidewalks and list the exact condition and location of each, if they would ask the City Council to provide funds for their repair and order the owners assessed for the cost. They agreed. Block organizations and a group of high school youngsters shared in the survey. At this date most of the sidewalks have been repaired or replaced, and a problem which once gave block groups great difficulty is now handled effectively with a minimum of effort.

While professionalization brought greater efficiency, it also relieved block groups of a number of functions they had performed for the benefit of the community. Great care had to be taken to divert the energy thus released to other constructive activities, to prevent a relaxation of effort and therefore of interest, and to impress on the people of the community that the neighborhood program depended for success on their advice, information, and action.

With experience came other changes in the approach to block problems. Residents here and there began to take more individual responsibility when they saw conditions needing correction. Having learned something about procedures, it became possible for them to act alone and immediately on problems which once had to be thrashed out in block meetings. And as their horizons broadened, they came to see their neighborhood as part of a larger community. Interest and activity spread to take in the problems of the city.

ORGANIZATION AND METHODS

Experience also brought changes in structure and methods of block organization.

In the beginning, for block organization purposes, the community had been divided into twenty zones of equal population (later reduced to sixteen), each with a "zone coordinator" responsible for organizing his zone block by block. Names of interested individuals within the zones were made available to the coordinators who tried to involve some in block leadership and all in block meetings. The coordinators met fortnightly to report on zone and block meetings, exchange ideas, receive information, and work out new approaches to problems of organization.

After a year of experimentation, the weaknesses of this operation were evident. Too much responsibility and time were required of the zone coordinators. They could not give adequate training to block leaders who had little confidence in what they were trying to do and very little contact with one another or identification with the conference. People did not want to attend block meetings unless there was a clearly stated purpose for them, and they could not be interested in a continuing group unless there was a sense of problem. It was clear, moreover, that the various areas within Hyde Park-Kenwood had different problems and that flexibility in approach and methods was essential.

The zone coordinators worked out a reorganization plan under which they abolished the zone system and divided the community into three areas on the basis of similarity and common problems. Mass meetings were then held in each area during which the problems were identified and three or four selected for study and action. At these meetings citizens were asked to attend training sessions for block leadership. Fifty-nine signed up.

Each of the three areas appointed an area executive committee and representatives to a seven member Block Steering Committee charged with coordinating block efforts.

Herb Thelen had long advocated "community clinics" to train

block leaders and help them with the problems involved in the first stages of block organization. For fifteen months, beginning in February 1952, such clinics were held regularly. (See Chapter 8.) Two former zone coordinators were made co-chairmen of the Block Steering Committee, leaving Thelen free to concentrate on leading the clinics and to serve as adviser, general guide, and trainer. His chief aide in these tasks was Bettie Belk Sarchet, a former graduate student who became his associate in the Human Dynamics Laboratory.

By 1953, when a large group of block leaders had been trained and a number of block groups had been developed, the program was again reorganized to meet newly emerging needs—helping leaders with a continuing program and broadening the interest of block groups in community-wide problems. While the clinics continued for another six months, the area type of organization was abandoned, and the original small Block Steering Committee was expanded to include all block leaders.

The new Block Steering Committee met monthly to exchange information about block projects, learn about developments within the conference and the community, coordinate projects involving more than one block, and provide leadership training when needed. An executive commttee elected by the block leaders concerned itself primarily with planning for the meetings of the Block Steering Committee, expanding the block program, and tying it more closely into the general conference structure.

Individual block groups varied widely—in history, size, membership, form of organization and attitude, as well as in maturity and type of projects undertaken.

They came into being in several ways. A concerned resident called the conference about a specific problem. If no organization existed in his block, he was invited in for a talk, told how block groups had handled similar problems, and encouraged to explore with a few equally concerned neighbors the possibility of organizing his block. Sometimes members of successful block groups urged friends in other blocks to take the initiative or, on moving into a new and unorganized area, put their block experience to use in getting their neighbors together. Where problems indicated the need for action and concerned individuals did not come forward, the conference staff tried to find possible leaders through contacts with other blocks, PTA's, churches, and similar groups and to stimulate interest by inviting them to the clinics or Block Steering Committee meetings. In every case, leadership had to be found within the block, and organization was based on concern over concrete problems.

Experience showed the need for careful planning in advance of the first block meeting by a small committee of three or four residents of the block. The most effective beginning was to agree on a date for a meeting, make personal calls on neighbors to urge attendance, at the same time mentioning some of the problems of the block and encouraging them to add to the list. The agenda for the meeting itself must be framed with enough flexibility to allow for change if necessary but with sufficient guidance to keep the group from wandering. A member of the temporary planning committee usually chaired the first meeting, pending a decision about permanent organization and the election of officers.

At one such meeting, Robert Jones, the host, was in the chair. He was a genial man, obviously pleased to have thirty-five of his neighbors in his home. He had greeted them cordially as they arrived, called the meeting to order as promptly as possible, and asked everyone to introduce himself, giving address as well as name.

"We are here tonight," he continued, "because we are interested in improving our immediate neighborhood, if we can. Before we get into a discussion of our problems, it might be helpful to hear Mr. Lockhart, leader of the —— block, which has successfully tackled problems similar to some of ours."

Mr. Lockhart told of the work of his block, relating its efforts to those of other block groups. He summarized the total program of the conference, the role of block organizations in it, and introduced Elsie Krueger, the conference block director, as the staff person who had always been available to his group for information and advice.

Jones thanked them both for being there and continued. "When several of us called on you to invite you to this meeting," he said,

"we found there were a number of problems that concerned you."
He listed them on a blackboard. "Are there any others?"

Mrs. King spoke of the garbage in a nearby alley. Mr. Reed felt
that something should be done about an intersection which had
no stop sign. These were added to the list.

"Since we can't work on all the problems at once, what priorities would you suggest?"

The group decided to begin with four: the disposition of a large
apartment house rumored to be for sale, an overcrowded building,
abandoned cars which were taking up much-needed parking
space, and a tavern said to be selling liquor to minors.

"Before we do anything," Mr. Jones went on, "we will have to
get the facts. Who would like to serve on the Building Committee
and the Tavern Committee? Who will undertake to get the location and description of the abandoned cars and report to the
police?"

Volunteers presented themselves and agreed to take the necessary action before the next meeting. Mrs. Krueger of the conference staff offered to report the garbage and traffic problems to the
appropriate city departments if Mrs. King and Mr. Reed would
supply detailed information.

"At our next meeting," Mr. Jones went on, "in addition to deciding further action on the basis of the committee reports, we
should begin to consider certain organizational matters. For example, what geographical boundaries should we set for ourselves?
How formally or informally do we want to organize? How often
shall we meet? How will we take care of our expenses? These are
all questions we should be thinking about in advance of the next
meeting. When should it be held?"

It was set for two weeks from that night. Mrs. Valerian volunteered to send out notices and others offered to call on those of
their neighbors who had failed to come.

Coffee and cookies were served after the meeting adjourned,
and neighbors stayed on to talk.

A new block organization had begun. Mr. Jones and the small
planning committee had done the kind of job block leaders were
encouraged to do.

They had invited all the people who lived on the block—by personal visits—and a good many had come. The chairman had kept the meeting moving and had drawn everyone into the discussion of problems and the decisions on action. The evening had resulted in an increase in information about the community; the beginning of friendly and useful communication among neighbors; the development of methods by which block problems could be solved cooperatively; the relief of anxiety through the knowledge that it was shared and that something concrete was to be done about it; first steps toward actual improvement of the block.

Through appointment to committees, participation in decisions, and discussion of the problems to be considered at the next meeting, people had been committed to coming again. Plans had been made to reach all those who had not been present. Many had met their neighbors for the first time, had talked with them during the social hour, and had found the experience pleasant.

In the months that followed, the block organization grew in strength and accomplishment. Its members worked on a variety of projects. They kept in touch with the activities of other blocks and of the conference as a whole. As simpler problems were solved, the block took the initiative in inviting neighboring groups to join in larger projects.

Not all block organizations were so successful nor did they operate in the same way.

Boundaries were usually decided by each block organization on the basis of common problems. In the Kenwood area of large single-family homes, block groups covered three or four square blocks. East Hyde Park, a section of sixteen blocks, united in a single organization because its problems were area-wide. A few groups began with a single large apartment building or one side of a street and occasionally spread out to cover a larger area as their interests expanded. Most organizations, however, involved the residents of buildings facing each other on opposite sides of the street.

Some blocks laid down ground rules for membership: agreement to maintain certain standards, the payment of dues, ownership of property. The conference, however, constantly urged the inclusion in block meetings of *everyone* in the area selected—tenants and landlords, those who lived in apartments and in single family homes, old-timers and newcomers, potential and known troublemakers as well as "good" citizens. Attendance at meetings varied from 6 to 150.

The frequency of meetings also varied. Some, in the early stages of organization, were held weekly or fortnightly. Other groups met monthly, two or three times a year, or only on special call.

Methods of financing activities similarly differed from block to block: token monthly dues, passing the hat when necessary, contributions for special projects, sales and carnivals for major improvements. One enterprising and imaginative group sponsored an "International Cookie Fair" featuring the display and sale of the favorite sweets of seventeen nations representing the countries of origin of the block's residents.

Blocks which had responsibility for common property and a continuing project, such as the establishment and operation of a playground, usually found it useful to organize formally, with charter, constitution, and bylaws, and the regular election of officers. Some formally voted on a full complement of officers and committees, while others asked for volunteers. Infrequently a chairman seemed to serve in perpetuity because he wanted the job and campaigned to be sure he held it or because no one else wanted it and he continued in office by default.

The conference advocated leadership by team. This way of spreading responsibility not only involved a larger number of people, thus increasing the knowledge and resources available to the block organization, but gave more assurance of a continuing program.

There was variation, too, in the attitude toward social activities. Some block groups regarded the idea with loathing, while others —finding from experience that such activities played an important part in encouraging friendly relations between neighbors—operated on a part work, part social basis. Sometimes the social time was limited to a coffee hour before or after meetings. Sometimes street dances, picnics, Hallowe'en parties were given either to raise money for special projects or just for fun.

An evaluation of the conference block program by a competent research team (in "Block Groups and Community Change" by Bettie B. Sarchet), showed a high correlation between success and the methods used. The effective methods were defined as

1. Orderly problem-solving procedures.

2. Use of own resources before calling for help.

3. Work on short-term projects even where the over-all objectives seem impossible to attain.

4. Shared leadership.

5. Continuing effort to keep membership inclusive of everyone on the block.

6. Provision for social as well as achievement rewards.

BLOCK GROUPS AND THE CENTRAL ORGANIZATION

The services of the central organization to the block groups increased as the conference staff grew. Volunteer leaders continued to help, but chief responsibility for the program was assumed first by one block director, then by two.

These professional staff members stimulated the conception of block groups and stayed with them through birth, growth, and continuing development. When block organizations declined and died in spite of every effort to keep them vital, the block directors searched out ways to bring about a stronger rebirth.

Their first service was putting interested individuals in touch with neighbors who might be willing to join in planning for a block organization. For this purpose they maintained a block-by-block file of conference members and volunteers, people suggested by them, and individuals who had been active in the community in other ways. They sat in on the initial session of these neighbors to help plan an effective first meeting, and attended their block meetings regularly for the first months and periodically thereafter to provide information and lend support. They urged block leaders to attend the training sessions and the monthly meetings of the Block Steering Committee. Between these meetings they kept in touch with block leaders, offering encouragement and guidance, reporting on developments concerning their block and on action taken by the office at their request.

Block members came into the office for help on a wide range of problems.

They didn't know how to design and produce a flyer that would bring people out to a meeting of special importance. The block director displayed samples, helped choose the wording, and had the sheet mimeographed by the conference typist at nominal cost.

What did the block director think of the newsletter they were planning to send out? Excellent! Could the office have additional copies to guide other groups?

They wanted to prepare an information sheet on who was responsible for what in keeping the block clean and what the neighbors themselves should do. Such a sheet had already been prepared. The leader was given a kit of materials on this and related problems. (See Appendix.)

A disturbing rumor was circulating; what to do? The advice was always the same: Pay a friendly call on the person involved, explain the purpose of the block organization, get the facts.

Negroes were moving into the block and panic was spreading. The block directors dropped everything to help plan a meeting, find people whose effectiveness could be counted on, and to be on hand themselves.

When necessary, inquirers were referred to other agencies or to other staff members for advice on how to attain specific objectives. If the problem required an approach to public agencies, leaders of private organizations or large property owners, the executive director, with the advice and approval of the board and any special committee that might be involved, took responsibility for action on behalf of the entire conference. This was especially true of requests for new facilities and services. In such cases, block groups frequently pointed out the need, conducted surveys, and got residents to sign petitions. These were used, together with other supporting evidence, by the central organization in obtaining necessary improvements. Thus the prestige of the conference and the wider channels of action provided through its office made the work of the block groups more effective.

For their part, the block groups were encouraged to provide the kind of information and cooperation that would ensure coordination of effort and maximum effectiveness for the conference program.

They were asked to notify the block directors in advance of all meetings so that there could be public announcement in the community newspaper (thus increasing attendance) and a staff member or volunteer observer could be present.

They were urged to send representatives to the Block Steering Committee to (1) participate in leadership training and the development of new block groups, (2) help develop program materials and methods, (3) share program ideas with all blocks and receive full information about conference activities (to be relayed to their block organizations), (4) have the opportunity through the Block Steering Committee to make recommendations for action and policy to the board of directors, (5) participate in community-wide projects.

They were invited to help in the wider program.

The Building Department is cooperating in the conference effort to prevent deterioration by making a house-to-house inspection. Block groups can help by notifying every property owner in the block that. . . ."

We have been informed that a building at the following address has been sold to ——. If you have any additional information, please notify the conference office.

Block groups differed greatly both in services received and given.

Most of them asked for guidance whenever new problems arose and welcomed the services the conference offered. A few, who sought no help, were frequently most in need of it, and the block directors tried to find ways of providing assistance and sharing in their discussions without giving offense. Some came to the conference only for technical information and did not need or want staff attendance at meetings. Others were in almost daily communication with the block directors, sought guidance at every step, and insisted on the presence of a block director at all meetings.

Staff members had to exercise self-restraint and firmness to keep from taking on responsibilities that should be left to the block or encouraging unhealthy dependence on the parent organization. Speaking of the role of the professional, Irving Horwitz, one of the block directors, said: "If he becomes too involved personally, he discourages the participation of others. His purpose should be one of guidance in terms of supplying services and information and developing self-reliance rather than of participating actively in the block proceedings. He should learn to listen, to understand, and to feel the sense of the group before making any suggestions. Even then, it is better to be asked for information than to volunteer ideas."

Several blocks behaved as if the conference were not in existence. These had organized themselves without any assistance and resented the suggestion that they cooperate with the conference. Certain others, brought into being by the conference staff, became alienated for one reason or another: disapproval of action or lack of action by the central organization; fear of domination by the conference; insistence on engaging in generalized activities not directly related to the block program; the use of methods opposed by the conference; refusal by the conference to allow its name to be used to further the private projects of individuals.

Because of these differences, there was considerable unevenness in the degree of cooperation and communication from block groups. While the record for the most part has been reasonably good and is continually improving, certain blocks failed to communicate with the conference on any matter, to participate in community-wide projects when called upon, or to send representatives to its meetings. Of the 52 block organizations active in February 1958, an average of only 40 were represented at the monthly meetings of block leaders.

This failure handicapped the development of individual block groups, the spread of the movement, and the effectiveness of the larger conference program. Without communication it was impossible to develop understanding. Without understanding, there could be neither intelligent cooperation nor enthusiasm for "the cause." Without these, support of the conference through membership could not be obtained. Without a broad membership base, the prestige and usefulness of the conference could not reach their fullest development.

A good share of the blame for the failure to identify with the conference could be laid to the central organization itself. Time and personnel were so limited that conference leaders did not always tell the block groups what they were doing, give adequate attention to the continuing personal contacts the block program demanded, nor produce news releases with the required frequency. The problem of communication was further complicated by the turnover in block leadership and in attendance at the Block Steering Committee meetings. It was especially difficult to deal with misunderstandings about the authority of the Block Steering Committee when there was lack of agreement on policy.

GROWTH AND SPREAD OF THE BLOCK PROGRAM

For the first two years, all the organizational help and training for the block program was provided by volunteers, professional and lay. Through heroic efforts they helped to initiate block activity in sixty block strips. (A block strip is one side of a street. This designation was considered more meaningful statistically because of the variation in size of block organizations.)

It was impossible, however, for volunteers to provide the continuing services and contacts the newly emerging leaders required or to keep detailed accounts of progress and problems. Beginning with the early meetings of the zone coordinators, there were repeated pleas for the employment of professional staff, but the conference budget was too limited to permit it.

In the summer of 1952, the half-time services of Beverly Brown were made possible through a grant by the Wieboldt Foundation to the University of Chicago's Human Dynamics Laboratory for training and research in block organization. After Miss Brown left in December 1952, Alice Schneider donated her services until the conference was in a position to employ Shirley Mankin for twenty hours a week. This was obviously inadequate to meet the need for staff help, but the program continued to grow. By August of 1953 there were 165 block strips organized into 37 groups.

In that month Donald Miller was employed as the first full-time block director, while Mrs. Mankin continued for a brief time as community projects adviser responsible for coordinating projects involving several block groups.

The program kept outgrowing the ability of the staff to keep up with it. Before another year was out it became evident that a single staff person could not begin to cope with the demands of the burgeoning movement. A new development made the situation crucial: the city had approved a redevelopment effort in Hyde Park that would dislocate hundreds of families. Anxiety was widespread. The need for effective communication with community residents seemed almost impossible to meet. While block organization had begun in many sections of the community, failure to consolidate gains was weakening the movement. The number of organized blocks (205 strips in 47 organizations) was misleading since it gave no real picture of the degree of organization or effectiveness. Many groups had been inactive for some time.

Transiency seemed an insoluble obstacle to block development. Leadership moved away and was replaced with great difficulty or became discouraged over constantly shifting and declining attendance at meetings. It was difficult to reach individuals and groups with whom contact had not yet been established, a problem found among the privileged and economically stable as well as in areas of high transiency and low income. Another difficulty, common in areas where there was no in-migration of Negroes, was lack of a sense of problem, even in the face of serious deterioration, and thus lack of willingness to organize. Yet wider and more effective coverage of the community was essential to the attainment of conference goals. Professional staff help was imperative.

It came. Grants from the Schwarzhaupt and Wieboldt Foundations were received and put to work at once. Two block directors—Elsie Krueger and Irving Horwitz—were employed in the fall of 1954 to take over from Donald Miller. They divided the conference territory between them and assumed responsibility for the blocks, organized and unorganized, within their geographical boundaries. With the guidance of Block Steering Committee leaders, they began the slow, painstaking task of strengthening weak groups and helping to organize new ones on the soundest possible basis. Their careful monthly reports on every block group gave a bird's eye view of problems, failures, progress, and successes.

Of problem blocks they wrote gloomily:

"Small weak group, attempting monthly meetings with poor showing. A change of leader might help."

"No activity for six months. No communication."

"Group disorganized and inactive."

"Unable to find interest in block group. Attempting to form area-wide group around interest in maintaining parkway."

Or they were cheered by signs of reviving interest and new activity:

"Block reviving activity. Reassuring. Concerned with demolition sites."

"New block chairman. Communication improved. Working on building maintenance problems."

"Gained cooperation in sidewalk repairs. Housing violations abated. Good leadership."

"Regular monthly meetings. Cooperation excellent. Working on zoning problems."

"Active group at work on tot-lot and building violations."

"Strong leadership. Group concentrating this month on parking lot problems."

"Improved intra-block communication. Involving new people."

"Held clean-up. Appeared at Council hearings on Building Code."

The formation of the East Hyde Park Council was especially heartening. This area had resisted organization for years. Its structures were for the most part in excellent condition. Many of the residents lived in elevator buildings, and the higher people were removed from the ground the less interested they seemed to be in the community. There had been no Negro in-migration. Residents in several of the blocks had met once and had then disbanded for lack of recognizable problems at the block level. Now east Hyde Park had organized on an area basis, its leaders—Martin Cohen, Frances Bentley, Martin Lieberman—were closely tied to the conference, and the group had begun active work on sidewalk and lighting problems.

Formerly inactive block groups reorganized along similar lines. A number of blocks were spurred into birth or rebirth through invitations to learn about and share in the urban renewal planning for the community. (See Chapter 16.)

In 1957 there was an average of 20 block meetings a month. When urban renewal plans were considered, there were sometimes as many as 35 or 40.

By the fall of 1958 the block program covered 85 per cent of the Hyde Park-Kenwood community. Fifty-six block groups, covering 350 block strips, were active, and four new groups were in process of formation.

Certain conditions were found to be favorable to the development of a block group, according to the evaluation of the block program by Bettie Sarchet in "Block Groups and Community Change." These are "(1) homogeneity of population with regard to social class, social position, and housing, (2) stability of population, (3) pressures due to problems of maintenance or due to anxieties about the neighborhood, and (4) problems which lend themselves to solution at the block level." However, the study also showed that it is not impossible to carry on a block program in the absence of the first two factors if the other conditions are present and the proper methods are used.

The influence of the conference block movement has been felt far beyond Hyde Park-Kenwood. People concerned with community problems in other parts of Chicago and in cities throughout the United States have shared in training sessions, attended block and staff meetings, studied instructional materials and methods, and returned home to set up similar programs.

CHAPTER 8

Developing Leadership

"Our block has something new to report," said a block leader enthusiastically to a group of leaders at one of the "community clinics" of the conference.

"You remember I reported several months ago that we were disturbed about the grounds of one of the apartment buildings? The rest of us had beautified our lawns, cut the grass, and cleaned up the litter around our places—and here was this one building looking awful, the grounds covered with weeds, the grass not trimmed for ages."

"Hadn't you spoken to the janitor several times about cleaning it up?" asked the clinic chairman, "and didn't he tell you he was too busy and to stop bothering him?"

"That's the one." The block leader nodded. "Of course he *was* busy; he has several buildings to look after. We couldn't keep on pushing him to clean up; it only made him angry. Finally we had an idea. We called on the man and said we knew how busy he was and would like to help him, so we were planning to come over during the week end and work on the grounds.

"We did—and the place looks wonderful. But that isn't all," he went on happily. "The janitor now finds time to look after the grounds himself. What's more, *he* has become a good neighbor

87

and shares with us in block work. And the rest of us learned something mighty important from the experience, too."

"I wish our experience had been as happy," said another block leader. "Ever since one of the buildings in our block changed hands, there has been such a steady decline in services that a number of the tenants are threatening to move. We are trying to persuade them to sit tight for awhile in the hope of working this out with the management. Can the rest of you give us any ideas?"

"Maybe our experience will help," said Mrs. Shire. "The tenants of the large building in which our block organization started were upset because they felt the management had not discharged its responsibilities. The management, on its side, had grievances against the tenants who, they felt, demanded a lot but did not themselves do their share of keeping up the premises. First we got the tenants together and they spelled out their responsibilities. Then we had a meeting with the management's representative and told him we understood his problems and wanted to do our share. We promised to do a long list of things—like keeping buggies and bikes out of the hallways, sweeping the porches regularly, keeping our dogs off the grounds, even planting the lawn if the manager would provide the tools and seed, and so on. He was pleased and promised that the management would do almost everything we wanted. Since then the hall stairways have been newly carpeted, the apartments are being decorated, the janitor has stepped up cleaning services, and we have a real sense of accomplishment."

"We have a different kind of success story to report," said the man to her right. "Last week the playground we've worked on for so long opened officially, even to the snipping of a ribbon by the alderman. It was a lot of work—took 40 of us to do it—get the necessary permission from the owner, clean up that dirty lot, build fences and equipment, raise money for the things we couldn't build—but you should have seen the faces of the kids when the playground opened!"

"Could you give us some help?" asked a woman in the rear. "Our children need a place to play, too. There's a vacant lot in our block, but we're not sure how we ought to proceed."

The discussion leader suggested that the two might wish to

compare notes. "It would be very helpful to other blocks," he said, "if the procedures followed in creating this playground were set down, together with any special suggestions the block group may wish to pass on from its experience." The block leader volunteered to do it.

For many months the "community clinics" provided opportunity for this kind of exchange. They were started for the purpose of training block leaders. Leadership training, however, had begun with the earliest days of the conference.

The first group to receive formal training were the "zone coordinators" responsible for seeing that blocks within their zones were organized. The methods of block organization and the training of leaders in their use were worked out through the cooperation of the conference and the Human Dynamics Laboratory of the University of Chicago.

In the spring of 1951, two training sessions were held to transmit to potential block leaders the leadership techniques gleaned from over a year's analysis and testing.

The zone coordinators' seminars, the training sessions, and subsequent block experience laid the base for the "community clinics" begun in February 1952 to provide training for functioning block leaders who needed help as well as for the fairly large number of potential leaders who had become available. Certain of the zone coordinators and block leaders, now trained resource people, joined with Herb Thelen and Bettie Sarchet in conducting the clinics and eventually led them with little or no professional help.

Every three weeks for a year, and monthly thereafter until June 1953, the clinics met at the Unitarian Church. The program followed the same general outline in every session.

Each clinic began with a welcome and an explanation of the block program's purpose. It was designed, said Thelen, to reduce anxiety, stabilize and improve the neighborhood, educate the community.

The executive director followed with a brief report on the work of the conference, the problems it was currently facing, and important new developments in the community and the city.

Block leaders then told about the work of their groups since the last clinic: problems faced, attitudes encountered, successes and failures. Questioning brought out information about effective methods as well as those which should be abandoned. The group learned, for example, that it was fruitless to debate about ideas or differences, that approval of a neighbor's origin or philosophy was not essential; working with him to get the street cleaned was.

The exchange of information among block leaders generated enthusiasm, increased confidence, bolstered morale. The leaders and student leaders helped and reinforced one another. Those in successful blocks were spurred on by the approval and praise of their associates. Those who were less successful or just starting out learned that it was possible to solve problems like theirs and were thus encouraged to go on.

The next section of the clinic was given to the training of small groups in special skills: how to start a block organization; how to hold a successful meeting; how to get improved services.

Those who were interested in starting new block groups shared in a session concentrating on "practice calls" on different types of neighbors. They "called" first on a person who played the role of a neighbor easy to persuade, interested in the community and happy to learn a constructive program was about to be launched. Next they "visited" a hostile character who was opposed to being organized, who didn't want to know his neighbors any better, who thought the community was on its last legs, and who planned to move anyway. To get him to agree to come to a block meeting, even reluctantly, was no small task. Students and resource people analyzed the methods used in both calls, suggesting how the approaches might have been improved and the points at which the resistance of the hostile one seemed to be breaking down. Success in getting people to the first meeting was in sight when they could be persuaded to share their ideas about the problems of concern to them and made to feel that their advice and help would be valuable to the group.

Other practice sessions were devoted to make-believe block meetings. Here prospective leaders learned the pitfalls to avoid and the most effective techniques for involving people, keeping the meeting going, arriving at decisions, taking constructive action, interesting people in coming again. (See Chapter 7 pages 75–77.) Where the meeting wandered, they learned how to bring it back to the point. Where it lingered on a problem past the point of productiveness, they were shown how to move it along by a concise summary of the discussion, reference to other items on the agenda, or the suggestion that a committee be appointed to bring in recommendations. The importance of getting the facts was emphasized not only as essential to any kind of constructive action but as a way of dealing with rumor- and panic-spreaders within the block group. Where it was difficult to decide on a course of action, even after the facts were in, the alternatives were presented, together with the possible consequences under each.

Still another section of the clinic provided information and know-how to those who had specific questions about next steps in action programs, the services of public agencies, the functions of community organizations, whom to call for what kind of help.

At the end of the clinic, the entire group reassembled to hear reports on problems raised, information received, and fruitful ideas developed in each of the sections.

Participants filled out forms about their experience and needs and, after the clinic adjourned, conference leaders talked with the most promising of the newcomers, encouraging them to start block organizations and offering further help.

Many visitors came to the clinics from other sections of the city and the country and from many parts of the world. Their enthusiastic comments on this demonstration of "democracy at work" brought block leaders new pride in their efforts and a deeper awareness of their significance.

When over a hundred leaders had been trained and the community clinic had served its purpose, it was replaced by the Block Steering Committee. All block leaders, or representatives appointed by the block groups, were considered members and urged to attend its monthly meetings. The training of new block leaders was delegated to a subcommittee, but the development of leadership continued through the regular exchange of information and ideas.

The executive group responsible for planning the block leaders' meetings arranged different types of programs to meet the changing needs of block groups and the conference organization. Sometimes these were devoted to reports of activities within the blocks and discussion on what to do about such problems as poor attendance at block meetings, slum operators, littered streets. When necessary, subcommittees were appointed for specific tasks. Conference committee chairmen and staff members appeared at meetings to provide information on what was being done about special community-wide problems and to suggest ways in which block groups might help. When anxiety, rumor, or the solution of specific problems indicated the need, experts were invited in to give the facts: a police officer on crime; the high school principal on the school situation; the head of the Hyde Park Youth Project on delinquency; the ward superintendent on street cleaning and garbage collection; a botanist on lawns and block beautification; planners and public officials on redevelopment and conservation.

Block leaders were also helped by materials developed over the years: a chart defining the functions of public and private agencies; sample block newsletters and meeting notices; leaflets and reprints on various aspects of conference work and on effective methods of dealing with specific difficulties. Each time the successful experience of one block or of the conference office showed the way to solve problems shared by other block groups, an account of the procedure followed was prepared for distribution. These mimeographed directions came to be known as the "How to do it" sheets. (A list of informational materials, together with samples, appears in the Appendix.)

A slide sequence with commentary on the assets and liabilities of the community and the history and work of the conference was made available for showing at block meetings. Of special help was the training manual, "Neighbors in Action," begun by the first Block Steering Committee and taken over by Herbert A. Thelen and Bettie Sarchet under a grant from the Wieboldt Foundation to the Human Dynamics Laboratory. The handbook deals with such practical suggestions as how to get started in block organization, what to say when calling on people, how to get them to come to the first meeting, how to plan meetings, and how to keep block groups going.

Difficulties and failures in training methods became clearer as the growth of the conference made it possible to employ two block directors to work closely with block groups and watch leaders in action. Periodic training sessions, they found, were helpful to those who had some potential for democratic leadership but seemed to make little impact on others. Too many who participated in these sessions failed to call initial meetings or continued to chair meetings just as they had before.

Frequently the leaders who most needed help did not get to the training sessions at all. Even potentially good leaders, however, needed more than a training session or two to cope with such difficulties as the over-verbal or antagonistic person, getting the group down to business, and starting on new projects.

Three other types of training were available: (1) orientation meetings in which the conference staff gave groups of new block leaders a briefing, answered questions, and supplied materials; (2) individual consultation on specific problems with different staff members; (3) observation of effective block meetings in action. In addition, selected meetings of the Block Steering Committee were set up around organizational problems where weakness was most apparent.

The development of block leadership was a never-ending process. The best of the leaders moved on and up in the conference organization. Sometimes leaders moved to other blocks or other cities, leaving a gap difficult to fill. In blocks which had struggled feebly along under the handicap of one-man leadership, the groups declined and died until new and able leaders could be identified to bring them to life again.

The problem was further complicated by the difficulty of involving the new people who came into the area. Different in background or social and economic status from the older residents, sometimes distrustful of their new neighbors, sometimes fearful of taking the initiative because of their newness, they could not be persuaded to take leadership or to share in the meetings if others did. It was equally difficult to persuade old-time residents, who felt little bond with the newcomers, to try to work with them in a block program. To ferret out leaders to get a new block going or an old one reactivated, staff members used every contact possible, sometimes talking with dozens of people over periods varying from one to six months.

With potential leaders, the training process had to begin again. Ideally this process should begin before the first block meeting and include thorough information on community problems, orientation on the work of the conference and the need to support it, as well as training in leadership skills.

The need for leaders was not confined to the block effort. Every phase of the conference program called for leadership, and able new people were constantly being sought. They were found in any number of ways.

At block meetings certain individuals, not necessarily the leaders, showed imagination and sensitivity with difficult group members or had a gift for quietly stimulating others to act; Mrs. Williams had done an outstanding job of organizing a tot-lot, and would be a natural for the Recreation Committee; Robert Mason's demonstrated interest in research might be useful on the Planning Committee.

Conference members, in attending meetings of other organizations, met individuals who were leadership material because of their ability to think clearly, make careful judgments, or encourage constructive participation.

One committee member sometimes suggested another: "Joe Schneider has just moved into the neighborhood. He's a young lawyer, interested in the community, who might be willing to help out on the Legal Panel."

The Nominating Committee talked with educational and religious leaders, heads of business and service organizations, as well as with conference block and committee members in search of suggestions.

Anyone who showed sufficient interest and initiative to call the office for information, help, or advice, might be a leadership possibility. An office volunteer or a committee member who handled himself well in different situations might make an excellent committee chairman.

There was Babette Brody, a housewife who learned about the conference through K.A.M. Temple. She offered to help and began with office tasks. A short time later she became the conference observer at the housing court. Once or twice a week for many months she went to court, following every housing case in the conference area, keeping the office informed of developments and, when necessary, acting as liaison between the inspectors, the corporation counsel, and the community. Her knowledge of the functioning and problems of the courts and the Building Department became so thorough that, after the conference formed its Legal Panel, she served as one of the consultants. With closer acquaintance, other talents appeared. She had imagination and a flair for writing. She became chairman of the Public Relations Committee and a member of the board of directors.

There was William L. Frederick, research director for the Council of State Governments, a quiet, scholarly person not much given to participation in community affairs until he happened to attend a block meeting in 1953. He volunteered to work on a block project and from then on his rise was swift. The group elected him to its executive committee, then as its chairman. His contributions to meetings of the Block Steering Committee, at which he acted as his block's representative, led to his election to the board of directors. During this service, conference leaders and staff noted his objectivity, his balanced approach to problems, his careful weighing of facts before reaching conclusions, and his ability to clarify complicated issues. In January 1956, when planning for the urban renewal program was well under way and it was essential to create citizen understanding and participation, Bill Frederick's qualifications were needed. He was made chairman of the Planning Committee, one of the most important posts in the organization.

Many leaders similarly developed from within the ranks of block groups.

Victor Towns, a railroad dining car waiter, first became interested when he attended a meeting on urban renewal in a block adjacent to his. Thereafter, he visited the conference office every time he was in town to work out ways of reactivating his own block group. Through a tremendous job of establishing communication and preparing and distributing newsletters and fact sheets at his own expense, he built a strong and effective organization and saw to it that complaints were handled with dispatch. Vic Towns became chairman of the Block Steering Committee.

As a result of the experience and knowledge acquired in the conference operation, a number broadened their interests and horizons and extended their leadership to other causes in the community and the city. The records are full of examples, but it is possible to give only a few.

Henry McGee, a supervisor in the post office, became concerned about deterioration in the block in which he had bought a building. He got his neighbors together and formed a block organization. Setback after setback only spurred him on to greater effort. His leadership qualities became evident at meetings of block leaders. He became chairman of the Block Steering Committee, a member of the Real Estate Committee, a member of the board of directors, and finally a vice-chairman of the board. Other groups began to seek him out. He became a director of the Hyde Park Neighborhood Club and the Kenwood Redevelopment Corporation. Today he is one of the ablest and most useful leaders in the community.

Douglass Turner was another who rose from the ranks. He had begun as a block leader, become a widely sought resource person for other blocks, co-chairman of the Block Steering Committee, a member of the board, and one of its vice-chairmen.

"Strange," he said one day, "most of my leisure now seems to be taken up with community work. In the days when I had much more time I wouldn't have thought of spending it on PTA problems, for example. Now that I've become so active in the conference, I seem to feel more responsibility for general community affairs."

Doug Turner's involvement in the conference did more than change his views and his leisure-time habits. It changed his career. He had been a teacher, a vocational adviser, and a real estate broker. His work with the conference led to an offer of employment by the Chicago Commission on Human Relations. Today he is director of its Community Services Department.

Frank Zundel is another young man whose development within the conference opened up wider areas of service. He first became interested when he attended a meeting in a neighboring block. A conference scout relayed his name to the office. Soon after his own block was organized Frank Zundel became block chairman and eventually chairman of the Block Steering Committee. His obvious gifts for dealing sympathetically with people in difficult situations led the conference staff to suggest to the Chicago Land Clearance Commission that he be employed to handle the commission's relocation services in connection with the Hyde Park redevelopment program (discussed in a later chapter). Within two years he became administrative assistant to the executive director of the commission.

Experience with the conference led to other changes of vocation. Charlotta Evans, a block leader who had worked in personnel jobs, became block director for the South Shore Commission, a new community organization. Edgar Orloff, another block leader whose experiences in Hyde Park-Kenwood sharpened his concern about race relations, left his work as a newspaperman to become public information officer of the Governor's Commission on Human Relations. Albert N. Votaw, also a newspaperman who served on the Public Relations Committee of the conference, became director of a North Side community organization.

Since the day in late 1951 when Calvin P. Sawyier, a bright young lawyer, accepted the chairmanship of the Conference Enforcement Committee, his public service career has brought him wide recognition as well as increasing responsibilities. He began his work with the conference by creating a panel of lawyers to provide the community with advice and guidance in dealing with violations of the building and zoning codes, a panel he still heads. In this capacity he worked with city officials in the Law Department and other public agencies. He became a vice-chairman of the conference. The South East Chicago Commission, formed in 1952, later asked him to head its enforcement committee and also elected him to a vice-presidency. He took leadership in drafting amendments to city codes and new legislation which have since become law.

Some of the leaders were self-made people with natural intelligence who had never had an opportunity for higher education: a laborer whose good judgment and performance as a block leader put him on the Nominating Committee; a widow with four children, supported by public funds, who led her neighbors in improving conditions on her block; a domestic worker who was selected for leadership in the membership drive.

Those who became leaders of the conference were drawn from many races, creeds, and national backgrounds. Although they came from different economic and social groups, the majority were naturally middle-class, middle-income, and more or less well educated since they reflected the community in which they lived. Among them were experienced leaders who needed only to adapt their talents to the new cause; people with recognized ability who had no experience of leadership; and the much larger group with neither special skills nor leadership experience who had tremendous potential for development. In one way or another all of these people came to be leaders of the conference.

And, increasingly, as professionalization replaced some of the earlier volunteer efforts of the conference, its leaders began to take a place in activities relating more and more directly to city-wide improvements.

CHAPTER 9

Organizational Growing Pains

INTERNAL ORGANIZATION AND THE DEMOCRATIC PROCESS

The infant organization grew in all directions at once. New and changing problems demanded such growth. The founders of the conference, recognizing the need for flexibility and freedom to experiment, had not handicapped the conference with a rigid organizational structure. The first bylaws permitted wide latitude, and these were amended whenever necessary. Periodically, programs and structure were examined and improved.

If, for example, citizens were to do an effective job of helping the city deal with violations of building and zoning ordinances, they needed legal information and guidance. A panel of twenty-five volunteer lawyers was formed.

The Committee on Maintaining an Interracial Community was set up to work out new approaches to stabilizing the area on an interracial basis.

As specific community facilities—such as schools and parks—became serious problems, the subcommittees which had dealt with education and recreation were reconstituted to become major committees of the conference. Their original parent—the planning-working group known as the Community Organizations

99

or Community Facilities and Services Committee was dissolved, since its other subcommittees no longer had functions to fulfill.

Another planning-working group—the Community Survey Committee—was similarly abandoned in 1953. A standing committee was unnecessary; specific surveys could be conducted when the need appeared.

When the South East Chicago Commission (see Chapter 13) proved better equipped to deal with police affairs and real estate interests, the conference relinquished its committees on crime and police protection and real estate. Several years later, when the real estate problem demanded serious attention by the conference as well, a strong new committee was created.

By 1952 the conference had nine functioning committees; by 1957–1958 there were sixteen. The original four planning-working groups had become seven: Block organization (the Block Steering Committee), Planning, Maintaining an Interracial Community, Real Estate, Public Schools, Parks and Recreation, Enforcement (or Legal Panel). The programs evolved by these groups and approved by the board of directors were implemented by the staff and hundreds of volunteers with the help of nine administrative committees: Executive, Nominating, Budget, Advisory, Finance, Membership, Public Relations, Publicity, and Personnel. In addition, temporary committees and subcommittees were created from time to time to deal with special problems.

The board of directors increased in number from the original Steering Committee of 22 to 33 and then to 36, plus all committee chairmen who were asked to serve ex officio if they had not been formally elected to the board.

The speed of the organization's growth, and the advent of a new community organization in 1952 created grave internal questions for the conference.

What kind of representation on the governing body would ensure the maximum democratic participation consistent with informed action?

How much limitation should there be on the authority and responsibility of conference committees, and what should be their relationship to the board of directors?

How could the different parts of the conference be coordinated into an effective operating whole? How should the vital problem of communication between committees, block groups, the board and the staff be handled?

There were no simple answers.

Questions of democratic participation in the affairs of the conference and adequate representation of different groups on the board of directors were especially difficult. The Nominating Committee, made up of four members of the board and three chosen from the community at large, tried to present to the membership for election a slate of nominees representing the different economic, occupational, racial, and religious groups, the several geographical sections, and the various interests in the community. Members were given an opportunity to add to the slate by petition, and information about the background and qualifications of each nominee was mailed to the membership before the election. To ensure turnover, a three-year limitation was placed on the term of board service.

While board members were expected to serve as individuals rather than as representatives of special organizations, interests, or groups, it was felt that their outside associations would enable them to contribute experiences and points of view that would add greatly to the information, understanding, and joint wisdom of the board. Unfortunately, it was not always possible to secure this kind of representation. At first local businessmen were reluctant to serve. Until 1956 repeated invitations to members of the University of Chicago administration were also declined. While well-educated, middle- and upper-middle income people, both Negro and white, had been well represented from the very beginning of the conference, the same could not be said of certain newcomers to the area—particularly Negro workers of lower-middle income who had little formal education and who were just beginning to own property. This was not for lack of trying. Leadership from within this group rarely came forward.

An outstanding exception was a Negro millwright who became a conference leader. He said, "I know just the kind of people you are talking about—I'm one myself. I never saw the inside of a college except to paint a wall. Like me, most of the people you're trying to reach were raised in a slum and managed by guts and hard work to make down payments on a house or apartment building. I just don't think you can get the kind of representation you want from this group—not yet anyway. Most of them would be ill at ease on the Nominating Committee or the board. You wouldn't get their point of view simply because they wouldn't be willing to talk. Most of them are laborers, tired at night, not used to thinking about anything but making ends meet. They just aren't able to think in abstract terms.

"I don't know how you get my sort of people involved," he added, "except by the intensive organizational work the conference staff put into my block. I do know that a real educational job will have to be done before they are placed in policy-making positions."

His view was shared by other Negro leaders.

Another troubling question had to do with representation by block groups. Were they tied into the conference structure as closely as they should be? Was their thinking adequately represented on the board of directors? Some felt not, in spite of the fact that a high proportion of those elected to the board each year were block leaders.

It was suggested that block groups be given power to elect a certain number of representatives directly to the board or that the Block Steering Committee be allowed to do so, without reference to vote by the conference membership. A special committee set up to review block organization structure in relation to board membership advised against this: block groups did not have to conform to any standards; anyone could attend block meetings and share in decisions for block action; any group calling itself a block organization was entitled to representation on the Block Steering Committee. This informal operation was important as a means of encouraging participation. The Block Steering Committee was essentially a channel of communication and therefore did not require a tightened organization.

"Integrating the block groups more closely with the conference might be accomplished," the committee stated, "(1) by giving the conference some control over the block groups and (2) by giving the block groups some legislative or elective power in the conference. . . . The administrative difficulties in chartering and enfranchising block groups and the change of emphasis which might result," the study concluded, "would seem to outweigh the advantages of making the block groups a formal part of conference structure."

In the end the Nominating Committee dealt with the question of representation by encouraging everyone in the community to share in the quest for board members. Articles soliciting recommendations appeared in the *Hyde Park Herald,* in organizational bulletins, and in the conference newsletter which went to all members. Block leadership was given special consideration in selecting nominees.

Other recurring problems had to do with the desire of certain committees to take independent action, and their belief that policy decisions of the board should invariably follow their recommendations. Sometimes the board failed to approve committee recommendations because they might imperil some other aspect of the conference program. They might also needlessly alienate public officials or jeopardize the conference's tax exempt status—for example, sending delegations to "demand" action by public officials, holding mass meetings to put forward special points of view, picketing City Hall, petitioning state legislators on particular legislation. Negotiations in the name of the conference on matters of general public concern could be damaging if carried out by over-aggressive uninformed representatives too personally involved to be objective. These problems were aggravated by the the creation of other agencies, the development of a planning program for the community, and the need to correlate the work of all groups. (See Chapter 15.)

A major cause of difficulty lay in the structure of two of the conference committees—the Public Schools and Block Steering committees. Unlike other conference committees whose members were appointed by the conference chairman and who were supposedly committed to the total conference program, these two drew their membership from other groups.

The Public Schools Committee was made up of representatives elected by the local PTA's, representatives of the school administration and, in the early days, any others the committee wished to add. By 1953 the committee included representatives from the six schools serving Hyde Park-Kenwood and representatives from four schools in the neighboring Woodlawn and Oakland communities. Most members were not members of the conference, were not informed about all of its efforts, and some did not live in the area in which the full conference program was concentrated. Their primary allegiance was to their individual schools. These people, who knew most about the schools, were the logical members of the Schools Committee and it was important to unite them for the purpose of meeting community-wide school needs.

The committee was outstandingly effective. (See Chapter 12.) A number of its members were unusually able, hard-working people, concerned about the seriousness of the school situation and militantly determined that action should be taken quickly. They felt hampered by restrictions on their power to act. The committee believed that it should elect its own chairman; that it should deal directly with officials of the Board of Education on all matters related to school policy, and that when the conference board rejected their recommendations it was due to "lack of confidence" rather than the need to balance their proposals against other considerations.

The difficulty seemed to be concerned not with goals for the schools, but with methods for attaining them. At one point, for example, the Schools Committee considered sending a delegation of two hundred to impress the new school superintendent with the community's interest in more and better schools. The board recommended instead that a small representative group call on the new superintendent, listen to his ideas, talk over the community's school problems, and ask for help, perhaps indicating that a group of two hundred had wanted to visit him as evidence of community interest. This minor matter was quickly settled, but sometimes disagreement flared into anger and once individual members suggested that the committee withdraw from the conference.

A specially appointed committee studied the structure and functioning of the schools group; its recommendations were adopted by the board. A major change was the addition of two members—a conference vice-chairman and a school authority not involved with any of the local schools. These, plus the chairman of the Schools Committee, provided three members of the committee selected directly by the conference and responsible to it who would be expected to create understanding of the larger conference program and the role of the committee in it. The advisory nature of the committee was clarified.

The Block Steering Committee was made up of members chosen by the block groups. For some time this created no special problems. When the demolition and redevelopment of certain areas were proposed, however, controversy began. Leaders of affected blocks brought their concerns to the Block Steering Committee and, through a misunderstanding of the committee's function, pressed for a vote on general policy matters. Agitation developed with the refusal of the board to allow the majority vote of block leaders present at any meeting to decide policy for the entire conference. The board was accused of top-down rule. It was said that the conference was a two-headed organization with the board and office on one side and the block groups on the other.

Members of the board, on the other hand, pointed out that the Block Steering Committee could not reasonably be expected to make policy. Not all members of the conference lived in organized blocks. Thus any policy made by the Block Steering Committee would not represent the conference membership, nor would it represent all the block leaders, since many were not present at Block Steering Committee meetings. In voting, were block leaders representing themselves alone or the opinions of the members of their block organizations? If the latter, how was that opinion arrived at? Even if block leaders knew and conscientiously tried to share with their block groups the issues facing the community as well as the facts about particular proposals, the fluctuating attendance at block meetings made it impossible for everyone to be sufficiently informed at any given point to decide policy intelligently. Moreover, the majority of the block leaders, as well as their constituencies, were not members of the conference, their primary interest was in the block in which they lived, and they could not therefore be expected to make judgments for the wider community.

Questions of grave import could not be settled by a public opinion poll or a majority vote outside the informed central governing body. "The conference itself would never have been formed if we had sought the opinion of the majority of the community," said a member of the board. "While the board of directors must always weigh community opinion, it is the function of leadership to guide as well as to follow. Democracy does not mean that everyone must decide everything. Certain responsibilities have to be delegated."

The board of directors held joint meetings with its committees to create understanding of the function, role, and responsibilities of each group. It was made clear that the board was the sole policy-making body. It relied on all the committees for guidance and recommendations, but retained the right to make final decisons. It reserved the right, too, to work with the executive director on all contacts with top officials. Block groups could do whatever they wished in the name of their own blocks. The PTA's could take individual action on behalf of each of their separate schools. But no committee could act on behalf of the conference unless the program of action had been approved in advance by the board. Each committee was invited to draw up a statement of function and program to be submitted to the board for approval.

Coordinating the activities of the many committees, block groups, the board and the staff and developing communication between them presented great difficulties.

An increasing number of questions demanded thoughtful consideration by a central coordinating group before any action could usefully be taken.

If, for example, real estate transactions resulted in the illegal conversion of an already dilapidated, overused building and a complete change in occupancy from white to Negro, which of five different groups should take action—the block groups in the affected area; members of the Legal Panel; the Planning Committee; the Real Estate Committee or the Committee on Maintaining an Interracial Community? Should they work out a joint approach or should the conference act alone? Obviously nothing but harm could come of an uncoordinated effort with each group taking independent action. It would hardly do for the block groups to seek the cooperation of building owners on a friendly, neighborly basis while at the same time city inspectors appeared as the result of pressure by the conference office. Nor would it be wise for the Committee on Maintaining an Interracial Community to call on building owners who had already been seen by block people. To have the Legal Panel press for correction of costly violations might be a needless waste of money if the Planning Committee took the position that the building should be demolished. And so on.

As new agencies joined in the struggle for community improvement and far-reaching physical changes were planned, the need for effective coordination became even more urgent. The schools people wanted more schools, the recreation people more parks and playgrounds, certain block groups more housing, other block groups more green space, still others more parking facilities, while the Planning Committee and the board faced the problem of weighing the many needs and supporting a program which would provide an adequate balance of them all. (See Chapters 15 and 16.)

Most of the early problems of internal organization could have been resolved more readily had there been adequate communication. In theory, the chairman of the Block Steering Committee and the staff were the communicating links between the block groups, committees and the board. Through their attendance at board and committee meetings and their office experiences, they were expected to filter down to block groups information on the work of committees and to bring back to the board and other committee chairmen the suggestions of the block organizations. This did not always work. When there was only one staff member it was impossible for her to attend every meeting. Some block groups never reported. The committee chairmen did not always keep their own groups fully informed. People were sometimes absent from the meetings at which their chairmen did report and acted without knowledge of what had gone before. Frequent and full communications by mail were expensive.

As difficulties were identified, steps were taken to remedy them. To supplement the staff, observers from the Block Steering Committee were asked to cover block meetings. Leaders absent from Block Steering Committee meetings were brought up to date through the minutes of the meetings and a special block newsletter. The chairmen of different committees made periodic visits to meetings of block leaders to report in detail on their programs. The board minutes were summarized for block leaders and on occasion the board held joint meetings with individual committees. All committee chairmen were selected with greater care and were made members of the board of directors. Several vice-chairmen were added to the list of officers, with special responsibility for working with certain of the committees. In addition, where the work of committees seemed closely related to one another, direct liaison was established between them through the exchange of membership. Thus the chairman of the Schools Committee served on the Planning Committee, together with a representative of the Parks and Recreation Committee. Representatives of the Block Steering Committee were placed as observers on each of the program committees. In a further effort to improve understanding, the board meetings, always open to the membership and local leaders, were held in a different section of the community each month.

Slowly the gaps were filled. Although coordination and communication continued to be problems, both improved greatly.

THE ROLE OF THE PROFESSIONAL STAFF

As other communities began to form similar organizations, they turned to the conference for advice and help. One question frequently asked dealt with the qualifications of professional staff members. What kind of training should be sought by community organizations just getting under way?

The professional staff of the conference through the years had

had education or experience in a variety of areas: race relations, teaching, housing, social work, political science, real estate, and administration. They might have come from planning, community organization, group dynamics or related social science and education fields. In general, a broad education and some knowledge of municipal government were helpful. Where new and unpredictable developments were constantly taking place, however, character and personal qualifications were far more important than professional skills. Flexibility, good judgment, imagination, objectivity, patience, almost inexhaustible energy, the ability to learn from experience and to work creatively with others, a deep interest in people, leadership qualities, and dedication to the goals of the conference were essential. If a person had these or a reasonable combination of them, technical knowledge and general information could be acquired.

In the early days of the conference, however, neither personal qualifications nor the required skills were clearly defined. Staff members had to learn as they went along. Since there were no precedents to follow, it was necessary to adjust to each new crisis, to think quickly over the range of possibilities and to arrive at a decision. Should the Executive Committee be called together to advise on action or should the office take responsibility for trying to reconcile a conflict situation? Was the crisis symptomatic of a deep-seated problem that required committee study and recommendations for long-range handling? Should outside agencies be called in to help or would this encourage publicity which might hurt community morale? With committees demanding immediate attention to problems of seemingly equal importance, how could priorities be assigned without creating resentment? Gradually the role of the staff and the pattern of their responsibilities took form.

The professional worker in the conference (at first only the executive director and later other staff members) had four major responsibilities. The first of these responsibilities was sharing in policy making and program development. The staff worker was expected to know the problems of the area and to make recommendations for their solution on the basis of the best advice he could get.

The second responsibility—implementation of the program—involved a variety of activities. Some of these called for giving leadership in setting up committees and guiding them and the board in carrying out the program, while others demanded individual handling. Working relations with public officials had to be developed. To achieve cooperation, the community had to understand the nature of its problems, the goals of the conference, the steps needed to reach those goals, the tools available, and the part it might play. Once understanding was secured, it was necessary to involve people in the actual work and to stimulate volunteer leadership. Methods had to be found to deal with all of these —education, involvement, leadership development. (See Chapters 8 and 10.) It was also essential to interpret the policy laid down by the board of directors to volunteers, to committees, to the wider community, and to city-wide groups. And program implementation called for a high degree of coordination. One of the major responsibilities of the professional staff, therefore, was to see that the work of one committee was related to that of the others and to help in the reconciliation of different approaches through clear and competent explanations of the considerations involved.

The third major responsibility was administrative: budgeting for the program, frequently helping to finance it, seeing that informational materials were prepared and distributed, advising committees and the board (sometimes when such advice was not sought), deciding which aspect of program activities should be given priority in time and money within the framework of board policy and, as this became necessary, selecting, training, and supervising professional staff members.

All of these roles had public relations implications, but the staff had additional public relations functions as well—and this was their fourth role. They were expected to keep people informed and inspired through continuing personal contact, frequent written communications, attendance at any number of meetings, and speaking before interested groups.

No person could play each of these roles with equal vigor and success. This was simply the ideal everyone reached for.

In the process of reaching, the worker had one other role to play—that of the learner. All members of the conference staff had a great deal to learn. Indiscreet remarks and their repercussions taught them the value of discretion. They learned that to most outsiders the professional staff person *is* the organization he represents and that he must be careful about speaking as an individual on community matters lest his personal opinion be taken for the position of his board. They could not permit themselves the luxury of discouragement in public, for if they did not believe ways could be found to conquer seemingly insoluble difficulties, how could others be expected to believe it? They evaluated and re-evaluated their mistakes in the hope that they might distill from errors in judgment or strategy the wisdom they had to have to guide future decisions and actions. They studied the problems and programs of other organizations in an effort to work as effectively as possible with them, and to keep abreast of developments in fields related to theirs.

They had to learn to view their own program objectively. In this they never really succeeded. Along with their frustrations and ulcers, they developed a tremendous pride in the accomplishments of the conference and an undeviating loyalty to its objectives. Their enthusiasm was evident to all and had the advantage of drawing people into the cause—but there were disadvantages as well. They had to keep fighting the danger of smugness, self-satisfaction, and arrogance. With other groups constantly turning to them for guidance, they had to keep reminding themselves that they still had a lot to learn.

DEVELOPING RELATIONSHIPS WITH PUBLIC AGENCIES

Hyde Park-Kenwood was singularly fortunate in its aldermen. Throughout its history the conference had been able to count on their support and guidance.

Building effective working relationships with public agencies and appointed officials, however, demanded endless time and patience.

The political environment of Chicago had been shaped by a long tradition of patronage before competence. Whether the mayor has been a Republican or a Democrat, a city employee's ability to carry his precinct has had much more to do with his job tenure than his ability to supervise a street-cleaning crew or his vigor in prosecuting a slum landlord.

Too often even decisions of law enforcement agencies were based not on the facts but on the need to repay political favors or to side with members of the home team.

Conscientious city department heads, finding it difficult or impossible to get rid of incompetent employees, often had no choice but to try to put them in jobs where they could do no harm. They could not be dismissed because they brought the party too many votes on Election Day.

The close relationship between city services and party politics also often led officials to bend over backwards to avoid offending voters even when they were acting against the public interest.

It was no wonder that many officials looked upon citizens' groups not only as nuisances but also as natural enemies. The reforms and improvements these organizations insisted on were in conflict with the code and rules it seemed necessary to follow to attain political success.

In some instances the attitudes of citizens' organizations served only to widen the breach. Too often city services and the conduct of government received no praise even when it was deserved. Instead citizens subjected officials to a barrage of criticism, attacks in the press, irate calls on the mayor. The dedicated public servants—and there were a number—sometimes suffered vilification along with the others, and this only added to the conviction that citizens were ignorant and unjust, a necessary evil that had to be tolerated. Nor had direct experience with most citizens' organizations given public officials much reason to rely on their accuracy or good sense. The complaints of citizens' groups were sometimes so vague as to make it impossible for authorities to act. Their demands for improvement frequently seemed unreasonable to harassed administrators who felt they were doing as well as possible under limitations of budget and personnel.

The resentment grew inward because it had to be hidden. Citizens in groups were also voters, and public officials could not afford to offend them. So an uneasy truce prevailed. When representatives of citizens' organizations arrived at certain of the city offices to complain, they were received politely, listened to courteously, given vague promises, and quickly ushered out. Sometimes these visits resulted in minor improvements; more often not, and when they did not antagonism grew.

Most of the citizens' groups viewed government departments with unconcealed cynicism. It was not uncommon to hear people who had no firsthand knowledge of the problems or operation of the city government discourse at length on "corruption at City Hall." Citizens who continued to demand improvement seemed to do so with no real hope of success. Expecting the worst, they usually found it. Not infrequently they resorted to threats: if the commissioner or director of this or that did not take immediate action, they would "call in the papers," "set up a 'mass demonstration,'" "throw the rascals out" at the next election. They were, in a very real sense, defeated by their own attitudes for, by looking upon city officials as adversaries, they did not encourage them to become the partners they should have been.

Many officials, sometimes even the most courageous and competent, were part of the same defeat. They were not highly paid, and salaries could not in any case make up for the constant criticism directed their way both by those threatening the public interest and by the citizens they often tried to protect. Expecting criticism, they were antagonistic to suggestions of citizens' groups. The widespread belief, openly expressed, that they were incompetent or dishonest made those who were, defensive and hostile, and angered and embittered those who were not. Whether or not they merited the respect of the public, many were aware that they did not have it, and their respect for themselves suffered.

Conference people were unaware of these undercurrents when they set out to make official contacts. Well-meaning friends were generous with advice on the best approach. "Make it clear from the beginning that you intend to see some changes made." "Make them understand that you mean business." "You won't get anywhere at all with ——; go over his head to the mayor." "The only thing they respond to is pressure and force. Threaten them with what you'll do if you don't get results."

Conference leaders, however, believed that people should be approached with the assumption that they wanted to discharge their responsibilities and that failure to do so might be caused by factors outside their control on which they needed help.

It was in this spirit that all calls were made.

A delegation was berating the police captain as the executive director waited to see him for the first time. When she was finally ushered in, the captain was on his feet, flushed and angry, a "what-in-heaven's-name-do-*you*-want?" expression on his face.

"I came in to get acquainted," she said, "and to tell you how impressed our organization was with the magnificent way your officers handled that teen-age racial fight."

He sank slowly into his chair and was silent for a long moment.

"Do you know something?" he said finally, "I've been a police officer for thirty years, and this is the first time a citizen ever told us we'd done a good job.

"We get enough criticism to drive a guy nuts, but praise—no. People expect around-the-clock protection, but are they willing to pay more taxes to get it? They expect the police to risk their lives for them, but where are those same people when attempts to raise the low salaries of our men are voted down by the City Council? Do we have the respect of the public?—you know the answer to that. Is it any wonder we have such a hard time getting men? Give me one good reason why anyone in his right mind would want to be a policeman!"

The pent-up bitterness had poured out in a rush. He pulled himself up sharply. "I shouldn't be shooting my mouth off," he said. "You don't want to hear my tale of woe."

"On the contrary," was the answer, "people just don't know about your problems. They are worried about crime, and they can't be expected to act intelligently if they don't have the facts. The organization I represent believes that you and your men want to do a good job. If anything stands in the way of it, this is a responsibility the people of the community must share with you."

114

They talked for more than an hour, exchanging information on the operation of the police department, the functioning and program of the conference, and developing their first plans for a cooperative approach to community problems. In the months and years that followed, a mutually productive relationship was established. (When the South East Chicago Commission was formed in 1952 it took responsibility for direct contact with the police department on all questions relating to crime, and thereafter the conference worked through the commission and in cooperation with it on these matters.)

Establishing relations with the district police officer was simple compared to the problems of working with most city departments, and especially with the Building Department. The inner organization of this department was more complicated, its responsibilities were greater, and it was constantly being harassed by city-wide as well as local improvement associations. Moreover, the head of the department was reported to be even more allergic than other officials to citizens' groups—"damned busybodies," he was said to call them privately. "Their complaints," he once said, "go into the wastebasket as soon as we get them."

It was no wonder that the request of the executive director of the conference for an appointment with the building commissioner, though granted, was greeted with something less than enthusiasm. The commissioner was wary. In spite of the friendly approach, he obviously suspected that his caller had something up her sleeve, and he fenced skillfully.

"I'd like to work more closely with your group, as with all organizations," he said, "but there is such a shortage of personnel that it's impossible. We can't handle the complaints we are already getting—and a lot of them aren't even legitimate—just drag my men out on wild goose chases."

"We could help you there and reduce your burden," was the reply. He was told about the block groups, that complaints would be checked before they were reported, that the conference could provide witnesses to help his inspectors in court cases. The conference recognized that the problems were tremendous, but believed the citizens and their officials should form a working partnership to solve them. "As a public servant, we assume you share this view. The question is, how do we work together to get results?"

The problems on both sides were explored and some possible areas of action considered. At the end of their talk the commissioner had unbent but was not convinced.

"Let's talk about it again," he said heartily.

"I'd be glad to," was the answer, "but we don't want to take your time unnecessarily. "Why don't you just put us in touch with those members of your department who handle the different building and zoning matters and, as a first step, let us arrange to deal directly with them unless questions of special urgency demand your attention?"

He agreed.

From then on, through his administration and those of two successors, cooperation grew. It was not easy sailing.

In spite of surface cordiality, officials at the Building Department frequently resented the inexorable follow-up on every case the conference reported and the equally constant pressure for effective action. Experience with individual citizens—"respectable" people who saw nothing wrong in offering bribes to inspectors and police officers or "making a fast buck" by exploiting slum properties—had given them no reason to trust citizens, and they suspected all citizens groups, including the conference, of acting from hidden motives. Every new request for action was privately examined for the "angle." What was the organization or its staff really "after"? Was pressure being exerted because of the desire to put a personal enemy out of business? to make a better showing than a rival organization? to get the owner's property away from him at a bargain price? Such suspicion, of course, was never the reason publicly given for not acting effectively on complaints. "We are responsible for covering the whole city and can't give special service to community groups," they said.

Since this was also the publicly expressed attitude of certain other city departments, the director of the conference asked a highly respected city official for advice. "There can never be too much 'pressure' on a department to do its work," he said, "because pressure to do work ceases when the work is done . . . In a relatively inefficient and partially corrupt city government, the amount of special attention to politically favored areas is tremendous. No matter how much pressure you try to exert, you would never get more than a fraction of what goes to the favored area of a really powerful group or politico; and you *never* hear a squawk about that kind of pressure."

In spite of attitudes which hampered progress, there were some advances. Officials of the Building Department came to respect conference representatives, to value the help of the organization, and to rely on it in many ways. Conference records on Hyde Park-Kenwood cases were considered so reliable that they were sometimes used in staff meetings of the Building Department and in official discussions with the mayor in preference to those kept by the department itself. The accuracy of reports on building violations led certain of the Building Department employees to refer individual complaints from the Hyde Park-Kenwood area back to the conference for checking. The conference always came to officials with facts. Its criticism was constructive. Officials knew, too, that conference representatives tried to understand their problems, to cooperate in solving them and, when controversial issues arose, to give them a fair chance to put their own house in order.

While other groups went to the press and to the mayor to complain indignantly, conference representatives went instead to Building Department officials and said: "We don't like what is going on any better than they do. Now what can we do about it—together?" When they did go to the mayor—as they sometimes did if the commissioner said he was powerless to act or did not agree that he should—it was always done with the commissioner's knowledge and usually with his cooperation.

When an inspector turned in a "no cause for complaint" report on a building widely known to have dozens of violations, the conference resisted pressure to make the suspected bribery a *cause célèbre*. Instead, a letter went to the building commissioner stating that "Your inspector must have gone to the wrong address. Our office has exact information about the following violations.

. . . Would you be good enough to have another inspection made?" The violations were found, and inspectors exercised greater care in future. Later, evidence against certain inspectors was privately presented to their chief. Officials understood, however, that if the public interest demanded it, the conference would notify citizens through the press, as it did on a number of occasions.

Cooperation with the conference led to new practices in the Building Department. To prevent undesirable building alterations based on misrepresentation, volunteer conference architects, who knew the actual condition of properties, were allowed to inspect architectural drawings related to proposed conversions in Hyde Park-Kenwood; no building permits were granted over the objections of the conference. Using the forms and methods developed by the conference, the Building Department set up a service for other neighborhood organizations.

The conference cooperated in other ways as well: by interpreting the work of the Building Department to community residents; by securing citizen cooperation in house-to-house inspections; by backing every effort to strengthen the department with money, personnel, or organizational changes.

Dealings with public employees were not always successful. When failure in relationships occurred, however, it was usually caused by faulty advice rather than by the spirit of the approach. The first such failure developed from the desire of the conference to work out a human relations program in cooperation with the local schools. The chairman of the Public Schools Committee, acting on what she thought was good advice, went directly to the superintendent of schools who instructed all the principals in the area to cooperate. They did, but their hearts were not in it. It was later discovered that their lack of enthusiasm was due to resentment because they had not been approached directly. The harm was finally undone, but valuable lessons had been learned: going over the heads of potential or actual colleagues was to be avoided if at all possible; it was important to draw into partnership the people responsible for the day-to-day operation of projects as well as their superiors.

The relationship with school people was strengthened by the growing realization that the conference could help them to attain their own goals for the schools. For many years they had fought for additional facilities and services which they had been unable to secure until they received united community support through the conference. When school principals and district superintendents needed improvements, therefore, they learned to share their concerns with the Conference Schools Committee and to look to the committee for support and help.

As the conference program grew, friendly working relations were established with a wide variety of public agencies and departments: the Department of Law, the office of the housing and redevelopment coordinator, the top personnel of the Board of Education as well as with local school administrators, the Chicago Land Clearance Commission, the Chicago Housing Authority, the staff of the Chicago Plan Commission, the Chicago Park District, the Chicago Commission on Human Relations, and the new official agencies as they were formed.

Through the distribution of information sheets and talks before large and small groups, the conference tried to create understanding of the function, operation, services, and responsibilities of the various city departments as well as the responsibilities of citizens.

Public agencies sought the advice of the conference on possible citizen reaction to plans and proposals and relied on its suggestions for procedure.

In some instances, even the political climate was affected. Said one official: "The appointment of a well-qualified person who had no connection with the political machine as —— was possible only because the citizen interest created by the conference made it politically desirable to raise the standards of city performance."

And another commented: "The fact that Irving Landesman sought and won election as judge of the municipal court on the basis of his record for strict prosecution of building and zoning cases in Hyde Park and Kenwood was a complete switch from the old days when prosecutors failed to crack down on violators for fear of losing votes or offending influential political friends of the violator."

A combination of methods was undoubtedly responsible for many of the successful developments in Hyde Park-Kenwood. Conference leaders, however, remained committed to the cooperative approach, convinced that it established an atmosphere in which genuine sharing was possible and thus brought about advances that probably could not have been achieved in any other way.

An educator, heartily concurring in the conference approach, commented: "Even basically weak and ignorant officials would like to be good and strong officials. Demanding that they play their proper roles, through making them understand over and over again that this is what is expected of them, is more likely to make a good government than the ballot box ever can. In the process officials learned that the proper performance of their duties could be rewarding to them after all. Moreover, the conference approach released tremendous energy and worthwhile experience in city departments with fine officials who were thrilled by citizen interest and welcomed the opportunity to act in accordance with their beliefs."

RELATIONSHIPS WITH PRIVATE AGENCIES

Relationships with private city groups were characterized by friendly helpfulness on both sides.

In the case of the Metropolitan Housing and Planning Council, the conference received more than it gave. In the early days, before the conference knew its way around, the council was its mentor and guide on building and zoning laws, the intricacies of Building Department policies and operation, and the obstacles to improvement in the inspection, trying, and judging of housing cases. Sometimes it lent the weight of its experience to cases of special concern to Hyde Park-Kenwood. The conference, in turn, tried to keep the council informed of local developments.

The Citizens' Schools Committee relied heavily on members of the conference for help in spreading information on school conditions, financing problems, and the necessity for adequate bond issues.

The Association of Community Councils similarly relied on the conference to share its experiences with member groups, the majority of which struggled along without staff.

A number of city agencies, public and private, felt responsible for coordinating activities in a variety of fields, and conference representatives were thus called upon to appear at too-frequent meetings.

Increasingly, new community organizations in different parts of the city turned to the conference for advice and help. The additional burden on the staff was balanced by the satisfaction they gained from this widespread recognition of the program they administered and the high regard in which it was held.

Within Hyde Park-Kenwood itself, however, the regard was not so universal. While other areas were hailing the work of the conference, general acceptance in its own community was a long time coming.

Perhaps part of the reason was lack of time for essential personal contacts, an inadequate public relations program, the difficulty of overcoming the hostility caused by early mistakes.

A number of the churches and temples, the Hyde Park Neighborhood Club, the Hyde Park Cooperative Society, and the welfare groups had been friendly and cooperative from the beginning. Although a few of the member organizations of the Hyde Park Community Council made no secret of their opposition, the conference received and accepted an invitation to membership in the council in the fall of 1950 and thereafter regularly sent representatives to its meetings. The PTA's were gradually brought into cooperative action on community-wide school needs through the Schools Committee of the conference.

Long hours were spent with representatives of the Oakland-Kenwood Planning Association in the effort to straighten out a jurisdictional disagreement. The association considered all of Kenwood its territory and with some reason, since it was the first organization on the scene. Historically it had dealt primarily with zoning matters, had a number of successes to its credit, and looked upon the building and zoning program of the conference as a usurpation of its prerogatives. The conference, on the other hand, pointed out that the Oakland-Kenwood Planning Association was limited by part-time staff, was less zealous in the apartment sections of Kenwood than in protecting the large homes, and did not have a comprehensive community program. The association finally agreed to the conference proposal that both organizations report building and zoning violations in Kenwood, exchange information on all Kenwood cases, and work together through the courts when indicated. But, although both the conference and the association tried, and their directors were in frequent touch, the relationship did not become cordial or productive. This continued to be the case until the Oakland-Kenwood Planning Association was dissolved in 1953.

The leaders of the Hyde Park Planning Association were so convinced that the conference was to blame for the increase in Hyde Park's Negro population and so persuaded that its very existence threatened the interests of the large real estate owners and businessmen who were their members that they refused to have any contact with the organization. After several years had passed and the association had gone out of existence, some of its former members came into a cooperative relationship with the Conference through a joint effort to secure more street lighting. Herb Thelen had been right when he had urged: "Let's quit trying to convert people. Let's just work with them and their groups where we can—along their own lines and in terms of their special opportunities, responsibilities, and interests."

Approaching the businessmen on this basis was one of a combination of factors which finally produced closer ties with their associations.

A few local businessmen had approved of the purposes of the conference even in the early days, but they either did not attend the meetings of the businessmen's associations or had little influence in them. Others continued to regard the conference as a pro-Negro, extreme left-wing group.

In the first three years of its existence, the conference had made several unsuccessful—and sometimes ill-considered—attempts to reach the businessmen as individuals and as groups. On three occasions, members of the businessmen's associations declined invitations to accept nomination to the board of directors.

Some time later, however, when specific projects were proposed, businessmen cooperated immediately and effectively. The Kenwood Chamber of Commerce shared fully with the block groups and a conference committee in Kenwood clean-up campaigns. Leaders within the business associations, convinced that improved schools were vital to their own interest as well as to the community, helped persuade school authorities to seek an adequate bond issue by pledging the wholehearted support of their groups. Businessmen joined the conference in successful efforts to secure new street lighting.

Several factors undoubtedly influenced the change in attitude which made cooperation possible.

The work of the conference had begun to attract national attention, and the recognition it received—through awards, laudatory articles in newspapers and magazines, radio and T.V. programs, books and pamphlets—gave the organization new stature in its own community. Businessmen began to take pride in the fact that Hyde Park-Kenwood was leading the nation in a pioneering attempt at conservation.

The spread of block groups and their efforts to preserve the neighborhood helped to change the attitude of some who had formerly been hostile.

The conference was also helped by the fact that Sydney Stein, Jr., a senior partner in a leading investment counsel firm, had become its second chairman. He had considerable prestige in the financial center of the city as well as in the Hyde Park-Kenwood community. It was unthinkable that a person of his stature would be associated with an organization of questionable goals. "Jim" Stein was considered a practical man of affairs rather than a "do-gooder," and when he spoke "as a businessman" of his personal reasons for working with the conference, he was listened to with respect.

He was succeeded by another influential businessman from the downtown area—Elmer W. ("Jiggs") Donahue, a lifetime resident of Hyde Park and a director of one of the community banks. His fellow bank directors included the former president of one of the businessmen's associations and the Hyde Park Planning Association. They knew and respected Jiggs Donahue as a responsible man of conservative political and economic views.

Newspaper reports on the rapid spread of Negroes into many formerly all-white communities in northern cities were appearing with increasing frequency. The rate of population change was obviously slower in Hyde Park-Kenwood than in the two communities immediately south which had already lost the majority of their white residents. The suggestion that efforts of the conference, as well as the presence of the University of Chicago, might have something to do with keeping white residents in the area now began to seem altogether reasonable.

In 1953, when a businessman who had been hostile to the conference was asked to accept nomination to the board of directors, his fellow members of the businessmen's association assured him that their organization would consider it an honor to have him serve. The incoming chairman of one of the business associations, in his installation speech, spoke of the importance of cooperating fully with the conference and was applauded. Local businessmen began to appear at conference meetings, and several took places on committees and the board. Beginning in 1955 they participated in the financial campaigns of the conference and a number made individual contributions to its budget.

Friendly understanding had been established, and thereafter, even when the conference and the businessmen's groups took opposing stands, as they sometimes did, the relationship continued to be cordial and cooperative.

CHAPTER 10

Marshaling Resources

INFORMING AND INVOLVING PEOPLE

The most valuable of the assets of Hyde Park-Kenwood were its human resources—its 72,000 people, many of whom were rich in knowledge, skills, talent, and energy. If conference goals for the community were to be attained, money would be needed, of course, but the people would have to do the job. Success or failure, therefore, would depend primarily on the extent to which the people of the area could be interested and involved.

The need for their involvement was evident. Their daily actions as individuals—what they did about their own homes, what they said to their neighbors—would contribute either to improvement or decline. The state of their morale—their pessimism or optimism —would determine whether or not they remained in the area. The effectiveness of the conference with public agencies would depend on the numbers and strength it could muster. And finally, a vast reservoir of manpower, skilled and unskilled, was essential to do the tremendous amount of work that needed doing.

Conference leaders had deep faith in the ability of people to make intelligent decisions if they had the facts and a sense of direction. These were available—the facts of community change, the conference goals for the community, what should be done and was being done about problems—but how should this information be communicated? Once people were informed, how could sufficient interest and enthusiasm be created to lead thousands of them to a desire to be involved? How could this desire be fostered to make involvement meaningful both to individuals and the community?

Conference leaders did not know, but they were willing to experiment. Over the months and years they tried most of the known methods and experimented with new ones.

Personal calls were made on friends and neighbors. The Welcome Wagon lady, who visited all new residents, was given materials for distribution. Countless letters were written: to lists of people whose names were provided by interested individuals and groups; to newcomers to the area; to those who attended meetings at which conference people spoke. Articles were prepared for church and PTA bulletins and the local and city press.

Materials were produced and distributed. They dealt with the history and activities of the conference, current developments, municipal ordinances applicable to community problems, the city services available, recreational facilities and services, and the handling of specific community problems. (See samples in Appendix.)

To raise morale, attention was called to encouraging signs of improvement, of confidence in the community, of public recognition: new buildings going up, new laws passed, a court case won, a playground created, a tribute to the work of the community.

Speakers, recruited by the Public Relations Committee, accepted every invitation to appear before community groups, large or small. The conference itself arranged or encouraged meetings—on the blocks, within regional areas, covering the entire community. Their specific purposes varied, but the central idea was invariably the same: to inform and involve the people.

Communicating information, difficult as this proved to be, was simple compared to the problem of getting people sufficiently involved emotionally to want to take action. To encourage such involvement, conference meetings were carefully planned. Problems, issues, and events known to be of immediate concern to large numbers of people were made to come alive through socio-dramas or skits presented in such a way as to bring about emotional identification on a very personal basis. If, for example, the lack of outdoor play space was a serious cause for worry, a skit might show three mothers discussing the problem.

"I'm afraid to let Susie out of my sight," one would say. "I can't let her play in the street; I can't keep her in the house all the time; and the park is too far away to get to on foot."

"Johnny ought to be with other children, where they could play together," said another. "He's getting too ingrown."

"I'm worried, too," the third said, "but I understand we can do something about it."

(Every mother in a similar situation could see herself in this.)

The next scene would show the same three women in blue jeans turning a littered lot into a playground.

A wide variety of problems were posed in this way, sometimes with a dramatization of possible solutions, sometimes as the starting point for a discussion on what ought to be done. Whenever possible, the active participation of the audience was sought through discussion or question and answer periods. This was possible in block and area meetings, where there were manageable numbers.

At annual meetings, however, attendance was so large that direct participation was usually out of the question. Ways had to be found to create a sense of participation through emotional involvement with the problems and people on the stage. This presented difficulties. The annual meeting was the one occasion of the year for the conduct of business affairs, and certain formal requirements had to be met. There had to be an election of new board members and reports on the work and financing of the conference. In addition, it was essential also to take a collective look at the most serious problems of the community and share with the membership the difficulties as well as the opportunities ahead. At the same time, the annual meeting presented an opportunity for contact with new people who had not yet been exposed to the conference. The information function, therefore, had to be performed in such a way as to capture the interest of newcomers while satisfying the desire of the "in" group for as complete knowledge as possible. It was perhaps even more important that the annual meeting should build confidence and hope for the future. To do this there had to be a delicate balance between attention to the problems, which were admittedly formidable, and the inspiring story of pioneering in which community residents were sharing.

The type of presentation and the emphasis on different problems and achievements changed from year to year. Sometimes reports were enlivened by role playing. On one occasion, a straight report by the executive director was followed by the staging of a sample meeting of block leaders, who directed questions of high community interest to a panel of top public officials. At other times, the annual report to the community was interrupted by descriptive skits as problems, situations, and accomplishments were acted out in song and dance.

Catchy titles hinted at the theme of meetings: "Stay South, Young Man: or Pride without Prejudice," advertised an annual meeting whose top scenes dealt with the advantages of living on the South Side of Chicago over moving to the suburbs and with dedication to the maintenance of an interracial community. "The Little World Serious," or "It's Hell To Make History," looked back at the troubled present through the perspective of an imaginary future and showed how history had been made. "Now That They're Down, What's Up?" touched on the demolition of certain sections of the area and plans for rebuilding and renewing the community. The scenes combined seriousness of purpose with gaiety and humor. The people of the community saw themselves as human beings with many strengths and the normal weaknesses. They were able to laugh at their frailties and inconsistencies, while they glowed over their courage and accomplishments. And, at the end, they went out into the night on a high note of inspiration.

In 1955 a new feature was added to annual meetings with the establishment of Good Neighbor awards. These were instituted to build morale and encourage positive action by publicly honoring individuals for selected contributions to the community. The public was invited to send in nominations, and a panel of judges chose the janitor, homeowner, businessman, apartment house owner, and policeman whose conduct and activities set an example for others. The awards engendered considerable interest.

Every effort was made to secure the largest possible attendance so that increasing numbers of people could be reached. Flyers and posters advertising annual meetings were widely distributed. Stories were written for the press and community bulletins. Announcements were made at block gatherings and at every meeting at which conference representatives spoke. Sometimes dedicated conference members arranged car-pool or baby-sitter services to ensure the presence of interested friends and neighbors or not-yet-involved acquaintances. Those who went to the meeting one year and were amused or moved or inspired spoke enthusiastically to others who went the following year, and so the word spread. Attendance at annual meetings swelled to over a thousand.

Questionnaires were distributed to learn about the background, occupation, skills, and interests of everyone who came in contact with the conference. "Tell us how you can help the community," they were urged, and given check lists which described the opportunities for service in the blocks, on committees, and in the office. The membership form similarly invited applicants to check the areas in which they wished to work.

A card file, classified by skills and training, was maintained: Architects, Artists, Lawyers, Office Workers. Under the latter there were subdivisions covering bookkeeping, phoning, stenography, and typing. New people were put to work as quickly as possible.

Every method of reaching people was tried, although not all were equally effective. Real involvement came primarily through personal calls by friends, individual concern over particular problems, emotional response to experiences in meetings and in personal contacts, and through constructive activity. Of them all, sharing in the planning and the work was by far the most significant. Providing ways in which people could function meaningfully as part of a team thus became a vitally important and time-consuming part of the conference operation.

VOLUNTEERS AT WORK

The volunteers *were* the conference. They did all of its work for the first eight months and continued to do most of it as the organization grew. The employment of a staff simply made it possible to use more and more volunteers, to fit jobs to people more efficiently, and to coordinate their efforts with increasing effectiveness.

The people who did the work of the conference represented a cross section of the community: lawyers, planners, architects, writers, university professors, social workers, teachers, ministers and rabbis, artists, photographers, students, factory workers, elderly ladies with no more family responsibilities, busy mothers, secretaries. These were the people who organized the conference, served on the board and committees, gave technical help and advice, worked on their blocks, did the surveys, solicited funds, investigated, spoke, typed, mimeographed, ran errands.

If any job needed doing, somehow people were found to do it, and they responded with heart-warming enthusiasm and devotion.

Speakers wanted to tell the conference story to community groups? Marjorie Andrews, Russell Babcock, and a score of others were glad to do it.

Property owners needing advice on building alterations? Conversion plans to be inspected? Architect William Keck or Theodore Thomas was called in.

Important court cases coming up? Would Cal Sawyier, Ed Rothschild, Al Teton or any one of the twenty-five members of the Legal Panel work with the corporation counsel's office and appear in court at the specified time? They would indeed.

Exhibits needed for special meetings? Margaret Via, Rusty Wilson, or Goldine Shaw took charge of the designing and art work, rounding up a corps of assistants to help.

What to do about a brochure on the conference? Carl Petersen produced the copy, arranged for art work, farmed out the printing of 10,000 copies, and had them delivered. No charge.

Who would explain to the block groups issues and proposals relating to the renewal of the community? All the members of the Planning Committee would—Eri Hulbert, Maynard Krueger, Sandy Liveright, Bill Frederick, James Braxton, Willard Stout, Pete Shire, Ruth Denney, Martin Cohen, and a dozen others.

A film-slide presentation would help to interest people in the conference. Bettie Sarchet, Clyde White, and Mildred Mead collaborated on script, cartoons, and photographs.

There was no money to enlarge and decorate the conference office. A call for help went out, and twenty people turned up during the week end. Among them were the principal of the Kenwood School and a Pullman porter; the assistant curate of St. Paul's Episcopal Church came, and a personnel manager, an actor, a stenographer, a file clerk, several housewives. They plastered, scraped, sanded, painted, swept, scrubbed, washed windows. A local contractor supplied the lumber, and three of his carpenters built partitions and shelves. A scientist turned amateur electrician connected up the new buzzer system. The paint was donated as well as the electrical equipment and additional furniture. The transformation was completed at no cost whatever and without a single day's loss of service to the community.

Annual meeting time? Scores of volunteers would be put to work.

What problems and ideas should be stressed this year? A special committee would ponder with the staff and then call in script writers, and a sparkling script would be hammered out.

The director? Thelma Dahlberg, of course. A call for the cast would go out: to Roland Bailey, Tom Jenkins, John Ballard, Tobie Harris, or to many, many others: "Will you sing, or dance, or play a speaking role?" And the quick answer: "Sure, when do we rehearse?"

Production people would be telephoned. A head usher would be named and asked to round up fifteen or more helpers. The Public Relations Committee would plunge into action.

And thus everything would be set for another annual meeting.

Frequently children were put to work licking stamps while their mothers discussed committee business. Color pencils and scratch pads were always available to entertain children if the stamps ran out. Visitors were sometimes amused to see a cooing baby watching from its carriage as its mother turned the mimeograph machine handle or pushed the carriage with her foot while she typed or took notes.

A daytime visitor to the small conference office would find from one to fifteen volunteers working at assorted tasks.

Mrs. Abraham Meyer and Mrs. Freda Sahud, both in their seventies, might be preparing the newsletter for mailing. They knew they were not just folding sheets of paper. They were part of a company of people who were making it possible for the community to learn what was going on—the writers of the newsletter, the volunteer who cut the stencils, the people who made the news, those who ran the sheets off on the mimeograph machine, the volunteers who would do the addressing, stamping, and mailing.

Over at the file drawers, Thelma Rosenthal, Amy Meyer, Florence Clark, Jeanne Orlikoff or Sam Iden might be checking lists and planning new ways to reach people in the next membership drive. Or Marian Despres might be telephoning dozens of people about serving as solicitors in the finance campaign.

Any one of the Schools Committee chairmen—Peggy Preskill, Ruth Otto, Emily Waldman, Vera Margolis, Ethel Shufro—might be talking to the executive director about a letter that was to be sent to school people, or about the presentation to be made at the budget hearings of the Board of Education.

Miriam Elson, Gustavus Swift, or Jean Block of the Parks and Recreation Committee might have come in to go over the list of requests to be presented to the Chicago Park District. Or Adah Maurer might be there with copy for the new recreation directory.

Madeline Hudson or any one of a hundred others might have come in to report evidences of building violations, while over in a far corner several block leaders might have their heads together as they planned with the director of the Hyde Park Neighborhood Club for a teen-age recreation program.

Marianne Tax and Mike Rothschild, high school students, might ride up on their bikes to deliver brief reports on the progress of the sidewalk survey, or a group of Girl Scouts who helped out several afternoons a week might be getting instructions on the distribution of "clean-up" information to businessmen.

Work was not confined to the daytime. All over the area committees and groups met in homes, in churches, and at the conference headquarters, and several evenings a week volunteers could be found at the office as late as 11 p.m.

Everyone could serve in some way, and staff members tried to involve people in tasks that would challenge them and keep them working in behalf of the community. Major responsibility for this volunteer operation rested with the administrative assistant to the executive director, and it was handled with great skill first by Pat Selmanoff and later by Wanda Van Goor.

"I never saw anything like it," said a visitor who was studying the conference. "I wouldn't have believed it possible that so many people would continue to work with dedication and enthusiasm when they don't get anything for it—not even their names in the papers!"

It was not true, of course, that there were no rewards. Most of the volunteers found real satisfaction in their work. They saw themselves grow and develop. They were making important contributions to a cause they believed in. They felt themselves part of something bigger than themselves, something in which they were needed and wanted.

The use of volunteers also created problems. Volunteers could not always be counted on to get a job done in time. Under the circumstances, how much of the work could safely be left to volunteers and how much had to be done by staff?

It was true that schedules had to be met and delays could injure the program. But without the interest and personal involvement of people, something much more important would be lost: the excitement of sharing in a great adventure, the experience of solving problems together democratically, the sense of community and neighborliness that was slowly being recreated. These, which were at the heart of all the striving, had to be preserved and strengthened. Moreover, there was a tremendous amount of work to do, and it could never be done by hired hands alone.

So each year more and more time was given to making more

and more people feel—what was certainly true—that they were the most important force in the movement for community improvement.

Over and over again newly formed community groups asked the same question: "How do you continue to keep so many people involved?"

The answer was simple. The conference had discovered no new truths. Experience had taught that working successfully with volunteers was very much the same as working successfully with people anywhere.

Continued participation depends upon reward, and the kinds of rewards that bring satisfaction vary with volunteers. These might be concerned with self-expression, recognition, feeling useful and important, meeting new people, the acquisition of knowledge, the opportunity to use leisure time for social ends.

Volunteers must see the relationship of the job they do, however small, to the total effort. And even in the most routine job, the volunteer could be given an opportunity to share in considering the various ways of doing it. Staff members learned the importance of encouraging volunteers to share in making as many decisions as possible, of treating them like the intelligent and responsible human beings they were. People not only liked to be consulted, but it was important to *listen* to them; in particular cases they might know more than the staff.

Volunteers must be made to feel the usefulness of their contribution. Has it resulted in improvement to the community? Has it provided a service otherwise impossible, or has it saved the conference money or released limited funds for essential uses?

A little success goes a long way in maintaining interest, and the jobs people are given to do must therefore be within their skill and experience. Even small successes encourage volunteers to tackle other jobs.

Volunteers must be given a chance to grow and learn; continued involvement demands new challenges.

Volunteers work best in a friendly atmosphere where they are part of the working family, and where they are each regarded as individual human beings with recognized strengths whose services are warmly appreciated.

However busy the office was, it was important to the continuing involvement of volunteers to keep them informed about developments in the conference, whether or not these were directly related to their own work.

The time given to seeking out volunteers and working with them harnessed tremendous resources in energy, enthusiasm, and skills, and released unsuspected gifts in the service of the community.

In the process of participation, a heartening number of individuals were greatly changed. They became better informed about their neighborhood. They learned about the problems and functioning of their government, and with understanding came more responsible citizenship. Increased knowledge and experience developed greater insight. Slowly, almost imperceptibly, the quality of participation changed. Before taking action on isolated conditions, people wanted to know their causes, to see them in perspective, to make a reasoned attack on the problems behind the conditions. As they learned and thought and worked, their confidence in themselves grew and their attitudes changed. Apathy, lethargy, and pessimism were replaced by hope for the future. People began to believe they could make their community what they wanted it to be.

The list of volunteers grew and kept growing. In 1958 over two hundred served on the regular committees alone. Additional hundreds were active in and out of the office on every program of the conference, while several thousand worked on the problems of their blocks.

FINANCING THE ORGANIZATION

In the fall of 1951, a gathering of volunteers was briefed by Marian Despres on the campaign to raise the $12,200 budget of the conference.

During a two-week period, each of 140 volunteers would call on five to ten people to tell the conference story and ask for contributions. They would be given kits of materials containing brochures about the conference, answers to questions that might be asked, a copy of the budget, contribution blanks, and an instruction sheet. Each solicitor would report every few days to his team captain, one of the fourteen designated for this purpose. The office, with the help of other volunteers, would seek contributions from community organizations. In addition to the larger gifts, there would be membership dues—$3.00 for an individual and $5.00 for a family—and, in late November, the block groups would cover their blocks in the effort to enroll members in the conference.

This was the beginning of a finance-membership drive, the first concentrated campaign for contributions and dues, planned and directed by conference chairman Sydney Stein, Jr.

Up to late 1951 there had been no really organized effort to get funds. (For information on the earlier financing, see Chapter 5, page 51.)

To meet the first budget of $11,500 (1950–1951), an appeal had been sent to two foundations. The conference was pioneering in a new field, they were told, and needed time to develop community support. Foundation grants would buy that time while making it possible to carry on the program. Both foundations responded favorably. The Field Foundation would provide $5,000, and the Chicago Community Trust $1,000 as soon as the conference secured a tax-exempt ruling.

Some of the balance came from community organizations, which responded to an appeal by mail. The Council of Churches and Synagogues donated the offering received at the special Thanksgiving service conducted jointly by their congregations. But most of the balance was raised through "parlor meetings." These required little preliminary organization. Conference leaders simply asked people of means to invite to their homes those of their friends who might be willing and able to make substantial contributions to the conference after they understood its purpose and program. All that was required was the time of the conference chairman and executive director or any others who could present the story compellingly. The first parlor meeting, held at the home of Dr. and Mrs. Stanton Friedberg on November 1, 1950, brought in $1,950.

There were people, however, who considered it unhealthy for the conference to rely on a limited number of large gifts even temporarily. If this dependence continued, they argued, the withdrawal of a few gifts might seriously impair the program. People would be more involved in work they shared in financing. The influence of the conference, its effectiveness in obtaining improvements, would be tremendously increased if public authorities could be told that thousands of people paid dues to support the program. Even small payments from large numbers would provide more money than could be obtained each year from the comparative few who could spare or would be willing to give larger sums.

There was opposition to this point of view. When the need to finance the conference was first broached, it was felt by some of the people concerned with block organization that emphasis on the payment of dues might discourage active participation. This feeling continued to be so strong that in February 1951 the Executive Committee reaffirmed the position that the conference should not have a membership fee but "should encourage individuals both to participate in the work and make financial contributions to it," at the same time voting to give membership cards to everyone who contributed time or work. There were then 1200 "members."

The drive for membership dues, as part of the finance campaign in the fall of 1951, thus represented an important change in policy. Everyone could still participate and was encouraged to do so, but membership from then on depended on the payment of at least three dollars to five dollars a year.

Each year the size of the budget increased as community problems grew and the program expanded to meet them, and each year the conference sought new ways to strengthen its fund-raising efforts. Although it was necessary in 1953–1954 and for each year thereafter to secure foundation grants, the major emphasis and the goal of the conference was to work toward full support of the program by the community.

The composition of the Finance Committee was changed to provide the proper balance of hard workers and people of prestige and influence. The finance drive was divided into sections, each responsible for different groups within the community.

The Membership Committee, with the help of the Block Steering Committee and the office, worked out plans for house-to-house calls on all nonmembers during a two-week period, year-round solicitation by selected individuals, the appointment of a membership chairman in each block, letters to all members and friends of the conference, a graduated scale of membership contributions ($3.00 individual, $5.00 family, $13.33 share-the-cost, $25 . . . and so on up to $500).

Special Events committees ran a movie benefit each year or, on one occasion, a rummage sale.

In securing funds, personal calls—particularly by friends, acquaintances, business associates, or professional colleagues—were by far the most effective. If time made this impossible, personal notes were advised. General form letters, it was found, scarcely covered their cost. Movie benefits and the single rummage sale had value far beyond the income they produced ($2,000 to $4,700 per year from the movie benefits, $1,100 from the rummage sale), because they involved hundreds of people who would otherwise not have been reached.

It was strangely difficult, however, to involve people in membership. There seemed to be a curious reluctance on the part of the most dedicated conference workers to ask other volunteers for money or to take time at block and committee meetings to enroll members. While block groups were urged to share in the annual membership drives and a number did, too many block leaders resisted the idea or participated only halfheartedly. Some felt fund raising was an unwelcome distraction when there was so much work to do; others that attendance at block meetings might be adversely affected if people got the idea that the solicitation of dues was to be part of the meeting; still others saw no way of "selling" the membership idea—they recognized the need for money to carry on the program but, with everyone in the community receiving the same service from the conference, what reason other than ideological could be used to persuade people to join?

Undoubtedly part of the difficulty was overcoming the tradition that placed emphasis solely on participation through work, the idea that sharing in a block group carried with it no obligation toward the parent body.

There was also failure in communication. Many people expressed surprise when they heard there was a membership fee— no one had ever told them. It was shocking but true that 60 per cent to 80 per cent of those who attended block and committee meetings were not members. One reason, of course, was that the need for funds was rarely mentioned at meetings and when the chairman did so, reluctantly and almost apologetically, he quickly passed on to the business of the meeting, making no arrangements for follow-up. Another difficulty was the failure to obtain, for later follow-up by the Membership Committee, the attendance lists of block meetings.

The rate of membership renewals—50 per cent—was also cause for concern. While new members were being added all too slowly, not enough attention was being paid to retaining old ones.

Renewal notices went out on schedule, were followed by a reminder and a friendly letter, and the names of "delinquents" were then given to telephoners or to block leaders, but personal follow-up was too limited and sporadic to be effective.

By 1956, the number of people involved in the conference had grown to 7,000, but only 2,000 were contributing to its support. In 1956 and 1957, when community developments demanded still further expansion of the program, the Finance, Membership and Public Relations committees joined forces in a renewed struggle to strengthen the membership and financial base of the conference. For the first time the full board of directors and all the committee chairmen were drawn into the effort. They were asked to contribute liberally themselves, to enroll every committee member in the conference, and to share responsibility for securing membership renewals by making personal calls when routine notices failed to get results. The Block Steering Committee applied itself with greater vigor to reaching members of block groups. The graduated dues structure was abandoned to return to annual dues of five dollars per family and three dollars for an individual. The membership drive was separated from the finance drive and held in the spring, while large donors were approached in a special finance campaign in the fall.

The most comprehensive membership drive in conference history was held in March 1957. More than five hundred community residents participated in the two-week campaign. Training sessions for campaign workers, which had begun with the first drive in 1951, were planned even more carefully to prepare callers for the block-by-block and door-to-door solicitation. At four one-hour workshops in different sections of the community, trainees were shown, through informative and amusing skits performed by amateur actors, the kinds of responses they might get. In the discussions which followed, guided by skilled group leaders, methods of approach were suggested, and workers were given instructions and the answers to any questions they might have.

A kick-off meeting the day before the door-to-door calling was launched added to the enthusiasm and *esprit de corps*. An extensive publicity drive supported the campaign. Every member of the conference received a sticker announcing "I BELONG—HYDE PARK-KENWOOD COMMUNITY CONFERENCE"—and was asked to display it prominently, both to publicize the conference and to save campaign workers an unnecessary call. Thousands of copies of a special newsletter were distributed to residents of the area. The day before the formal opening of the drive, posters were distributed to local businessmen by Boy and Girl Scout troops. Campaign workers were on duty during the drive at booths in the Hyde Park Cooperative and churches and temples to accept membership applications.

The membership drive brought in more than a thousand new members.

In the meantime, an attempt was made to strengthen every phase of the finance drive. Lists of prospective givers were prepared with greater care, and consistent follow-up was provided. A more vigorous approach to new groups was planned. All those already supporting the conference were encouraged to increase their contributions.

A special Advisory Committee, headed by David Zisook, a prominent realtor, was responsible for securing the advice and financial aid of owners of substantial real estate in the community. Thus an important new source of funds was tapped, bringing in contributions ranging from $50 to $1,000.

In 1957 for the first time the conference employed a professional fund raiser to collect the balance needed to close the year without a deficit. Working with conference volunteers on a movie benefit, she sold advertising space in a program book and secured "sponsors" for the occasion. Some three hundred volunteers joined in this effort which netted $4,700 from the benefit and an additional $4,000 from the program book.

The Public Relations Committee, now made up solely of individuals professionally active in the public relations field, provided the expert knowledge of its members on specific phases of financing. Under the leadership of Herbert Bain, its chairman, new and improved materials and publicity were produced. Letters of appeal were framed by a direct mail expert. A regular flow of stories appeared in the press. For the first time a budget for public relations expenditures was provided which made possible the monthly publication of an attractive, printed newsletter.

Each year conference leaders had decided the amount that was needed for the current program and then had made heroic efforts to meet the budget. If a deficit threatened, stringent economies were undertaken to prevent it, and in only one year was a slight deficit recorded. Each year the income obtained within the community increased—from under $5,000 in 1950–1951 to over $35,000 in 1956–1957. The budget, however, showed even greater proportionate growth.

The 1952–1953 budget, providing for an executive director, an office secretary, and a half-time block director, had been increased in the middle of that year to something over $15,000 to add vitally needed office space. The full amount had come from the community.

It was obvious, however, that the program was badly handicapped by inadequate staff. An immediate doubling of the budget —to $30,000—was essential.

Foundation grants totaling $7,250 received during the 1953–1954 fiscal year, together with increased income from the community, helped to make possible the employment of a full-time block director and an administrative assistant and the payment of additional office expenses.

One year later the community's first redevelopment project was taking shape. The necessity to deal with the fears and anxieties of families facing relocation or concerned about future improvement projects and to involve the community in planning for the renewal of the area were added to the problems of deterioration and changing population. Additional foundation grants were obtained to employ a second block director, a director for the building and zoning program, and another secretary-clerk. Of the 1954–1955 budget of $39,500, which provided for a staff of seven, $18,500 came from foundations.

And still the program grew and had to grow. There was no other alternative to defeat. Although a 1955–1956 budget approximately the same as that of the previous year was approved, the board of directors at the same time decided that an all-out effort had to be made to obtain, for each of the five years ahead, annual budgets of about $60,000. The next few years would be critical. A combination of forces had brought Hyde Park-Kenwood to the beginning of a far-flung urban renewal program which had the support of city, state, and federal authorities. If it was to succeed, there had to be an increasingly vital citizen action program to prevent further deterioration as the urban renewal process was set in motion and to deal constructively with the practices and pressures militating against an interracial community. To do this the necessary staff had to be attracted and retained. Another professional worker, additional secretarial and clerical help, adequate office space, equipment, and materials were needed to strengthen every one of the conference programs.

Again foundations were asked to help. Grants were received, the conference undertook an emergency drive to increase the income from the community; operation under the expanded budget began in the spring of 1956 and has been continuing.

To provide more office space, a double store on 53rd Street, in the center of the community, was leased in 1956 for a three-year period. The conference staff—numbering ten—was now made up of six professional workers (the executive director, an administrative assistant, two block directors, the director of the building and zoning program, the director of a new real estate program) and four secretarial and clerical workers. Another professional position (coordinator for a tenant referral office) was added in 1957. This staff coordinates the work of hundreds of volunteers; responds to innumerable complaints, inquiries, and requests for help from within and outside the community; and serves a board of thirty-six directors, two hundred committee members operating through sixteen committees, fifty-six block organizations covering 85 per cent of the community, and some 3,800 members.

Of the $64,000 budget for the year 1957–1958, $22,000 came from foundations and $42,000 from the community.

Foundation grants over the years were made by the Chicago Community Trust, the Division Fund, the J and S Foundation, the Field Foundation, Inc., the Emil Schwarzhaupt Foundation, Inc., and the Wieboldt Foundation.

The directors of the conference were not happy about the heavy reliance on foundation aid and came to it because there seemed no other way.

"We sincerely believe," they wrote one of the foundations, "that when the pressing needs of the years immediately ahead are met, the conference will be maintained fully by the community it serves, and that our request for additional foundation support can be amply justified by the nature of the demonstration under way in Hyde Park-Kenwood. Other communities will be able to profit from our experience and thus will not need the larger funds that experimentation and the development of methods demand.

"We are convinced," they continued, "that the single factor most vital to stimulating effective programs of this kind throughout the country *is one successful demonstration that it can be done.*"

The foundations agreed and supported the conference because it was pioneering in a new and uncharted field, and other communities had much to learn from the experiment.

In the meantime, volunteers and staff continued to work at increasing the income from local sources to ensure the continuing operation of the program.

CHAPTER 11

The Effort To Stop Blight

While the danger of spreading blight was clear, for some time conference leaders had no real conception of the tremendous obstacles in the way of stopping it. The full scope of the problem became evident only after months of frustrating experience with the city's inspection and enforcement procedures.

At first, however, the conference concentrated largely on what was considered the most important line of defense—an alert and informed citizenry. At public meetings, community clinics, and block gatherings, through the columns of the *Hyde Park Herald*, in private discussions with block leaders, through mimeographed information and instruction sheets, community residents were coached and briefed.

They were told about the zoning regulations affecting every block in the area, minimum housing standards, the conditions under which conversions were permitted, defective porches and stairs, inadequate fire escapes and sanitary facilities, defective wiring or plumbing, improper garbage and trash disposal, rats and vermin. They were given complaint forms, guides for determining violations, and explicit instructions for acting on them. (See Appendix.)

A constant concern was how to bring about constructive watchfulness while guarding against snooping, vigilantism, and grudge complaints.

"The best practice in dealing with all violations," block leaders were advised again and again, "is to call on the offender, tell him about the block group, and invite him to attend meetings. . . . It is important to be friendly and enlist his cooperation."

The violator, it was pointed out, might be plagued by problems on which he needed help. If he had paid too much for his building, for example, and the high monthly charges were driving him to overcrowding, perhaps refinancing could be arranged. Or, if he could not afford the full outlay for required repairs, it might be possible to help him secure a loan.

When friendly efforts did not get the desired results, however, formal complaint was urged. The identity of complainants was protected, but anonymous as well as vague reports were discouraged.

"The city cannot act unless it has exact information," people were told. Overcrowding? Why was it suspected? What was the size of the dwelling unit? How many occupants? Did each unit have its own bath? How many shared each bath? "Would you be willing to testify in court if necessary?"

Residents were especially urged to watch for signs of illegal conversion (physical alterations without a Building Department permit).

"It is easier to prevent violations than to correct them," they were told. "If you see lumber or plumbing fixtures being moved into a building, or carpenters at work, call the conference office at once."

The conference would then advise an immediate visit to the owner (who might have a permit to remodel) or, when necessary, would ask the Building Department to make an inspection and have the work stopped if it was being done illegally.

The conference office asked residents to report new developments on every building promptly. In turn the complaining individual or block group was informed of action taken by the conference and the Building Department.

The interest and vigilance of residents led to the prevention of countless violations.

Through block organization neighbors became acquainted with the properties on their blocks. If a building went up for sale, they called on the owner or real estate agent to urge the selection of a buyer who would maintain the property decently.

Whenever they could get the names of prospective buyers, block groups invited them in to discuss the future of the buildings in which they were interested and to get their cooperation in the community program.

In central Kenwood, an area of beautiful single-family homes, residents went much further. When houses were advertised for sale, they undertook to find purchasers who would maintain them properly, and a number of homes were sold through their efforts.

A building which had changed ownership was watched with special vigilance.

The office phone rang continuously.

"This is ———. Some workmen appeared this morning at ———. A lot of hammering is going on; and just now about six bathtubs were delivered."

Later, a return call from the conference office. "The Building Department says they have no permit to convert. The police are on their way. If work begins again after the police leave, let us know at once."

Thus the vigilance of residents, combined with the prompt cooperation of the Building Department and the police, resulted in the prevention of scores of illegal conversions and the stopping of many others after work had already begun.

Word of the citizen action program spread to many parts of the city, and the conference began to receive calls from prospective purchasers of property.

"I'm interested in the building at ———," said one man. "It now has six apartments, each with eight rooms, and if I bought it I'd want to add two apartments. Would your organization object?" He was told that the conference could not object to legal changes and that good conversions could be an asset to the community.

He and others like him were encouraged to talk with the block groups or visit the office for professional advice.

Some callers were told their plans were illegal and that any attempt to convert would set off community action. Others, confused by misrepresentations, called to get facts.

"The real estate agent told me I could move two separate families into the twelve room house at ——," reported one man, "but he seemed evasive about the law. I want to put in another kitchen for a friend's family since the house is too big for us to swing alone. Would that be all right?"

No, it would not; the area was zoned for single-family use.

And another call, this time from a speculator who, on three occasions, had been prevented from carrying through illegal conversions.

"Say, lady," he said, "what has your outfit got against me anyhow?"

The reason for the community effort was explained, the determination to prevent slums, etc.

"I getcha," he said. "O.K., so I'll quit."

The executive director had just begun to glow with gratification when the blow fell. "How much of the South Side have you got sewed up?" he asked. "I can operate in plenty of other places."

On occasion property owners appealed to city authorities for variations of the zoning ordinance so that they might use residential or business properties in ways other than those permitted in the ordinance. While support of these variations might sometimes be justified and the conference did, in fact, approve a few (such as the creation of a private parking lot in an overcrowded residential area), most of them would have been detrimental to the community either because of the use proposed or because of the danger of setting precedents for similar requests. Every such request, therefore, was carefully reviewed by a conference committee which considered the implications not only for the block involved but for the community as a whole. Conference representatives, accompanied by community residents and occasionally by the ward aldermen, appeared regularly before the Zoning Board of Appeals to present the community's reaction to variation proposals in the Hyde Park-Kenwood area. Thus many proposed undesirable changes were defeated, among them the re-zoning of an entire block from single family to duplex residences, the installation of large advertising signs in residential areas, the operation of an automobile repair shop on a residential street.

The majority of violations corrected through the years—as well as all of those prevented—were the direct result of citizen action. Of the cases which were reported to the city, those involving minor expenditures—the cleaning up of premises, the removal of fire hazards, installation of trash baskets, garbage collection and the like—usually resulted in compliance with the law. Official action, however, was inadequate to check the serious, slum-producing violations because of the weakness of inspection and enforcement services and the profitable nature of slum operations.

Slum owners resorted to every possible device to protect their source of income, including bribery and concealment behind trusts. No appeal seemed to stop them; tough cracking down by the city was demanded.

The problem was made even more difficult by what one community leader referred to as "that fearful dilemma—the conflict between good will and fast profit." America's market-oriented society seemed to put much greater value on "making a fast buck" than on community betterment. Thus sometimes pillars of society, "good" people who gave liberally to their religious institutions and other worthy causes, saw nothing wrong in renting single apartments to two or three families, tripling their income from rents, and at the same time cutting down maintenance. A religious leader said he had been advised by respected businessmen to put his institution's extra money into "some of these houses which are paying 300 to 400 per cent on their investment. And the people who gave this advice," he said, "gave it with all the fervor of those who know they are speaking good sense—something the hardheaded realistic American businessman can really appreciate."

Sometimes, in spite of these attitudes, there were rare victories through a combination of city action and social pressure, and

these were all the more cheering when the friendship and understanding of the property owner could be secured along with the
desired improvements.

In one such case, an old mansion, which had been converted
into a rooming house some years before and had a number of
violations, was sold to a new owner. The block people and the
conference staff, continuing to press for compliance with the law,
followed the case to court on three occasions. Finally the owner
telephoned to ask why he was being persecuted. He was already
putting all of his profits back into the building. An inspection by
the conference showed that he had indeed done a great deal of
work on the building, most of it inside and so not apparent to
neighbors.

The next day the conference office telephoned to congratulate
the owner on the work already done and to ask about his future
plans. This was the first property he had ever owned, he said,
and he would like to make it an asset to the community, but he
still had a plumbing problem. The office offered to help him. The
record states: "He seemed very grateful and again said he hoped
his building would be an asset to the community, so I suggested
that he become a member of the conference and work with us.
He seemed amazed to be invited and accepted with delight. This
week he sent in a check for $25."

Usually successes were much harder to come by. In spite of
months, sometimes years, of effort, failures were frequent.

In the beginning, conference leaders had been happy when the
city agreed to make an inspection of a slum property, believing
that once inspectors saw the seriousness of the violations the
building owner would be forced to correct them.

To their dismay, inspectors frequently reported "No Cause" for
complaint or "Compliance" when neighbors on the block knew
that violations continued to exist.

So the conference asked the Building Department for a reinspection and then tried to get the owner before the city's
Compliance Board—a device intended to give property owners
opportunity for a hearing and the chance to bring their buildings
into voluntary compliance without resorting to law—this in the

hope of avoiding the time-consuming court procedures. The Compliance Board process proved even more time-consuming. Since the board had no real power, owners could neither be fined nor forced to make repairs.

Conference leaders realized that they had been naïve. Their methods had worked well with local residents, with many owners and managers, with some city departments. But to deal with the real troublemakers—the deliberate exploiters and speculators—they would have to go to court.

They pushed the city to prosecute and went to court almost daily. Cases dragged. Continuances were numerous. Serious violations were seldom corrected. Judges felt that if in the end an owner complied with minimum standards that was enough, and fines were rarely assessed.

This meant, in effect, that slum owners could continue to operate unsafe structures for years, pretending to comply with the law by applying for the required remodeling permit and then getting continued extensions on the permit and never doing any work—all the while continuing to collect rents. When and if the authorities did bring the owner to court, he could be sure of getting off with no fine if he complied with minimum standards even at that late date.

The conference kept asking for one inspection and court case after another in the hope that the annoyance of repeated inspections and frequent court appearances might discourage violators —a vain hope. The money to be made through exploitation of buildings was too strong a counterinfluence.

But the conference kept going to court. One week its representatives would appear in court on a housing case against a slum operator; the next week, against the same owner, on a building case; several weeks later, against the same owner on a zoning case. The different types of cases (housing, building, zoning) were scheduled for different days of the week; property owners who feared that judges might recognize them as constant violators could easily ask for a change of venue. It was thus possible to appear six or seven times against the same owner and never be in the same court or before the same judge or the same city prosecutor. Moreover, housing violations could not be brought up on building or zoning days, with the result that the judge and corporation counsel saw only limited violations each time, and fines were consequently negligible or not assessed at all. Conference representatives were the only people involved who had the entire picture of violations.

They tried again. Visit after visit to the officials of the various city departments always had the same result. "We'll try," they would promise. "We'll instruct our men to check with the other departments before setting court dates and coordinate the work." And they did try. But many problems prevented their success, including an obsolete filing system in the Building Department. Another blank wall.

Frank Kenney, as chairman of the first Conference Enforcement Committee, had pointed up many of these problems. In 1951 he suggested that the enforcement program of the conference be enlarged by enlisting the help of the many lawyers in the community.

It fell to Calvin Sawyier, who succeeded Frank Kenney, to develop the program further. His first move as chairman—in February 1952—was to call together twenty lawyers and the conference's three volunteer court observers. Their suggestions formed the base of an enforcement program adopted by the board of directors at their next meeting. The conference, it was decided, would work on:

1. *The enforcement of present codes* (through following the conference methods already in use, plus (a) having members of the volunteer Legal Panel work with the city's lawyers, (b) pressing the corporation counsel's office to urge the court, in imposing fines, to count each day the violation continued as a separate offense, punishable by a separate fine, (c) pressing the corporation counsel to take serious cases into a court of equity so that injunctions which would stop violations might be obtained.

2. *A study of existing laws* to see whether the powers under them were being fully utilized.

3. *The introduction of new laws* to promote conservation, in cooperation with the Planning Committee of the conference and

with city-wide agencies—such laws for example as would enable the city to make repairs to private buildings when the owners failed to do so and to sequester rents for payment; set up a special housing court; permit conversions only if they did not contribute toward overuse of the building and of community facilities;

4. *The reorganization and revitalization of the Building Department,* through cooperation with private city-wide agencies.

Work along these lines began at once. Sometimes improvements came through the leadership of city or regional agencies. The Metropolitan Housing and Planning Council and the office of the housing and redevelopment coordinator, continually pressing for reforms, were responsible for some of them. In 1952 the South East Chicago Commission also became active in the struggle for an effective enforcement program. General public reaction to slum conditions, aroused by a series of articles in the *Chicago Daily News,* resulted in the formation of a Citizens' Committee to Fight Slums, spearheaded by the Metropolitan Housing and Planning Council, and this committee's recommendations, plus continuing pressure from the conference and other groups, led to additional reforms, including changes within the Building Department itself.

But often the conference acted alone. At first the executive director, with the help of volunteer court observers and lawyers and an increasingly vigilant community, tried to keep up with the growing program. When in 1954 foundation funds made extra help possible, Ozzie Badal and then Grace Tugwell became director of the building and zoning program. A secretarial assistant added in 1956 took over the record keeping, and a real estate adviser employed in the same year devoted himself to securing the cooperation of property owners and real estate firms in a preventive program. Mrs. Tugwell was thus freed for daily contact with the Building Department, the corporation counsel's office and the courts, as well as with community residents.

Through repeated discussions with top city officials, testimony at public hearings, united community action, the work of several agencies, and the preparation of new laws, a number of changes were effected.

House-to-house inspections in Hyde Park-Kenwood were conducted by the Building Department in 1951 and 1953.

A new building commissioner—General Richard Smykal—was appointed and directed by the mayor to develop an effective enforcement program.

The Building Department was helped to secure additional inspectors, under civil service, institute a training program, consolidate its files and, through microfilming, preserve its records against change or loss.

The corporation counsel's office transferred zoning cases to a special division which had its own investigators and appointed several lawyer members of the conference and the South East Chicago Commission as special assistant corporation counsel, without salary, to work with the city on the preparation and prosecution of zoning violations.

Amendments to the Building Code and the Zoning Ordinance, drafted with the help of the chairman of the Conference Legal Panel, were enacted into law. They restricted the conversion of buildings and the density of occupancy by prohibiting a more than 15 per cent increase in the number of dwelling units or occupants unless the parking requirements for new construction were met. They gave the city power to apply to the circuit and superior courts for injunctions or for any other orders necessary to bring buildings into compliance with the code or to have them demolished, repaired, or closed as dangerous and unsafe. They provided for mandatory fines ranging from five dollars to two hundred dollars for each day a violation continued after receipt of a notice from the Building Department, and for the assessment of these penalties against owners, lessees, occupants, or managers of buildings as well as against contractors, architects, or builders responsible for work contrary to the code or to permits.

This was progress. Of course, the provisions of the Building Code dealing with existing housing still needed modernization (and the Zoning Ordinance as well), but work on revisions was under way. The Building Code, originally passed in 1897, had by

1949 become a pyramid of amendments, and the corporation counsel held that a building must simply comply with the portion of the code in effect at the time it was built or altered. If proof of when it was built could not be offered, the assumption was that it should comply with the requirements of the 1897 code. The most unfortunate aspect of this lag was that the city was thus powerless to correct the most noisome condition brought about by illegal conversions: insufficient bathing and toilet facilities. Since early requirements for sanitary facilities were minimal, property owners who had partitioned large apartments into smaller units without adding plumbing to service three, four, and five families with children, could not be brought to account.

However, when city departments could be prevailed upon to use the powers they did have with persistence and determination, they were able to turn years of defeat on individual cases into victories, especially when their efforts were combined with the initiative and enterprise of conference members and staff.

On one occasion, with six apartments illegally converted to 26, the owner presented to the court an affidavit signed by a "former owner" stating that the building had been converted prior to 1932. The conference produced two witnesses—a former tenant in the building who had been asked to move in 1948 so that her apartment could be converted, and a woman who had visited the building and seen the conversion in process. In addition, the conference supplied the corporation counsel with a copy of an application to convert 6 to 18 apartments made by the former owner in 1948 to the Zoning Board of Appeals (which the board had denied). This proved that there had been only 6 apartments in 1948 and brought the conversion under the 1938 code which required one bath to each apartment. The judge ordered the owner to de-convert.

In January 1954, acting on a report from the conference that a Kenwood single-family residence had been turned into a rooming house, the Building Department notified the owner to restore the home to its original use. She did not, and the city filed an injunction suit. Nothing happened; the owner continued to violate the Zoning Ordinance. After repeated attempts to secure enforcement of the injunction, in February 1956 the city filed proceedings to show cause for contempt. Edwin A. Rothschild, a member of the Conference Legal Panel, summing up the city's case in his capacity as temporary assistant corporation counsel, asked that the defendant be imprisoned as an example to other violators.

The judge sentenced the owner to thirty days in jail—the first time such a drastic penalty had been imposed in a zoning case— and warned her that she would be recommitted for another jail term if she did not comply when her sentence expired.

The sentence, later reduced to one week, was served, the rooms were cleared out, and the community and the court went to work to find a buyer for the building who would use it as a single family home.

In November 1955 the city took receivership action for the first time in its history following pressure by the South East Chicago Commission and the conference. A receiver appointed by the court was authorized to collect the rents in a heavily converted four-story slum building and use the money, after mortgage payments, for necessary repairs. The receiver set his goals too low, but some improvement was made. The experience showed that receiverships could be a useful tool in enforcing the law if the court empowered the receiver to make no payments to mortgage holders until buildings were brought into compliance and properties were put on a sound management basis.

The conference was now beginning to have some success in persuading the city to prosecute conversion cases. In June 1955, for example, neighbors reported to the conference that two of the apartments in a six-flat building which had little open space around it were being converted without a permit. The Building Department promptly issued a stop order. The owner, unable to meet the off-street parking requirement, was sued by the city and forced to restore the building to its original condition.

While these victories were coming a little more frequently as 1955 came to an end, they were still the result of (1) the few new tools which had been added to the city's outmoded building and zoning codes and (2) increased activity on the part of the conference staff. On one case, successfully resolved after three years of work, the conference building and zoning director alone had spent 86 hours on 17 court appearances, conferences with witnesses and city officials, correspondence, record keeping, and telephoning. The city had not yet faced up to its responsibilities in enforcing the laws which it had on the books.

The reasons for the failure of the city's enforcement program were many and varied.

There continued to be little coordination within the Building Department. Inspectors sent out on housing, building, fire, or electrical complaints were not expected to look for violations outside their own bureaus.

Even the limited number of inspectors were being used ineffectively. Many of them had been given their jobs in reward for political services (although this was limited to some degree after civil service was instituted); there was reason to suspect all were not as reliable as they might be; and, with few exceptions, they had little interest in their work. Frequently they could and did sabotage the city's enforcement program through not finding violations where they existed, testifying that the owner had complied with the law when in fact he had not, delaying inspections to give owners a chance to complete illegal conversions, causing records to disappear.

Honest inspectors were still handicapped by inadequate training and by policies which put more emphasis on the number of buildings covered in a day than on the quality of the inspection. Moreover, they came to feel that their efforts were pointless. They were frustrated and discouraged by the frequent continuances which forced them to inspect the same premises again and again, by the attitude of judges who seemed indifferent if not actually bored when they testified, and by the dismissal of hundreds of cases against individuals known to be violating the city's codes.

Since annual inspection was made only of residential buildings over three stories high, the investigation of approximately 95 per cent of Hyde Park-Kenwood's structures depended solely on "complaints" of neighbors.

Violators continued to be allowed too much time to comply with the law.

Lawyers from the Department of Law usually arrived in the courtroom with little or no advance preparation and without the benefit even of a pre-trial conference with the Building Department. As a result, the prosecution had to depend on the information and integrity of the inspector who was the city's only complaining witness.

Since inspections were made in the daytime when men were at work and children at school, evidence of overcrowding was seldom found by inspectors or, when it was, could never be proved in court unless a witness could be found who had seen all of the occupants in the apartment and knew they lived there.

Violations of the single-family provision of the zoning ordinance were equally difficult to prove. A dozen or more people living together could claim to be related and, without careful investigation which inspectors were not authorized to make, the claim could not be successfully challenged.

The law did not provide means to control the growing practice of turning single-family homes in apartment house districts into rooming houses.

It was also possible to evade the law against conversions without a permit and the expense of physical alterations simply by putting beds into every room of an apartment.

The off-street parking amendment to the zoning ordinance, an important tool which might have stopped undesirable conversions, was seldom enforced.

Neither the Building Department nor the Department of Law gave sufficient attention to getting detailed information on ownership before cases went to court. Dismissals and delays were therefore common. Speculators could and did sell illegally converted properties and remove themselves from the scene between receipt of violation notices and the date of court appearances.

Building and zoning cases continued to be tried in the municipal court which had power only to fine violators. This court could not order repairs or compliance, issue injunctions or order the demolition or closing up of buildings. When fines were imposed, they were so small in relation to the profit a speculator might be making as to have no effect on his future action.

Small as fines were, judges frequently continued to suspend them if the owner complied, even if serious violations had been in existence for some time. A major factor in this leniency was lack of information. The judges were still not being given an over-all view of the violations in any building. Instead, each bureau of the Building Department continued to send its cases to the Department of Law separately, and these were handled in separate court cases. Nor was a judge given the complete history of violations in a building and so had no way of knowing that the charges before him might be identical to those on which the owner had been found guilty again and again in the past.

While the total picture did not look very bright as 1955 ended, several things had happened during the year which were destined to bring important changes.

The publisher of the community's newspaper, Bruce Sagan, had long been using the *Hyde Park Herald* to further the efforts of the conference in alerting residents to their privileges and duties as community members. In June 1955, Grace Tugwell of the conference office offered to prepare a weekly column containing a listing of building and zoning cases heard every week in municipal court, with names and home addresses of owners brought in for violating the city's codes and ordinances. The *Herald's* editor, Adelina Diamond, thus began a service which came to be something of a community institution and contributed greatly to the program of code enforcement. It acted as a deterrent on owners who had a tendency to allow standards to slip and was read regularly by city officials.

In July 1955 Irving Landesman was appointed assistant corporation counsel in charge of ordinance enforcement. His grasp of the problems and his resourcefulness in finding solutions made him a valuable ally in the conference's fight against blight.

A new building commissioner, George L. Ramsey, was appointed in September 1955 to succeed General Richard Smykal. Mr. Ramsey's first undertaking was to order a survey inspection of the entire Hyde Park-Kenwood area to supply the information needed for the urban renewal program under way in the community. (See Chapter 14.)

In May 1956 the conference submitted to the Building Department a list of thirty-three slum buildings on which action to date had been ineffective and asked the commissioner to institute inspections by teams of inspectors from the various bureaus within the Building Department and to coordinate the court cases on all thirty-three buildings. He agreed to put his department to work on the problem.

Among the buildings on the list submitted was a large tenement on which a survey by Kenwood residents had revealed overcrowding, sagging porches, loose wiring, broken plaster and windows, leaky plumbing, piles of junk and filth in basement and yard, and one bathroom for each three apartments shared by up to thirteen adults and children. Inspections confirmed these violations and turned up others. The cases were coordinated and all charges were brought before the judge at the same time. It was so unusual to be presented with such an overwhelming number of violations at one time that the judge made a personal inspection of the building. The owner was given five weeks to bring the property up to standard or face fines of $3,200 per day ($200 on each of sixteen charges). Extensive repairs were begun at once. During the weeks that followed, the director of the conference building and zoning program made three personal inspections and each time reported progress to the judge. In the end, with an expenditure of $20,000, the building was brought into compliance.

On another of these slum buildings the city for the first time used its power to force an owner to vacate the premises. This was an apartment building converted into a tenement, which had originally been called to the attention of the conference in 1953. Building Department inspections had confirmed numerous violations. Cases dragged through the courts until March 1954 when the owner had been fined $25 on one charge. A second charge had been dismissed in November of the same year. New complaints had been brought by the conference in 1955, and again the case had dragged on to a dismissal.

Early in 1956 the block leaders and the block director of the conference had made personal inspections. Photographs had been taken and these, together with a detailed report on conditions in the building, had been submitted to the building commissioner at the May meeting. By that time there were over fifty violations. Overcrowding, litter-obstructed exits, unusable sanitary facilities, falling plaster, rats, and vermin were a hazard to the community as well as to the tenants. When there had been no action by June, the block leader, impatient with what seemed to him unreasonable delay, turned the facts over to the *Hyde Park Herald* which ran a dramatic story with pictures.

The building commissioner acted immediately, employing a rarely used device—a board of survey, including a sanitary expert, a building expert, and a medical inspector from the Health Department—and sent this group out to inspect the building. A fire inspection was made simultaneously, and these findings were incorporated in the board of survey's report. Using the special powers provided by the new legislation, the building commissioner ordered the owner to vacate the property. The office of the housing and redevelopment coordinator, with the help of the community, provided relocation services for the occupants. And shortly thereafter the corporation counsel was granted a court order to close the building.

Coincidental with the closing of this building came the passage by the City Council of the new Housing Code, to become effective in January 1957. This was drafted by a committee of the Metropolitan Housing and Planning Council, on which Calvin Sawyier served, with the advice of city agencies. It defined the responsibilities of owners and tenants, limited both the number of persons permitted to occupy a dwelling unit and the sharing of sanitary facilities, provided for the gradual elimination of "community kitchens," and set forth standards of maintenance and repair. Most important, it created minimum standards applicable to every dwelling unit in the city regardless of when it was built. (The city has yet to enforce these minimum standards. The building commissioner points to the large number of people who would be displaced from overcrowded buildings and the lack of standard housing to accommodate them.)

With the passage of the Housing Code, and the prospect of the passage of a new comprehensive zoning ordinance (which went into effect in 1957), all the laws that were needed were on the books. The immediate future looked bright. The new commissioner seemed eager to solve the many problems facing him and, more important, it was obvious from the two slum cases just successfully concluded that the coordinated court case device for dealing with slum buildings would serve until more fundamental reorganization of the Building Department could take place. The building commissioner and the head of the ordinance enforcement office were working together to eliminate the endless delays in the scheduling of court cases.

As the summer months passed, however, it became increasingly clear that the remaining thirty-one slum buildings were not being handled in the manner that had proved so successful in the first two. These cases were being processed in the usual way. By the end of October, only six had been prosecuted, of which four had been withdrawn at the first hearing by the corporation counsel for lack of knowledge of ownership, one had been discharged, and one owner had been fined *$15 and costs!*

Disappointment and concern were compounded by the fact that during these same summer months speculators had begun to move into the area in greater numbers, buying up as much property as they could, some of it in good condition. Experience had shown speculators that slum operations were especially profitable in renewal areas where they could overcrowd, raise rents, and spend nothing on maintenance for the two- or three-year interim between the designation of the area for renewal and the actual purchase of property by the city. Then they could expect to get inflated prices based on the blown-up profit and loss statements they could present.

Drastic action was necessary if renewal plans were to be successful. The community had seen speculators turn good buildings into slums in less than two years; failure for two decades to enforce the city ordinances had been responsible for the blight in

161

Hyde Park-Kenwood and for the need to spend millions of public and private dollars on an urban renewal program. Now, even as that program was moving into its advanced stages, failure to discourage new speculators and slum operators from moving into the area by strict enforcement, was threatening its success.

In the fall of 1956, therefore, in preparation for a strong plea for action, the conference analyzed the 147 court cases from the area which had been processed in the municipal court over the preceding eleven-month period. The combined fines for 36 cases had been $1,525. Only four of these fines were over $50 and eight had later been suspended. Forty-four cases had been dropped by the city for various reasons; 11 had been discharged; and 56 were still pending, each having been postponed from one to ten times. Almost a year's work, thousands upon thousands of dollars of taxpayers' money in salaries to officials in the courts, the Building Department, the Department of Law, and some $10,000 spent by the conference in assisting these agencies, had gone into the securing of just about $1,000 in fines, and the bad buildings were still as hazardous, as overcrowded, and as great a threat to the community's goals as they had ever been.

Armed with a detailed record of the community's experience, including an analysis of the reasons for the city's failure to stop neighborhood decline, the conference met with Commissioner Ramsey, Irving Landesman of the Department of Law and the municipal judge who had presided during the eleven-month period.

The conference again pressed for team inspections of all slum buildings and urged the inclusion in each team of an assistant corporation counsel who would thus be well prepared for the case when it came up in court. Such a system would meet many of the conference objections to the code enforcement procedures then in use. It would enable the city to secure a complete picture of the condition of buildings, thus eliminating the practice of inspecting for isolated violations and presenting weak and incomplete evidence to the court. It would raise the standard of inspections—a hazardous condition might be overlooked by one man but not by several; raise the level of compliance, because

owners would realize for the first time that the city had unim-
peachable evidence against them; eliminate the numerous Compliance Board hearings and the average of fourteen re-inspections
necessary before bringing an owner to court; and it would be
conducive not only to speedy correction of hazardous conditions
but also to quick action against slum owners. And, finally, team
inspections would have a tremendously important psychological
impact on law-abiding property owners as well as slum operators.

Building Commissioner Ramsey, though impressed by the
seriousness of the situation, felt that such a program could not be
undertaken unless additional funds could be secured. It was
agreed, however, that the matter should be discussed with the
mayor.

The housing coordinator, who was also approached for help,
arranged a meeting with Mayor Daley which was held in February 1957. Sharing in it were members of the Building Department, the office of the housing and redevelopment coordinator
Irving Landesman of the Department of Law, the director of the
South East Chicago Commission, and four members of the conference. The conference proposed that a pilot project in the way
of special enforcement machinery be set up for the Hyde Park-
Kenwood area at once which, if successful, could be used for all
other renewal areas in the city as they developed. The objectives
of such enforcement machinery were:

1. To prevent the spread of blight and discourage new speculators from moving into the 80 per cent of the area still in good
condition.

2. To force out of the area those operators of slum buildings
already entrenched by making team inspections and bringing the
findings of all inspection bureaus into court as a single consoli-
dated case.

3. To make these findings available to the Land Clearance
Commission for use when negotiations for acquisition took place.

The mayor showed awareness of the problems facing the area
and the city, but conference members came away from the meeting with the impression that no immediate action was likely to be
taken. Fortunately, Mr. Landesman, in a post-meeting discussion

with the conference director and Mr. Ramsey, successfully urged that there be team inspections and coordinated court cases on at least a few buildings in Hyde Park-Kenwood. This was something, but it was not encouraging. The conference did, however, select ten slum buildings and ten deteriorating buildings from its mounting lists and sent the addresses to the Building Department.

Within a week of the visit to the mayor, a fire in one of the buildings injured ten firemen and made some eighty families homeless. Ironically, this was the same building (described in Chapter 4, pages 36 to 38) in which the conference had achieved its first victory over overcrowding. Five years later, overcrowding had begun again.

The manager of the building had moved eighty families, including thirty children, into the again converted three-story structure even before heat, water, and gas had been installed. Garbage had not been collected for three weeks. Six times within as many weeks the conference had reported the condition of the building to the city, and the Building Department had just been preparing to take action when the fire occurred. The community was outraged. Every newspaper in the city carried the story.

The mayor acted the next day to put the conference suggestions into effect.

"A special task force of five inspection teams will crack down on dangerous and substandard housing conditions," announced the press. "The mayor said each team will include two fire inspectors, a building inspector, a housing bureau representative, a health inspector, an electrical inspector, and an assistant corporation counsel. 'If the task force idea works out,' said the mayor, 'it will be used in other neighborhoods.'"

The number of teams was later expanded to seven, and a plumbing inspector replaced one of the two fire inspectors on each team.

Teams assigned to Hyde Park-Kenwood inspected fifty buildings in the next two weeks. Within a month suits had been filed against most of these fifty owners by the city. Within two months $30,000 in fines had been levied against ten owners who were so impressed by the mayor's intentions that they had brought their buildings into complete compliance even before they came to trial. By November 1, 1957, coordinated court cases on 64 team-inspected buildings had been filed in the municipal or superior courts, and fines totaling $51,645 had been levied in 54 of them (in contrast to the $1,525 in fines levied on 36 owners in 1956).

Community residents flocked to the hearings and were cheered by the results. Some of the familiar dodges of slum operators no longer worked. Several of the judges refused to allow more than one continuance. Exploiters of property, surprised and dismayed at the speed of court action and the unexpected severity of judges, were given pause.

Pleased by the trial run of the pilot project, Commissioner Ramsey asked for an increase in his department's 1958 budget to provide for the establishment of twelve inspection teams. The proposal, vigorously supported by the conference which enlisted the help of a number of community groups throughout the city, was approved by the City Council, and the team inspection system has now become a permanent part of the city's slum-fighting program. A separate "anti-slum" division was also set up in the Department of Law to work solely on building, housing, zoning, and urban conservation cases.

Unquestionably, inspection and enforcement services had been greatly improved, but the conference remained unsatisfied. They were not yet good enough. Although over $50,000 in fines had been levied, only $15,000 had been collected. Judges continued to suspend or vacate fines if an owner eventually complied with the ordinances. The fines themselves were not as large as they needed to be to convince slum operators that the days of quick and easy gain had passed. Further, the new program of code enforcement would not be completely successful until all the agencies dealing with blight and renewal coordinated their efforts—the Building Department, the Department of Law, the courts, the Community Conservation Board, the Department of Planning, the Chicago Land Clearance Commission, the Chicago Housing Authority—under an intelligent over-all plan.

Mayor Daley is aware that the success of Chicago's urban

renewal program depends on strict enforcement. His backing made possible the adoption by the City Council in January 1958 of a registration of ownership ordinance. Conceived by Building Commissioner Ramsey, this ordinance requires all buildings with three or more dwelling units to register with the Building Department the name of the owner and the agent designated as responsible for the maintenance of the property when the owner is not available, together with a physical description of the building, including number and location of all family and rooming units and the number of occupants.

As late as January 1958, a number of lives were lost in a series of disastrous fires in the community north of Kenwood. These occurred in buildings violating city ordinances where law enforcement had obviously been lax. The chief justice promised broad improvements in court procedures.

CHAPTER 12

Getting New and Improved Facilities and Services

SCHOOLS

By early 1951 overcrowded housing had begun to be reflected in overcrowded schools. One of the community's five elementary schools was already on double shift, another was expected to be shortly, and a third was operating at top capacity.

When the conference was first organized, its Public Schools Committee had concentrated on human relations in the schools. In 1951 a subcommittee on overcrowded schools was formed, and thereafter a major share of the activities of the Schools Committee was directed toward securing adequate facilities.

A description of one year's work might be helpful.

In 1953 the Schools Committee faced the fact that the previous school bond issue of $50 million would soon be exhausted. Even at the time of its passage, it had been insufficient to meet then current school needs. In the meantime, enrollment had grown until it exceeded capacity in every one of Hyde Park-Kenwood's five elementary schools. One school, which had acquired an addition the preceding year, again had twenty-five classes on double shift; another had outgrown temporary buildings erected less than a year before; and every one of the schools was threatened by half-day sessions, a pattern vigorously resisted by parents. The situation was even worse in the adjacent communities of Oakland and Woodlawn, whose four elementary schools had recently been included in the expanded Schools Committee of the conference. And the 1950 census figures showed that the largest increases in school population were yet to come. Some of the schools lacked such essential facilities as libraries, lunchrooms, home mechanics rooms, playground space. The one high school which served the entire area was not yet crowded but would be overwhelmed within a few years when the large elementary school group reached high school age, and no planning was being done to meet that crisis.

In February 1953 the conference urged the city-wide Citizens Schools Committee to take immediate steps to stimulate action toward securing funds for an adequate school-building program. While the search for more permanent solutions proceeded, the Conference Schools Committee and the local PTA's prevailed upon the Board of Education to adopt special temporary measures to alleviate overcrowding and prevent double shifts. Space was rented in Temple Isaiah Israel and the First Unitarian Church for two of the schools, and the eighth grade of a third was housed in the high school.

At the same time, the statistics and needs of every school in the area, together with general information related to the increase in school population, were being carefully documented. A community-wide meeting agreed on a series of proposals and selected a special committee representing the religious, business, educational, and civic bodies to call on the superintendent of schools.

The Board of Education was asked to create a planning unit which would prepare, in cooperation with local PTA's, other interested community groups, school administrators, and planning agencies, a master plan of each community's school-building needs for the next five to ten years. Joint planning of this kind would lead to informed and active lay groups throughout the city which could spearhead the financial drive for an expanded school program.

The committee asked that the capacity of elementary schools to be built in the future be figured at the reduced rate of thirty per classroom instead of the current average of thirty-seven, so that new buildings would not be forever tied to inadequate standards.

They urged the Board of Education (1) to ask the state legislature to authorize a referendum for a bond issue that would be adequate to modernize the city's schools and (2) to seek additional sources of revenue for the developing and staffing of an expanded school program.

They described the conservation efforts in the community and the importance of the schools to those efforts and asked that the Board of Education take advantage of an unparalleled opportunity to use the area as a demonstration that would serve as a pattern for other communities.

These suggestions were then related to school problems within Hyde Park-Kenwood. There would be a deficit of 1,171 classroom seats by September 1954 *if no additional pupils entered the schools.* The committee pressed for inclusion in the next year's budget of appropriations that would provide "for more school facilities north of 47th Street . . . in the Ray School District which would also relieve pressure on surrounding schools . . . for additional facilities in the Woodlawn area . . . for an addition to the Bret Harte School . . . for a new high school within the next few years."

The predictable growth of the community was not being planned for. The Board of Education had to recognize that larger incoming groups would have to be cared for in the next few years—and there had been no drop in the birth rate.

In January 1954 the Schools Committee appeared before the full school board. The city already had 11,000 elementary and high school pupils on double shift, the committee stated, and went on to deal with the increases in school population both currently being experienced and predicted and the problems these increases would be creating.

The statistics were presented by Dr. Philip M. Hauser to show that enrollment in the elementary schools in Chicago—public, private, and parochial—would increase by 67 per cent between 1950 and 1960, and that by 1965 the high school enrollment would have increased by 104 per cent. The number of classrooms required added up to a frightening total, and these estimates did not take into consideration "any increase in school population due to continued net in-migration of population."

At previous meetings with the Citizens Schools Committee and the Association of Community Councils agreement had been reached on the urgency of pressing the school board to take immediate steps to obtain another bond issue. Summaries of Dr. Hauser's statement and the presentation of the Conference Schools Committee had been sent in advance to these agencies and to community groups throughout the city. During the day-long hearings before the school board, representatives of one organization after another rose and stressed essentially the same points, in full endorsement of statements by the Citizens Schools Committee and the conference. In separate presentations, representatives of the PTA's in the Hyde Park-Kenwood, Oakland and Woodlawn communities, whose leaders had shared in framing the Schools Committee's statement, supported each of its requests both for attention to specific local needs and to the general city-wide program.

As a result, appropriations of $1,675,000 were voted for the school area served by the conference to meet all of the immediate needs pointed out by the Schools Committee and the PTA's: a completely new school for Woodlawn; an addition to the school in Oakland that would "provide more facilities north of 47th Street"; and additions to the Ray and Bret Harte Schools in Hyde Park. (The preceding year the Board of Education had authorized two developments which relieved pressure in Kenwood.)

During the next few months, the Board of Education analyzed Dr. Hauser's figures and studied school needs; the Schools Committee kept in touch with the superintendent and individual school board members who were struggling toward a difficult decision. These authorities knew better than anyone else that tremendous sums were required but they feared public reaction to any request for them.

"It is a terrific fight to get any financing measure passed," they said. "If we ask for too much we may be defeated by the people, particularly by the large real estate owners and businessmen who have always protested high expenditures and increased real estate taxes."

So the Schools Committee went to the community's people. Over seven thousand people signed petitions giving enthusiastic backing to the Board of Education in any proposals it might make that would result in an adequately financed school program and expressly stating that they would be glad to pay increased taxes to make such a program possible.

A meeting of business and civic leaders was arranged. Using charts and graphs, the Schools Committee chairman painted a vivid picture of the current unhappy school situation within the community; Dr. Hauser sketched the proportions of the crisis posed by the growing school population; a banker gave compelling reasons for businessmen to take leadership in encouraging and supporting an imaginative long-range school program. It was made clear that the interests of businessmen were directly related to the condition of schools, since good schools played an important role in keeping residents in communities and preventing the development of slums; that with deterioration business fell off, property values declined, bank deposits suffered; that the conservation efforts already under way, into which millions of dollars would be poured, would fail if the school situation were not improved.

At the conclusion of the meeting, members of the audience signed a scroll urging the Board of Education to show courageous leadership, to tell Chicago's people how much money was needed for additional classrooms and other school expenses, and offering to help educate citizens to the importance of supporting financial measures designed to raise it.

It was decided that the scroll, together with the signed petitions, should be presented to the Board of Education by a special committee made up of three bankers, Dr. Hauser, the director of the conference, and the president of the Hyde Park Community Council. This was done during a discussion in which the committee stressed the fact that the financial solvency of the city, dependent as it was on real estate taxes, was seriously affected by neighborhood deterioration. If residents left Chicago for the suburbs, the city lost desperately needed support for all services, including the schools. The maintenance of good school standards was an important part of the effort to keep taxpayers in the city. Any money that was needed to do this would be well spent.

At the invitation of the superintendent of schools the committee attended the next meeting of the school board.

"I had a rare and exciting experience last week," the school superintendent said to his board. "It was the first time in my experience that bankers urged an increase in taxes. They came in to present a scroll and petitions signed by seven thousand, pleading for adequate school financing, and pledging their support to such a program. They represent the Hyde Park-Kenwood community and I invited them to come today so you could meet them."

The Board of Education soon asked for a bond issue of $50 million to be spent in two years. The voters overwhelmingly approved the bond issue in April 1955.

By early 1958 the Board of Education, responsive to the record of need so thoroughly and regularly documented by community representatives, had made a number of new facilities available to the area served by the Schools Committee. Ten additional school buildings had been put to use: three newly constructed as separate schools; two older buildings purchased to alleviate overcrowding; and four additions to already existing schools. The Board of Education had also purchased a large vacant site for future school building and was renting the athletic field of a private college for playground use by public school pupils. In planning new buildings, school officials were now conferring with community representatives and local school administrators, a process which was creating understanding and resulting in greatly improved school-community relations.

The active building program, together with the practice of renting facilities, instituted at the request of the community, had succeeded in preventing or eliminating double shifts at most of the area's schools.

These successes encouraged school groups in other communities to follow the conference practice of appearing each year at the budget hearings of the Board of Education with well-documented, factual statements of school conditions to support their requests.

The Conference Schools Committee had not been alone in securing these advances. The individual PTA's, as well as the South East Chicago Commission after its organization, had also pressed for improvements. And, happily, the Board of Education was thoroughly committed to a school system with the highest possible building and service standards consistent with budgetary limitations. But it was widely recognized that the work of the Schools Committee in uniting the PTA's and other community groups in a single community force for better schools, its constant marshaling of facts to document requests, the informed and articulate leadership it had provided in presenting the community's needs to school authorities, and its understanding and help on the financing problems of the Board of Education had contributed massively to these developments.

In spite of these advances, still further facilities were sought— and needed to be. At the December 1957 budget hearings, the Schools Committee was again pointing out the need for additional classrooms.

Through the years the Schools Committee had also sought improved school services. Toward that end, subcommittees undertook a series of special studies.

They explored existing services for the atypical child in their own community and in the city and found great unmet needs. They recommended that special provisions be made for children whose learning or behavior patterns differed radically from the so-called "norm"—the ungraded, the trainable mentally handicapped, the socially and emotionally maladjusted, the "gifted," and those who because of language or background handicaps needed special orientation. The local high school's limited honors program for exceptional seniors now has been greatly expanded to provide special accelerated classes, beginning with the freshman year, on the basis of the elementary school record of students. Decelerated classes for students who are far below the class norm have also been introduced, together with a special course in "community civics" stressing orientation to effective community living.

Committee members explored ways in which the schools might use social service and mental health agencies to help pupils and their families. They held an institute and printed a "Community Guide to Health and Welfare Services for the School-Age Child and His Family," to provide parents, teachers, school nurses, and principals with information on sources of help for children whose special problems require it.

To make up for the lack of recreational services in the southeast area, the committee persuaded the Board of Education to authorize expansion of its after-school recreation program to include three of the community's schools.

PARKS AND RECREATION

During the first few years of its existence, the conference did not become involved in any large-scale efforts either to improve existing recreation facilities or to create new ones. The Hyde Park Community Council had already done some work in the field of recreation and was believed to be the logical agency to give leadership in planning for new or unmet recreational needs.

The Recreation Committee of the conference, therefore—first under the leadership of John Guinessy and later of Alvin and Rhoda Eichholz—devoted itself (1) to seeing that the recreation services of the community were available to all groups without discrimination (most agencies, it was found, had sound policies in this respect); (2) to helping block groups whenever necessary with the organization of tot-lots; and (3) to acquainting community residents with the recreation resources of the community, which was done each year beginning in 1952 by the preparation of a recreation directory distributed through the schools and community organizations. This program was considered adequate until unexpected developments led to the adoption of new measures.

In the spring of 1954 the community was aroused by a threat

174

to one of its most highly prized attractions. The Wooded Island in Jackson Park, a quiet spot of forested beauty surrounded by a lagoon, was to be taken over by the Army for military installations. Indignation was widespread. Surely it was possible for the Army to create installations without destroying limited park and recreation area! Citizens, including conference leaders, protested vigorously. The conference board of directors asked the Army to consider alternate sites. The Wooded Island proposal was finally abandoned.

Without prior consultation with the community, however, the Army and Chicago Park District then moved to another cherished park site—the Promontory. This tree-shaded expanse of land jutting out into Lake Michigan had long been a favorite area of quiet recreation for community residents. Before the community knew what was intended, work had begun. Sections of the Promontory were barricaded from public use, trees were felled, radar installations were brought in. Angered and outraged, community residents kept the conference phones busy.

Quite aside from the threatened loss of one of the community's chief assets and the preservation of its parks, the need for additional recreation space and facilities had now become a serious problem. More, not less, land was required to serve the increasing population. Something had to be done, too, about adding to and improving recreational services as well as stepping up the rapidly declining maintenance of public parks and playgrounds.

By this time the Hyde Park Community Council had gone out of existence and the Conference Recreation Committee had ceased to be active. A new Parks and Recreation Committee was therefore formed in March 1955. Mrs. Alex Elson, a former social worker, was appointed to head it. Assisted by Co-chairman John Ramey, director of the Hyde Park Neighborhood Club and by an able and knowledgeable group, Mrs. Elson lost no time in going to work.

At first most of the committee's effort went into trying to retain the threatened park land for recreational use. The Army had leased from the Chicago Park District about ninety acres throughout the city, and twenty-three of them were in Hyde Park-Kenwood's Jackson Park. Members of the conference committee held discussions with Park District authorities and army officials, suggested alternative sites, met with park and army personnel to study them, secured the cooperation of Congressional representatives, appeared at public hearings.

As alternatives to the Promontory they suggested the use of other sites in the community, the building of an artificial island offshore, compensation by the Army in land or money to replace recreational space taken for military installations. They asked that there be no further destruction of the Promontory's beautiful trees. Other individuals and groups supported these requests.

The authorities explored the suggested alternatives with representatives of the committee. For reasons of cost, the time involved in implementing them and the work already done, the Army felt that it could not withdraw from the Promontory site. It did, however, modify its plans. Fence lines were moved to allow more space for civilians; a hundred thousand dollars was paid to the Park District to have a lagoon filled in; the Army agreed to restore a sidewalk which had been removed from the outer rim of the Promontory, to refrain from cutting down any more trees, including a number of those already marked for destruction, and to have adequate landscaping done to hide the scars of the installations. The commissioners of the Park District also had a change of heart. They asked the Army to consider removing the installations to man-made islands in Lake Michigan within five years and to reach a decision well in advance of the expiration of current leases.

While the committee was still fighting this battle, it was faced with another emergency. Newly introduced bills in the state legislature proposed the construction of a convention hall in Burnham Park north of Hyde Park-Kenwood, threatening further loss of park land with subsequent overcrowding of recreational areas to the south. The city's planning agency opposed the idea on the grounds that it was bad planning, and private civic groups, including the conference, promptly rushed into action. (See Chapter 18.)

As it set up machinery to handle these crises, the Parks and Recreation Committee also settled down to its basic program. It had been charged by the board of directors with "implementing the conference's concern for the provision and maintenance of adequate recreational facilities and services in its area and for promoting the fullest use by the community of these facilities and services."

In addition to assuming the responsibilities of earlier recreation committees for producing the annual recreation directory and for providing instruction to block groups on creating tot-lots, the committee turned its major attention to studying existing parks and recreational areas and conferring with city agencies on their maintenance, improvement, and extension.

These studies and conferences revealed the gravity of recreational problems and the magnitude of the obstacles that stood in the way of their solution.

The administration and financing of the city's affairs were not centrally coordinated. Three separate organizations were responsible for public recreation: the Chicago Park District for large parks and boulevards; the Board of Education for play areas related to schools; and the Bureau of Small Parks and Playgrounds for small recreational areas. Each had a limited budget, a different method of obtaining funds, and a different salary scale for recreation workers. The Chicago Park District had special authority in its own right, floated its own bond issues, operated its own police force for boulevard and park patrol, and, unlike other city services, was not directly responsible to the mayor. All of the agencies had more demands upon them than they could meet; there was little communication or joint planning among them. The lack of centralization was inefficient and costly. (Consolidation of recreational facilities into the Park District and of the boulevard system into the city Department of Streets and Sanitation has since been approved.)

Reforming the structure and administration of the city's parks and recreation program would have to be undertaken not by the conference but by a city-wide organization. All the conference committee could hope to do was work through existing authorities to secure improvements.

The needs of older children and teen-agers were not being met. In spite of active programs of the Hyde Park Neighborhood Club, the YMCA, Jewish community centers, and the churches and temples, these agencies could not begin to serve all of the community's youngsters.

The Hyde Park Neighborhood Club had employed a street worker to reach the teen-agers roaming the streets and plan with them constructive leisure-time activities. Vacant stores were sought as centers for recreational programs. Block groups joined together to sponsor special recreation projects. The Welfare Council of Metropolitan Chicago had chosen the Hyde Park community for a three-year demonstration in the prevention and control of juvenile delinquency and, working in cooperation with agencies, individuals, and citizen groups, their Hyde Park Youth Project was in touch with problem youngsters and their families.

All of this helped, but space, equipment, and more supervision were needed. There were simply not enough active recreation areas in Hyde Park-Kenwood. While the community was ringed round by parks to the east, west, and south, these did not provide sections for active or supervised play. Boating had long since been discontinued. Bicycling was not allowed. There were not enough beaches: the South Side of Chicago with over 56 per cent of the city's population, had only one-third of the city beach facilities.

Even if complete facilities had been provided, there were other problems: the parks were not within easy walking distance of all community residents; all were cut off from the community by major traffic lanes, and one—with crossings only at isolated points—provided no safe access for an eight-block stretch.

The whole answer, therefore, could not be found in the extension of present park facilities. It was necessary to have internal parks and large internal playgrounds as well. The Kenwood community had one such playground—Farmer's Field—under the direction of the Bureau of Small Parks and Playgrounds. For some months, however, several of the block groups in the vicinity

178

had been troubled by the misuse of the field and the lack of adequate supervision. In addition, many young Kenwood children no longer played there because older groups from outside the area had displaced them. The teen-agers were victims of the Chicago Park District practice of building expressways and highways through park lands at the expense of the city's recreational resources; their overcrowded community north of Kenwood had lost its recreational facilities when the Inner Drive had been built.

Maintenance of the parks and beaches had declined so disturbingly that many long-time residents no longer used these public facilities. The beaches were grimy and dirt-ridden. The bathhouse at one of them was rotting and unsanitary. The drinking fountains were unclean, and there were not enough of them. Only about one hundred feet of beach space was in use and, since garbage was burned on the beach during the day, sometimes use even of this land was further restricted.

One of the lagoons in Jackson Park had become stagnant and odorous and was cluttered with an unsightly fill. Work on the permanent filling of another lagoon had stopped midway. Tottering bridges, long since condemned as unsafe, were still standing. The once lovely Wooded Island was bedraggled and neglected. The parkway along one of the boulevards was deteriorating from misuse and lack of housekeeping.

These conditions, as well as the basic unmet needs of the area, were brought to the attention of public officials. Committee members prepared documented reports for officials of the Chicago Park District, relying heavily on the guidance of Dr. R. N. Strong, an expert in park district history and administration; discussed these at length with the general superintendent and his technical staff; confounded the Park District commissioners by appearing regularly at their biweekly meetings—the first time any citizens' group had shown such interest in their operations; appeared at every public hearing to present testimony. To keep the Park District fully informed, the committee developed an orderly and responsible method of reporting park maintenance needs. Community residents were given forms on which they set down:

"Conditions noted. Date, time, and place observed. Name, address, telephone number of observer." Each committee member had a beat which he covered regularly.

The authorities were friendly and cooperative. They shared with committee representatives their immediate and long-range plans as well as their problems, gave them blueprints and maps of proposed changes, granted every request that seemed feasible, showed themselves willing to consider and reconsider suggestions the community put forward.

In three years this collaborative effort between citizens and public recreation agencies had produced highly encouraging results.

The pressure on Farmer's Field had been relieved by the development of a large new playground in Burnham Park, fully equipped with ball fields, swings, teeter-totters, jungle gyms, slides, picnic tables, drinking fountains. The program and supervision at Farmer's Field itself had been improved through the cooperation of the recreation director and volunteer recreation leaders drawn from the block groups.

Another large playground had been created in Washington Park to serve the congested southwest Hyde Park area.

An ordinance passed by the Park District commissioners in May of 1956 not only permitted bicycling in Hyde Park-Kenwood's three parks but in seventeen others in the city, and bicycle paths were being laid out along the lake front and through the parks.

Maintenance of the beaches, parks, and parkway strips had been greatly improved. The committee proudly reported to the conference board of directors that "The beaches are now beautifully clean." The entire beach area was being utilized, and arrangements had been made to have the beach housekeeping done in the early morning hours to prevent interference with bathers. A new sandsifter had been purchased and was in use; new signs had been put up; new drinking fountains and outdoor fireplaces had been added; willow trees had been planted for shade. The Wooded Island had a new footbridge and new lights and was being cleaned up.

All of these gains were encouraging but still inadequate. In 1958, in addition to asking for the further reconditioning and improvement of parks and parkways, the continued maintenance of high housekeeping standards, and the provision of such facilities as additional tennis courts and picnic benches, the conference committee was pressing for a broad, long-range program of improvement. This included planning for the financing of an internal park in north central Hyde Park (a project proposed under the community's urban renewal program); the use of bond funds to develop two promontories about a mile apart on the lake front with equipped and supervised beaches, boat harbors, and other recreational facilities; the preservation of existing recreational areas or their replacement in planning the location of new roadways.

STREET LIGHTS

Several blocks at once were sometimes plunged into darkness as the ancient, overburdened lighting system of Hyde Park-Kenwood broke down again and again. Even when it functioned at top form, the power was so limited that illumination was dim and spotty. Dark and shadowy expanses of areaway and sidewalk provided inviting hiding places for lawbreakers. Residents were afraid to go out at night, and these fears were heightened by periodic outbreaks of purse snatching and attack.

Some of the block groups took private action to light their streets. These, however, were viewed as temporary relief measures, not as a permanent solution. Citizens united in the conference had no wish to encourage the abdication of public responsibility.

Early in 1952 an increase in crime stimulated block groups to start a determined drive for community support in behalf of new street lighting. Petitions were placed in stores and circulated through personal calls. Over six thousand signatures were taken to the mayor. He promised a limited amount of new lighting for the following year.

The mayor kept his promise. In 1953, 275 new lights blazed

forth. Other installations followed until arterial arc lights had gone up in several sections of Hyde Park and in most of Kenwood.

Then the program came to a stop. Areas around the University of Chicago and in east Hyde Park which suffered most acutely from poor lighting were offered no hope of early relief. The Bureau of Streets and Sanitation, which was responsible for the lighting of streets other than boulevards, held that the remainder of its bond issues for street lighting would be spent in other communities. The Park District, which had set aside funds for the lighting of Hyde Park Boulevard some years before, now stated that this money would be inadequate to meet increased costs, and so had decided to do nothing until another bond issue could be arranged.

Yet meetings of block groups, urgent calls by the Fifth Ward superintendent, the concern of the University of Chicago administration, religious leaders, and hotel owners underscored the need for immediate relief. A new wave of petitions began to circulate.

After consultation with Alderman Despres, the conference brought together block leaders and political representatives to consider what might most usefully be done to persuade authorities to reverse their position. They decided that the most direct way out of the impasse was a call on the mayor by an influential group.

Not long afterward, in March 1956, the mayor received an impressive delegation led by the executive director of the conference: the chancellor of the University of Chicago, the president of the Council of Churches and Synagogues, the head of the Hyde Park Business and Professional Association, prominent hotel owners, the director of the South East Chicago Commission, the commissioner of the Community Conservation Board, the state senator, and the three elected representatives of the Fifth Ward—the alderman and both the Republican and Democratic committeemen.

"My only function here," said the Republican committeeman to the Democratic mayor, "is to prove that this is a nonpartisan group."

The group recognized that other areas also needed lights, but felt that it was in the interest of the total city to provide street lights in Hyde Park-Kenwood because (1) the city's first urban renewal program was under way there, all Chicagoans had a tremendous stake in the area, and the program could not succeed if present residents left because of fear; (2) under the urban renewal program the federal government would match on a two-for-one basis any money the city spent for major improvements in Hyde Park-Kenwood.

The university chancellor spoke of the difficulty of attracting and keeping students and faculty. The religious leader reported that attendance at evening services and church meetings had fallen off alarmingly. The businessmen were finding that evening store hours, instituted as a service, were becoming increasingly unprofitable. The hotel owners were having difficulty keeping guests and help, and offered to cooperate with the city by installing special lighting to illuminate areas surrounding their hotels.

An examination of a series of pictures of the area's streets at night revealed an over-all blackness faintly illuminated by lights coming from windows and porches which seemed to cast as much light as the occasional dim street lamps. Cars parked in the streets could scarcely be seen.

At the end of an hour's session the mayor was convinced.

The next issue of the *Hyde Park Herald* proclaimed:

Earlier this year (the Commissioner of Streets and Sanitation) had said that Hyde Park-Kenwood had already received a large portion of new lights, and would now have to wait until other areas of the City were serviced . . . But last Friday he said . . . "We are now ready to go ahead with lighting plans . . . We expect to have the streets around the University, east of the Illinois Central tracks, and in West Kenwood done by the end of the year."

Still unresolved, however, was the problem of lighting the boulevards.

The mayor had offered to talk to the Park District superintendent, but this did not necessarily mean there would be a change of policy, since the Park District was not responsible to him. After several months that produced no action, the conference arranged meetings between Park District officials and owners of large hotels and other properties fronting on the poorly lit boulevards. Out of these sessions came the following understanding.

The Park District would begin installation of Hyde Park Boulevard lights in the spring or early summer. While new lighting on Chicago Beach Drive would have to be delayed until federal funds provided for the further development of the Outer Drive currently under consideration, the Park District and hotel owners could improve conditions by beginning a cooperative effort at once. The Park District would install larger bulbs in the present lights, obtain more effective reflectors, and destroy places of concealment by thinning out heavy shrubbery. The hotel owners would make current available at no cost to the Park District and would start a drive to encourage all large property owners to cooperate in a private lighting program. By the end of 1957, hotels and institutions in the area had added enough private outside lighting to equal the total wattage of the public lights.

Meanwhile, the Bureau of Streets and Sanitation had started its program as scheduled. As 1958 drew to a close, all of Kenwood, except Drexel Boulevard, and most of Hyde Park had new lights. New fixtures were soon to be installed in south central Hyde Park, and not long thereafter it was expected that the single remaining sections in southwest Hyde Park and Kenwood would get them.

PART **3**

New Forces Are Committed To The Battle

CHAPTER 13

New Tools and New Resources

For the first two and a half years the conference struggled along alone, trying to meet the overwhelming flood of problems in a fingers-in-the-dike operation. Attempts were made to plug up every troublesome front by the work reported in the preceding chapters, but these were obviously only delaying actions.

What was needed were massive resources, public as well as private, and an imaginative and long-term planning program.

The conference had pressed for systematic planning with increasing urgency since its organization in 1949. In February 1952, after the Community Appraisal Study had failed to produce the hoped-for results, the Planning Committee recommended to the board that ways had to be found to embark on a planning program which included:

1. Study, correlation and collaboration in city-wide redevelopment and housing plans looking toward intelligent action on a city-wide basis.
2. Participation in and/or initiation of long-range planning for the Hyde Park-Kenwood community, with special emphasis on collaboration with groups serving a wider area (such, for example, as the South Side Planning Board).
3. Implementation of this planning by (a) stimulating the build-

ing of new housing and repair of the old; (b) working for the removal of blighted buildings, (c) urging certain types of re-zoning . . . (d) providing resources for aid in legal conversions; (e) following through on such aspects of planning as adequate community facilities, better business areas, adequate parking space, improved traffic control, relocation or elimination of taverns; (f) stimulating community interests, and securing community cooperation in planning by publicizing present and future plans.

A program of this scope, however, called for much more power and money, prestige, influence, and authority than the conference was able to muster.

These began to be available later in 1952 when added forces committed themselves to the community's improvement.

Early in 1952, at the suggestion of the Reverend Leslie T. Pennington, the Council of Hyde Park and Kenwood Churches and Synagogues tried to encourage six major agencies of the southeast Chicago area to join in a united attack on the problem of law enforcement. Meetings were arranged, and community problems were discussed.

Conference representatives held that an effective effort had to include not only "an enforcement program to protect what we now have" but "a planning and action program to encourage future developments that will result in the best possible community." They suggested that an evaluation be made of the program, effectiveness, and resources of each agency and what it might contribute to a total program.

The University of Chicago representative felt that the cooperative effort should be limited to law enforcement. He proposed the immediate formation of a new organization covering the communities of Oakland, Kenwood, Hyde Park, and Woodlawn, directed by a forty-five-man board and operating under an annual budget of thirty thousand dollars, toward which the University of Chicago would contribute one-third and the cooperating agencies the balance.

The Hyde Park Planning Association and Woodlawn, Inc. supported this proposal, while the Hyde Park Community Council and the Oakland-Kenwood Planning Association agreed with the conference that a broader program was essential and that the objectives and program had to be worked out carefully before the organization and financing needed to carry them out could be determined.

In March 1952 an outbreak of purse snatchings and attacks led the Hyde Park Community Council to call a mass meeting to consider what should be done. A resolution, prepared in advance for adoption by the meeting, authorized the appointment of a committee of five, headed by the chancellor of the University of Chicago, to explore ways of solving the crime situation. Other members of the Committee were Rabbi Louis L. Mann of Sinai Temple, Fred Sprowles, director of the Hyde Park YMCA, Mrs. Raleigh (Ursula) Stone, professor of economics at George Williams College, and Hubert L. Will, an attorney and a director of the Hyde Park-Kenwood Community Conference.

THE UNIVERSITY OF CHICAGO AND THE SOUTH EAST CHICAGO COMMISSION

Through the years, the University of Chicago administration had tried in a number of ways to protect and improve its immediate vicinity. It had built or bought housing for hundreds of university employees, helped to finance the purchase of homes for faculty members, tried to control the use and occupancy of surrounding property, helped to support such community organizations as the Hyde Park Planning Association, Woodlawn, Inc., and the South Side Planning Board, had been one of the major forces in bringing about, in 1939, a planning study of Woodlawn, the deteriorating community south of the university. These efforts had obviously been too limited to achieve their purpose. Deterioration had kept spreading, and the community surrounding the university had continued to decline with frightening speed.

Conference leadership had been greatly heartened, therefore, when in 1951 Lawrence A. Kimpton, the new chancellor of the university, stated that one of his high priority projects was to take the lead toward conservation of the South Side neighborhood.

Early in 1952, the six neighborhood organizations—including the University of Chicago—began the series of meetings described above.

The appointment of the university's chief executive as chairman of the Committee of Five brought him into concentrated study of the community's problems and eventually led to the university's commitment to a far-reaching community program.

For six weeks following the March mass meeting, the chancellor met with the Committee of Five almost daily to consider problems, explore possible solutions with experts, and arrive at recommendations to be made to a future community meeting. Law enforcement, the experts agreed, could not be dealt with in a vacuum. A broader program had to be envisioned.

The committee recommended that a new organization—the South East Chicago Commission—be formed, covering the Oakland and Woodlawn communities as well as Hyde Park and Kenwood, which would cooperate with already existing organizations in those areas. The University of Chicago would contribute $15,000 to a $30,000 budget the first year and $10,000 for each of the four succeeding years.

Why a new organization? Why not give the Hyde Park-Kenwood Community Conference sufficient financial help to enable it to enlarge its geographical boundaries, employ adequate staff, and expand its program and services?

Such an idea could never have been approved at that stage in community history. Reaction to the conference within the community, the university administration, and the Committee of Five was mixed and involved. Some believed it was doing a fine job as far as it went. They felt, however, that the problems the community faced were primarily economic and political and that the money and power needed to solve them could never be attracted by the conference because business, real estate, and major institutional interests did not have confidence in its motives, goals, or leadership. They believed that a new organization could handle the power side while the conference worked at the grass roots.

Suspicion of the motivation and conviction of the naïveté of

190

conference leadership played a major part in the decision. "The conference," said one member of the Committee of Five some years later, "actively welcomed new Negro families into the area. This alarmed many people because it seemed to us the problem was how to prevent engulfment. It was really to offset some of the activities of the conference on the one hand and to work cooperatively with it on the other that the South East Chicago Commission was formed."

In any case, the organization of the South East Chicago Commission was formally announced to the community on May 19, 1952, by Chancellor Kimpton on behalf of the Committee of Five, which referred to itself in its official report as "The Citizens Committee on Law Enforcement." Chancellor Kimpton was made chairman of the board of directors and the Executive Committee.

The new organization was to begin on a minimum program with two immediate objectives: the reduction of crime "by maximum utilization of those police facilities available to us," and strengthening the work already being done on the problem of illegal conversions by devising "a more comprehensive and effective approach."

The South East Chicago Commission conceived of itself as a super-organization coordinating and strengthening the work of existing agencies. All of the community organizations, however, with the exception of the Hyde Park-Kenwood Community Conference, later went out of existence: the Hyde Park Planning Association, the Oakland-Kenwood Planning Association, the Hyde Park Community Council. A new organization—United Woodlawn Conference—grew out of a merger of Woodlawn, Inc., representing property interests, and the Woodlawn Community Conference, a local citizens' group.

At its inception, the South East Chicago Commission began a concentrated effort directed at the reduction of crime, including the employment of a criminologist who worked closely with the police department. It began to work on building code enforcement, employing its own inspector to investigate deteriorated buildings and spearheading the prosecution of key cases against slum owners and unethical real estate operators. Its most important program, however, later developed in the field of planning and working with government officials on urban renewal.

In the spring of 1954, the University of Chicago and the South East Chicago Commission set up a planning unit housed at the university. A number of factors and influences led to its formation.

In 1952 the Metropolitan Housing and Planning Council had employed Reginald Isaacs (the guiding spirit in the Community Appraisal Study in which the conference had played a major role) to direct a study of community conservation, using the Kenwood-Hyde Park-Woodlawn communities as one of its "pilot-study areas." The three-volume study, entitled *Conservation*, published January 31, 1953, was partially financed by the University of Chicago. As part of that study, Harvey S. Perloff, who had been the first chairman of the Conference Planning Committee and was then director of the University of Chicago's Committee on Planning, prepared a report discussing university policy in relation to the larger community (revised and printed as a separate pamphlet—"The University of Chicago and the Surrounding Community"—in July of 1953).

Through the years other faculty members had pressed for long-range planning by the university. Now Perloff, building on the studies already made, found ample support for his thesis that the university community could be expected to deteriorate at an accelerating rate unless drastic measures were undertaken, that such deterioration would make it increasingly difficult to attract students and faculty, that the necessary action was unlikely unless the university took initiative and played a central role. The university had to concern itself, he said, with expanding and unifying its campus and providing desirable housing for academic, professional, and other middle-income groups, as well as with the redevelopment and conservation of the entire South Side. This called for two major contributions: "(1) the establishment of a planning unit to give direction to the total effort and to evolve specific plans and programs, and (2) the establishment and initial financing of an instrumentality to spark rehabilitation of properties and new construction in the community." The report was sent to university trustees, administrative personnel, and faculty.

Meanwhile, early in 1953, the conference had begun to invite the director of the South East Chicago Commission and the chairman of its real estate committee to meetings of the Conference Planning Committee, during which the need for university action was similarly stressed. In April of that year, Sydney Stein, Jr., the conference chairman, wrote to Chancellor Kimpton transmitting a statement of the planning objectives of the conference and urging the university to organize a planning staff. He also took advantage of every opportunity to discuss with University of Chicago trustees the need for the university to become directly involved in community planning.

Interest in the idea of a unified campus led to the appointment of an advisory group to Chancellor Kimpton which, in addition to university administrative officers, included three faculty members—Philip M. Hauser, Harold M. Mayer, and Harvey S. Perloff —all of whom had previous connections with the conference. The group suggested the setting up of a planning unit.

It was difficult for the university trustees to reach a decision on the university's role in the community. Some felt that once an area started to deteriorate its decline was inevitable and nothing could be done about it. Others believed that any money spent on a planning project would be wasted, and that as trustees responsible for finances they could not throw the university's money away. Still others, who lived in the suburbs, seemed too remote from the situation to assess its seriousness. But an informed few, supported by Chancellor Kimpton, kept insisting that the university had no choice, that whether or not it wanted to act it had to, since it would be unable to attract students, faculty, and funds if it existed in a slum. The trustees finally agreed.

The need for a planning unit had been further pointed up by the Chicago Land Clearance Commission in mid-1953. Following requests by the conference and South East Chicago Commission that the Chicago Land Clearance Commission survey a selected section of Hyde Park for blight to determine whether it could undertake redevelopment there, the Land Clearance Commission had declared that if such blight were discovered it would engage in redevelopment only if the project were part of a much larger plan aimed at the rehabilitation and conservation not only of Hyde Park but of the entire area served by the South East Chicago Commission.

Not long afterwards, the Field Foundation acted favorably on the application of the university for a grant to establish a planning unit. The foundation appropriated $100,000 over a three-year period on the understanding "that the university and the commission are committed to the development of a physically attractive, well-serviced, nondiscriminatory community where people with similar standards may live."

By April 1954 the Planning Unit had been established and staffed, with Jack Meltzer, a top-flight planner, as its director.

At last the vitally essential planning program, for which the conference had been striving almost five years, was under way.

PUBLIC AGENCIES AND THE NEW LAWS

In the meantime, the city of Chicago was also facing the problems of its declining neighborhoods. Blight had already overtaken many square miles around the center of the city, and a program to clear and rebuild a limited part of this area was under way. Slum clearance, however, was an exceedingly slow process. New slums might develop faster than the old ones could be redeveloped unless action was taken to conserve sixty square miles of middle-aged neighborhoods—half of Chicago's residential communities—surrounding the blighted areas.

In July 1952 the City Council adopted a resolution setting up the Interim Commission on Neighborhood Conservation which was later made a permanent body. The conservation and improvement of neighborhoods thus became a major objective of the city administration under Mayor Martin H. Kennelly. The new commission was advisory to the office of the housing and redevelopment coordinator, which was given responsibility for developing the city's conservation program.

Laws passed by the Illinois General Assembly in 1953 gave the city additional powerful tools in its fight against blight, and created new agencies.

One of the most important of these was the state's Urban Community Conservation Act, under which the Community Conservation Board was established in Chicago in September 1953. This bill grew out of recommendations made in the conservation study of the Metropolitan Housing and Planning Council.

The Urban Community Conservation Act declared neighborhood conservation (slum prevention) a public purpose which warranted the use of public powers and public funds. It granted municipalities the right to set up local machinery to prevent slums and rehabilitate "conservation areas" of not less than one hundred and sixty acres in which the structures in 50 per cent or more of the area were residential and had an average age of thirty-five years or more.

Conservation areas were defined as areas which might become slums by reason of "dilapidation, obsolescence, deterioration, or illegal use of individual structures, overcrowding of structures and community facilities, conversion of residential units into nonresidential use, deleterious land use or layout, decline of physical maintenance, lack of community planning, or any combination of these factors."

Under the act, the Community Conservation Board, appointed by the mayor with the approval of the City Council, was given authority to designate areas for conservation, approve community conservation plans, acquire, manage, and dispose of property in connection with the plans, including making repairs and bringing properties up to legal minimum standards when owners were unable or unwilling to do so. *It could use condemnation powers to eliminate standard as well as substandard structures when they interfered with the carrying out of the community's plan.* Local community councils of seven to fifteen members, the majority of whom had to be property owners, were to be nominated by the board and appointed by the mayor. These bodies were charged with advising the board in the preparation of conservation plans, assisting in their administration within the neighborhoods they represented, and approving plans before their submission to the City Council.

The office of the housing and redevelopment coordinator, which had been guiding the conservation program and briefing the Community Conservation Board, turned responsibility over to the new agency as soon as it was ready to assume it.

In 1953 also, private groups were empowered to act for conservation ends. The Neighborhood Redevelopment Corporation law, originally passed in 1941, had made it possible for private individuals to form corporations for the elimination of slum and blight in their communities. The law had never been used. Now an amendment, drafted largely by Julian Levi, executive director of the South East Chicago Commission, made its provisions applicable to conservation areas. Any three citizens could form a corporation to apply for permission to do redevelopment work in areas ranging from two to one hundred and sixty acres. The corporation could repair or demolish buildings, construct new buildings, and take other measures to conserve a development area. It could sell stock and obtain public or private financing for redevelopment projects. Before a corporation could acquire property by condemnation, however, it had to own or have the consent of the owners of 60 per cent or more of the property within the development area as well as approval of the proposals by the Neighborhood Redevelopment Commission, a public body appointed by the mayor with the consent of the City Council. Both this amendment and the Urban Community Conservation Act were declared constitutional by the Illinois Supreme Court in September 1954.

In 1953–1954, the city was also strengthening its enforcement program by new provisions. Amendments to the state's Revised Cities and Villages Act enabled the city to amend its ordinances to authorize liens for the demolition, repair, and enclosure of dangerous and unsafe buildings and the employment of injunctions requiring conformance with minimum standards of health and safety. Other amendments to the Municipal Code made possible severe penalties for violation of building and zoning ordinances.

During the same period, legislation was being enacted on the federal level.

Much of the Chicago thinking that had gone into the Illinois Urban Community Conservation Act became part of the recommendations of President Eisenhower's Committee on Housing Policies and Program released in December 1953. The recommendations, enacted into law as the Housing Act of 1954, called for a broad new urban renewal program to prevent and eliminate the causes of slum and blight. Under the provisions of the new law, the program of federal loans and grants established under Title I of the Housing Act of 1949 was broadened to provide help to communities for conservation purposes as well as for the clearance and redevelopment of blighted areas.

To become eligible for this new federal aid, a city had to give assurance that it would carry out a "workable program" directed toward removing the causes of blight and renewing its neighborhoods. Such a local program had to include effective codes and zoning ordinances, a master plan for the city's development, an analysis of neighborhoods to determine the need for rehabilitation or redevelopment, effective administration and enforcement, adequate financing resources, availability of suitable housing for families displaced by urban renewal activities, and active citizen participation and support. In addition, specific renewal plans for selected neighborhoods had to be approved by the newly created Urban Renewal Administration of the Housing and Home Finance Agency, and the city had to agree to pay its one-third share of the cost of renewal, either in cash contributions or in non-cash grants for public improvements—streets, lights, schools, parks, or other facilities.

To encourage private investment in urban renewal areas, Section 220 of the Housing Act made FHA-insured mortgages on liberal terms available for new construction and rehabilitation.

All of the new tools and new agencies described in this chapter —together with Chicago's existing public bodies—were drawn into the Hyde Park-Kenwood struggle to save itself.

CHAPTER 14

The Urban Renewal Program

By 1953 and 1954 the need for a comprehensive planning program was widely accepted. The University of Chicago and the newly created South East Chicago Commission began a pounding drive "to get the show on the road."

The Hyde Park-Kenwood-Oakland-Woodlawn communities were declared a conservation area by the Interim Commission on Neighborhood Conservation. A survey of a section of Hyde Park showed sufficient blight to justify public action. Neighborhood Redevelopment Corporations were established. Mayor Kennelly announced that an urban renewal plan would be prepared for the southeast area. The community's new Planning Unit established at the university began to work with city agencies on suggested plans.

When the federal Housing Act of 1954 became law, the office of the housing and redevelopment coordinator set out at once to satisfy federal requirements for a "workable program" by the city and to cooperate with the director of the Planning Unit in the preparation of an application for a federal urban renewal advance.

The next four years showed considerable progress—sometimes

much too slow to satisfy an impatient community, but nonetheless steady and solid.

Hyde Park's first redevelopment project got under way. The Chicago Housing Authority approved a public housing project in Kenwood. Federal money was provided to carry forward urban renewal planning for the entire Hyde Park-Kenwood area. The newly appointed Community Conservation Board employed the community Planning Unit to work out plans for Hyde Park-Kenwood, which the board now officially designated as Chicago's first conservation area. By November 1958, the plans had received the necessary city and federal approvals.

THE BEGINNING OF REDEVELOPMENT—HYDE PARK PROJECTS A AND B

The sections of blight and near-blight in the community had been delineated in the conference "Report to the Community," distributed in 1951. For the next two years, the conference noted with growing alarm the rapidly spreading deterioration of buildings in these areas, and the inability of the Building Department to take effective action.

Sections of north central Hyde Park were in the most urgent need of attention. Anxiety centered mainly around an over-crowded, dilapidated, vermin-infested firetrap of a tenement dating back to the Columbian Exposition, which had been aptly dubbed "Misery Mansion." This slum building had so infected surrounding structures that they, too, were in a hopeless state of decline. Demolition, not rehabilitation, was called for. The budget of the Building Department, however, was inadequate to demolish all of Chicago's worn-out buildings, and the city's land clearance agency had always operated only within areas of total blight.

In mid-1953, Harold M. Mayer, then chairman of the Conference Planning Committee, proposed a solution. Since an area had to be designated as slum and blighted before there could be action under the Illinois Blighted Areas Development Act of 1947, he suggested that letters be sent at once to the Chicago Plan Commission and the Chicago Land Clearance Commission asking that they examine a section within Hyde Park—"the area bounded by 54th Place, the alley east of Blackstone Avenue, 55th Street and Ridgewood Court" (covering some three blocks) with a view to including it in the map of blighted areas. The Planning Committee and the board of directors approved, and the letters were dispatched forthwith. At the same time, the South East Chicago Commission was asked to send similar requests.

This was the beginning of Hyde Park-Kenwood's first redevelopment program. The director of the South East Commission and the chancellor of the University of Chicago began to press for the project. They met with top public officials and, in November 1953, the Chicago Land Clearance Commission began a survey embracing an even larger area than the conference had suggested—53rd Street to 57th Street, Woodlawn Avenue to Lake Park. Within that area enough contiguous blight was found to qualify a project in Hyde Park for public assistance. Two separate sections were selected for redevelopment—one of 42.7 acres, which the Land Clearance Commission called Hyde Park A, and the other—Hyde Park B—of 4.6 acres.

Hyde Park-Kenwood had pioneered again. For the first time a community had itself invited a slum clearance agency to come in. And for the first time, to help save the total community from the bulldozer, the land clearance powers of a public agency were to be put to work in a neighborhood that was largely good instead of wholly blighted.

The area to be cleared and redeveloped contained the largest and most troublesome concentration of blight—it covered only 6 per cent of Hyde Park-Kenwood but included 41 per cent of the community's deteriorated dwelling units. Included in it, too, were twenty-three taverns, a high proportion of transient residents, and a "Skid Row." Its character and size allowed it to qualify for city, state, and federal help with a minimum of delay. And the relocation problem was not expected to be serious both because the population was predominantly white and therefore easier to rehouse and because the high rate of "floaters" would reduce the need for family-size housing units.

Before the site could be officially designated, however, a number of steps had to be taken:

1. A site designation report had to be prepared by the Chicago Land Clearance Commission. The Planning Unit of the South East Chicago Commission, on the basis of information obtained by the Land Clearance Commission and its own studies, prepared an analysis and recommendations. These suggested the boundaries of the site to be redeveloped and a plan for rebuilding it.

2. The site designation report of the Land Clearance Commission had to be approved by the Chicago Plan Commission and then in turn by the City Council and the Illinois State Housing Board.

3. A "redevelopment plan" giving the proposed land uses in greater detail had to be developed and approved by city, state, and federal agencies.

4. An acceptable redeveloper had to be found, and his plan for rebuilding the area had to receive official approval.

During each of these steps, proposals were given wide publicity.

Challenged by the vitality of the community and the prestige of the University of Chicago, five redevelopers submitted plans in what the *Chicago Tribune* hailed as an unprecedented display of interest by private capital. "No other project of this kind in the United States," said the editorial, "has ever attracted this kind of competition."

In March 1957 the City Council approved the plan of the New York real estate firm of Webb and Knapp, headed by William Zeckendorf. It had some changes from the redevelopment proposals approved by the City Council two years before.

Of the net project area of 35.1 acres (12.2 of the 47.3 acres in Projects A and B had been reserved for streets and alleys), the Webb and Knapp plan assigned well over half to residential use, approximately one-third for shopping and parking, and the balance for public and institutional purposes. The plan provided for the construction of up to 825 dwelling units: two-thirds in two elevator buildings eight stories high, to be sited within a super-block two blocks long and two hundred feet wide in the center of the project; the remainder in row houses (up to three stories high) to be grouped around the super-block. There would be a nine-acre shopping center, including ample parking space, separated from the residential area but integrated with it; park-playground areas adjacent to a school and a recreation agency, reserved for development by city agencies; a university inn and restaurant. Through traffic would be handled by the widening of two streets and the relocation of one of them.

Over $25 million was to be spent on the project. The redeveloper's cost would be more than $15 million; the public cost approximately $10 million (representing the difference between the costs of land acquisition, relocation, building demolition, and installation of site improvements and the amount for which the vacant land would be sold to the redeveloper).

Acquisition of the land and buildings by the Chicago Land Clearance Commission had been begun in May 1955. By the fall of 1958, all buildings but one (the fire station) had been acquired and only four remained to be demolished. On September 25, ground was broken for the beginning of reconstruction. With another three years required to finish building, Hyde Park Projects A and B would take seven years from inception to completion.

PUBLIC HOUSING

Plans for the first public housing project in the community were developed because of the interest of several of the block groups in and surrounding Hyde Park A and B.

In May 1954 the conference had approved the first tentative recommendations for Hyde Park A and B developed by the Planning Unit of the South East Chicago Commission with the understanding that in the total urban renewal plan provision would be made for housing that would meet the needs of different income groups.

The block leaders were not satisfied. How could there be intelligent planning for relocation housing, they wanted to know,

202

without information that affected the ability to find housing—race, income, the housing requirements of people to be displaced by the redevelopment project? Although the Land Clearance Commission, as acquisition proceeded, would determine the housing needs of the people to be dislocated from each building, the conference was persuaded of the importance of immediate action and prevailed upon the South East Chicago Commission and the University of Chicago to authorize a survey at once.

The findings of the National Opinion Research Center, which was engaged to do the job, were made public. Of the 892 families in the project area (exclusive of families in rooming houses) 72 per cent were white, 18 per cent Negro, 6 per cent Oriental, and 4 per cent Mexican or Puerto Rican; 4 per cent of the dwelling units were owner-occupied; there had been a 50 per cent turnover of families in the project area in the last two years, 25 per cent having settled there within six months; 45 per cent of the families had incomes under $3,500 and another 29 per cent had incomes between $3,500 and $5,000; of the families eligible for public housing who would be willing to accept such housing, 112 white and 80 nonwhite indicated that they preferred to continue to live in Hyde Park. The Planning Unit was directed by the South East Commission to work with public agencies toward a solution of the housing problem.

It was possible to use a comparatively vacant site at the southwestern border of Kenwood. To meet some of the needs for additional classroom space as well as low-rent housing, it was decided that the site should be developed jointly by the Chicago Housing Authority and the Chicago Board of Education. A housing development with 84 dwelling units was authorized by the City Council. The 600-pupil school was ready for occupancy in February 1958.

Should there or should there not be additional public housing in the community? Some of the residents vigorously opposed even this one, while others pushed even more vigorously for as many such projects as could be obtained. The public housing struggle had only just begun. (See Chapter 16.)

PARKING LOTS

Increasing car ownership in high density neighborhoods created one of the many serious planning problems. In 1951 Alderman Merriam had secured City Council approval of routing traffic on the one-way street system but, even so, with cars already lining both sides of narrow streets, parking as well as driving was difficult. In an area so heavily built up, where could off-street parking facilities be put? Private builders would have to make parking arrangements for future housing and business developments, but could public funds add to the necessary supply of parking facilities for existing structures?

When the city of Chicago began to build parking structures in downtown Chicago, financed by the sale of revenue bonds, Hyde Park business leaders together with the alderman and the director of the South East Commission started to negotiate for facilities in the 53rd Street business district. Although urban renewal planning was not yet under way, here was a possibility for public assistance that could not be overlooked. After the Planning Unit was organized, other suggestions for residential facilities as well were put forward.

It was not until June 1956, however, that the City Council approved the proposal to develop two parking areas in Hyde Park—one, primarily for business use, providing 178 parking spaces, to be built in the north central section where most of the buildings to be demolished were blighted; and the other, for approximately 160 cars, to be set up on a predominantly vacant site in east Hyde Park where the needs of residents would be served.

THE REDEVELOPMENT CORPORATIONS

At the same time, private interests were being encouraged to play a constructive role in the urban renewal program through the formation of neighborhood redevelopment corporations.

Soon after passage of the amendment to the Neighborhood Redevelopment Corporation law in 1953, the South East Chicago Commission arranged with three property owners in a badly deteriorated four-block section on the western border of Hyde Park for the organization of the Maryland-Drexel Redevelopment Corporation, the first such corporation in Chicago's history. A plan for the acquisition of property and the improvement of the section was drawn up, the consent of owners of 60 per cent of the property was obtained, and the proposal was approved by the Chicago Neighborhood Redevelopment Commission. The plan was never implemented, but this first corporation made an important contribution nonetheless. It provided the successful test case for an Illinois Supreme Court ruling on the constitutionality of the amendment to the redevelopment law.

The next two redevelopment corporations—in Kenwood and Northwest Hyde Park—were set up through the joint interest of block groups and the technical assistance and advice of Julian Levi, director of the South East Commission. These were followed by the East Hyde Park Neighborhood Redevelopment Corporation which brought together hotel owners and other large property interests in the area between Lake Michigan and the Illinois Central tracks.

Each of these groups worked closely with the Planning Unit on the development of the urban renewal plans for its particular area. In addition, they attempted to deal directly with immediate problems peculiar to their neighborhoods. The Kenwood group concentrated largely—and successfully—on a real estate operation through which desirable homeowners were attracted. The Northwest Hyde Park Corporation also set up a voluntary real estate service. Both groups worked through the conference and the South East Commission on such problems as general law enforcement, the prevention and correction of building and zoning violations, overcrowded schools, the need for additional public facilities and services. Representatives of the East Hyde Park Corporation induced large property owners to install private lighting to supplement the public lighting program and cooperated in the effort to secure municipal parking lots.

It was unlikely that any of these corporations, however, would engage in large-scale clearance or construction. Parts of both Kenwood and Northwest Hyde Park called for considerable demolition and rehabilitation, but the cooperating residents and institutions in these sections were not prosperous enough to make more than token investments. The funds already obtained from the sale of stock, and those likely to be available in the future, were obviously too limited to finance an ambitious program. East Hyde Park, where adequate funds might be obtained, was in comparatively good condition and did not require severe action.

The fifth corporation to be formed—the Southwest Hyde Park Neighborhood Redevelopment Corporation—had both an ambitious program and University of Chicago money to see it through. The organizational work was again done by Julian Levi, and the corporation plan was drawn up by the Planning Unit.

The plan provided for the acquisition, by negotiation or condemnation, of a 14.5 acre tract of land directly northwest of the university campus for demolition and resale to the university. To meet its need for married student housing, the university would erect five five-story buildings accommodating two hundred families, with provision for future construction of another three buildings to house an additional one hundred. The total cost to the university would be $4,300,000. Also part of the "development area" were forty acres surrounding the property slated for demolition, and here the corporation proposed to use its power to spearhead the modernization and rehabilitation of dwelling units and establish occupancy standards.

The necessary 60 per cent consents were quickly obtained.

At the same time, a group of property owners in the redevelopment area formed themselves into an association to fight the plan and took their case to court where it was dismissed on a technicality. (See next chapter.)

URBAN RENEWAL FOR ALL OF HYDE PARK-KENWOOD

Jack Meltzer and his staff at the Planning Unit had not made their suggestions for Hyde Park Projects A and B, sites for public housing and parking lots, and the redevelopment of Southwest Hyde Park in a vacuum. All these were part of a comprehensive plan for the renewal of Hyde Park-Kenwood which Meltzer began to rough out as soon as he became planning director in April 1954, at the same time as the more detailed ideas for A and B were being set down.

Ideally, as Meltzer knew only too well, the total plan should have been prepared before specific projects were acted upon, but conditions were not ideal. People were continuing to leave the community. Something had to be done quickly to remove at least some of the blight, secure new facilities, and restore confidence. And it was possible to begin without delay by securing the cooperation of agencies which already had public funds that could be made available. Meanwhile, the South East Chicago Commission and the University of Chicago had been officially invited to work with the Chicago Plan Commission on the preparation of an over-all plan (in close association with the Hyde Park-Kenwood Community Conference, said later releases).

With the passage of the Housing Act of 1954, the financing of an adequate urban renewal program became possible. Jack Meltzer and D. E. Mackelmann, deputy housing coordinator, lost no time in preparing an application for federal funds to conduct necessary surveys and planning. It was hoped that on the basis of studies conducted with these funds, the federal government would authorize substantial expenditures for renewal in the Hyde Park-Kenwood section of the southeast Chicago area.

While all of the southeast area needed attention (the Oakland and Woodlawn communities had even more serious problems of deterioration than Hyde Park-Kenwood and fewer resources to meet them), it was manifestly impossible to cover so much territory in the application for federal funds. Hyde Park-Kenwood alone made up an area equal in size and population to many cities. The government might well consider even this part of southeast Chicago too costly an undertaking.

Hyde Park-Kenwood was an obvious choice. Traditionally among the city's finest residential communities, it was still predominantly stable though seriously threatened by deteriorating factors. It offered greater hope than any other Chicago community for the success of an urban renewal program because of the stabilizing effect of the University of Chicago and other important physical resources and the high degree of citizen interest and leadership. And Hyde Park-Kenwood had already gone far beyond the beginning stages on the road to renewal.

The application to the federal government asked for a planning advance of $198,680 to be used for additional studies and the preparation of a plan. The end product of these studies would be "a determination of the capital improvements, site improvements, and other major expenditures necessary to undertake and implement the renewal of the area."

The City Council approved the application in February 1955, it was forwarded to Washington, and in June the federal government authorized the full amount, half of which would be made available at once, the balance after approval of a "preliminary project report." The money was to be administered by the Chicago Community Conservation Board, which had been given full responsibility for the city's urban renewal program.

The Community Conservation Board, then in the throes of organization and staffing, employed Jack Meltzer's Planning Unit to carry out the studies and prepare the final plan under the policy direction of the board.

The Planning Unit had already done a considerable part of the mapping and preliminary exploration on the basis of which tentative suggestions for renewal had been drawn up. Now Jack Meltzer, acting under contract to the Community Conservation Board, set out to translate his earlier findings into specific proposals and to determine the feasibility of the proposals. A number of additional and more detailed surveys were initiated through his own staff, the Chicago Department of Buildings and other city agencies, and subcontracts to private research firms, architects, and realtors. Public departments made available the pertinent data in their files.

A mountain of materials piled up, adding to the mass of research that had already been done: maps and data on housing and the condition of every structure, existing surface improvements and facilities, characteristics of the population, community-wide problems and needs.

The documents were analyzed as they became available and

provided the base for the "Preliminary Project Report" required by the federal government midway in the operation.

The federal Housing and Home Finance Agency reserved $25,835,000 of federal money for the Hyde Park-Kenwood project, to be made available *if* the final plan was satisfactory and *if* the city would provide its one-third share toward the estimated $39,500,000 that would be needed in public funds.

Throughout the planning, two general problems common to all planners had to be faced and resolved:

1. Community plans had to be related to plans for the city: traffic problems, for example, had to be viewed in the context of traffic plans for the entire city, including the new Calumet Expressway, the Outer Drive, and other major thoroughfares which crossed or bounded Hyde-Park Kenwood.

2. Plans for the community had to be related to practical possibilities of achievement. To what extent, for example, should planning rest on long-range goals and to what extent should it be directed toward an action program based on immediate needs and possibilities, including existing laws, economics, and political situations?

Operating in a middle-aged neighborhood with high land coverage was far different from starting on open land to develop an ideal community. Given existing conditions in Hyde Park-Kenwood, how could its strong points be emphasized in line with long-range goals, and major changes for necessary facilities be made, without doing too much violence to a heavily built up community and driving residents away? What kind of planning would both meet the community's immediate and long-range needs and, at the same time, be financially, socially, and governmentally feasible and desirable?

Varying with the sub-areas and more severe in some sections than in others, the conditions with which the plans had to deal added up to a formidable list:

Slum buildings—17 per cent of the area's structures—occasionally concentrated in whole blocks.

The threat of conversions, rooming houses, congestion and overbuilding.

Violations of building and zoning codes.

An increasing vacancy rate.

Overcrowded schools.

Lack of space for housing, parks, play areas, parking, recreation facilities, and the expansion of community institutions.

THE FINAL URBAN RENEWAL PLAN

The planners believed that their final plan resolved the community's renewal problems as satisfactorily as they could be in all the circumstances. On February 18, 1958, the plan was released by the Community Conservation Board for community discussion before final action by public bodies. It covered all of Hyde Park-Kenwood with the exception of Jackson and Burnham Parks, the Illinois Central Right of Way, and those sections being developed privately or by other public programs.

Proposals of the final urban renewal plan.

Of the 855.8 acres in the renewal area, 105.8 would be subjected either to total or spot clearance or clearance for community facilities.

This would involve demolition of 638 of the community's 3,077 structures, containing 6,147 of the area's 29,467 dwelling units.

Thus 4,087 families (41 per cent white and 59 per cent nonwhite) would have to be relocated over a five-year period.

Approximately 2,100 new dwelling units would be built (over 1,600 in high-rise and the balance in low-rise buildings). Most of the building would be done by private developers. While there would be an actual loss of 3,997 dwelling units, in fact Hyde Park-Kenwood would be restored to the approximate number there had been before conversions had overcrowded the area.

The 23,320 dwelling units which were to remain—80 per cent of the area's structures—were substantially good and required no public attention.

(According to a careful study of 150 selected structures by the Zisook Construction Company, it would be economically feasible to salvage buildings constructed after 1915 by repair and modernization without undue rent increases. Under Section 220 of the Housing Act, insurance on loans up to 90 per cent of acquisition and rehabilitation costs, at 4½ per cent interest and with long-term maturities, would be available. These terms would make it possible for property owners to bring buildings into conformity with the electric code, modernize kitchens and bathrooms and do other work for rent increases of $2 to $5 per room per month. Thus two important ends could be served: (1) the basic job of conservation and improvement could be done by the individual property owner on his own behalf, and (2) housing in older buildings, currently averaging $22 to $27 per room, could be made available to middle-income families who could not afford the high cost of new construction. [One-third of the community's families had incomes between $4,200 and $7,200, one-third above $7,200, and one-third below $4,200.]

To provide adequately for the estimated increase in school population by 1963, 85 new classrooms and additional school play space would be provided by the Board of Education.

Every house would be located within three blocks of a play area. 24.3 acres of recreational space, including 10 new park and playground areas scattered over the community, would be added to the present 31 acres of open space, only about 10 of which are now devoted to recreation. Park and play areas were planned to give maximum service: a neighborhood park in central Hyde Park, for example, would serve an elementary school, a recreation agency, and two churches as well as neighboring families.

The facilities of institutions would be expanded: George Williams College, the Chicago College of Osteopathy and Osteopathic Hospital, St. Thomas the Apostle Church, St. Paul's Episcopal Church, the Hyde Park YMCA, the Hyde Park Neighborhood Club, the Church Home for Aged Persons. Land would also be provided for the construction of a child-care and research center for disturbed children and for an art and cultural center.

In addition to the neighborhood shopping center in Hyde Park A, there would be two new convenience shopping centers; an existing center would be expanded; and local shops would remain at convenient locations throughout the community. Stores characterized by marginal operation and non-convenience uses would be eliminated, and the space thus freed would be used for off-street parking for the remaining convenience centers.

Major traffic would be routed around, rather than through, the area, with three streets designated for improvement as through carriers. (Studies had revealed that 65 per cent of the traffic in Hyde Park-

Kenwood neither originated in nor was destined for the community.)
All other streets would be turned to purely local uses.

The plan prohibited discrimination on the basis of race, creed,
or color in the sale or lease of the land or in improvements on it.

By November 1958 the federal government and the Chicago
City Council had approved the urban renewal plan, which had
undergone some revisions after further public discussion. For the
renewal of the area, exclusive of Hyde Park Projects A and B,
about $139 million would be made available: $28 million from
the federal government; some $10 million from the city of
Chicago (about $8.2 million of which would be provided in non-
cash grants for schools, parks, street-lighting, traffic and utility
improvements); and investments of about $100 million in private
capital for rehabilitation of structures and new building.

The real work of renewal could now begin.

DIVISION OF LABOR

All this did not come to pass without great effort on the part of
many agencies, inter-organizational difficulties, and widespread
debate. In the process, the major organizations had to learn to
clarify their separate functions and to divide labor and responsibility so as to use their special talents and resources most effectively.

The role of the Conference Planning Committee changed. Most
of its original objectives, as revised in March 1953, were being or
had been attained through various avenues and agencies.

The long-range plan for which it had pressed for years was
now being prepared by a skilled planning unit. The University of
Chicago had at last become a leading factor in the planning.
Work on the re-zoning program was being undertaken jointly
by the conference and the South East Commission. Major attention was now turned to implementing one of the cardinal concerns of the conference—that the planning be done "with the
collaborative effort of the people in the community."

A complex inter-organizational arrangement was developed,
through which each organization made its special contribution.

The planning itself was the responsibility of the Planning Unit. Jack Meltzer, its tireless director, initiated the necessary studies, analyzed them, formulated the plans, and interpreted them to community leaders and public agencies.

Julian Levi, the director of the South East Chicago Commission, was equally tireless in the role of gadfly and expediter. He took leadership with government agencies, initiated discussions with top official and political figures, went to Springfield and Washington, cajoled and pressured large property interests and businessmen's groups, pushed ceaselessly in every direction to translate ideas into action.

Chancellor Kimpton made himself available for public contacts whenever the power of university prestige was demanded, and the university exerted influence on property through its own real estate transactions, and on community morale through the impact of its own interest and involvement.

The conference role is described in a later chapter.

Top local responsibility for the conduct of the over-all renewal program was vested unofficially in a Committee of Six representing the University of Chicago, the South East Chicago Commission, and the conference.

Liaison with public agencies was handled primarily by Julian Levi. When problems arose which were too serious for resolution by Levi or which called for the exertion of greater influence, the full Committee of Six stepped in—for conferences with the mayor, the housing coordinator, or other officials and, in one instance, top representatives of the three organizations called on the President of the United States.

This operational set-up was intricate and time-consuming, but it was effective. It produced an urban renewal plan with the necessary community, public and private support to carry it out.

CHAPTER 15

New Problems and New Solutions

Developing a basis for this complex cooperation would have been difficult enough under the most favorable circumstances. The existence of a powerful new organization and the beginning of the urban renewal program added complications that often threatened to split the community.

It was inevitable that the entry into the field of a new community organization, using different methods from those in which the conference had pioneered and supported by power groups antagonistic to the conference, should create inter-organizational misunderstandings, jurisdictional problems, overlapping, duplication of effort, and confusion in the community and the city.

At first, however, there was no sign of difficulty. A genuine disposition on the part of both organizations to coordinate their efforts was evidenced by the appointment of Sydney Stein, Jr., the conference chairman, as the South East Chicago Commission's vice-chairman in charge of program, and the election of ten members of the conference board of directors to the commission's seventy-five-man board. Ursula Stone of George Williams College, appointed acting director of the commission until a permanent director could be found, was knowledgeable about community organization and worked in close daily contact with the director of the conference to develop methods that would maximize the resources and effectiveness of the two agencies.

Difficulty began with the appointment of a permanent executive and the evolution of the South East Commission program in directions which sometimes brought it into conflict with the work or goals of the conference.

The operation of the commission was complicated by the wide geographical area in which it functioned and the fact that the different neighborhoods within its area were in varying stages of organization and development. Woodlawn and Oakland, for example, which did not have strong community organizations, needed considerable service from the commission on all cases involving violation of city codes. Hyde Park-Kenwood, which had the conference and an experienced staff person in charge of a building and zoning program, was in a very different position. Yet when commission publicity stressed a building and zoning program as one of its major functions, announced the employment of a private inspector, and urged the reporting of all suspected violations, it was natural for the people of Hyde Park-Kenwood, as well as those in the other neighborhoods, to assume—if they thought about it at all—that the new organization had taken over this responsibility for the entire area. Commission personnel seemed to confirm this belief by receiving and acting on all reports. This resulted in confusion and duplication of effort and sometimes, in spite of the best efforts of leaders involved in both the commission and the conference, the two organizations seemed to be working at cross purposes. While conference people might be trying to get voluntary cooperation from a new property owner and to involve him in their block group, the commission's inspector, or a city inspector responding to a commission call, might appear on the scene. Unaware of the distinction between the organizations, newcomers to Hyde Park were confused and sometimes angered beyond the possibility of cooperation. Confusion in the community spread, taking in even conference block groups whose representatives went to both organizations for help and frequently received conflicting advice.

The conference became alarmed lest the commission's help,

well-intentioned though it was, endanger the successful functioning of both the block groups and the building and zoning program which were interdependent. Residents of the blocks were the conference eyes and ears; their vigilance had been responsible for such success as there had been in stopping illegal conversions. The interest of block groups in building and zoning matters had been encouraged and their involvement maintained by the conference practice of keeping them informed on the progress of every case, the constant reporting back and forth between block people, the office, and the city Building Department. A break in the link could have grave consequences.

The personnel in the Building Department was equally confused. Information on cases reported by one organization was sometimes sent to the other. Occasionally resentment against the commission flowed over onto the conference and vice versa.

A basis for division of responsibility and cooperation was finally worked out. All violations in the Hyde Park-Kenwood area would be reported to the conference which would follow its usual procedures with block groups and the city departments and would continue to take cases to court when necessary. Information on conference activities would be made available to the commission. When necessary, the conference could call on the commission's inspector for his services. If all the regular measures used by the conference failed to produce results and additional pressure and power were demanded, the conference would turn to the commission for help. A detailed explanation of this arrangement was printed in the *Hyde Park Herald*.

Activity by both organizations on behalf of the schools also caused complications. From the beginning, the conference had had a strong public schools committee which had already achieved considerable success in securing new school facilities and services. The commission became involved in school matters as well and sometimes acted without consulting the committee. When this action was in conflict with the work of the committee, antagonism occasionally erupted into open controversy.

To make it unnecessary for the commission to set up schools committees of its own in Oakland and Woodlawn, the conference expanded the boundaries of its committee's work to take in the schools in those neighborhoods. The commission would be kept informed of conference activities on behalf of the schools through the service of a commission representative on the Schools Committee.

To clear up the confusion within the community, the purposes, functions, and methods of operation of the two organizations were reviewed in a public meeting. Attempts were made to establish liaison between them.

The conference, which had disbanded its real estate committee when the commission established one, invited two representatives of that organization to attend the monthly meetings of its Planning Committee. The commission invited two conference members to serve with two representatives from the University of Chicago and two from its own ranks on a committee of six to advise its Planning Unit. Members of conference committees began to confer with the director of the Planning Unit.

These steps were of limited usefulness. The real difficulty lay much deeper—in the different philosophy, approach, and methods of the two organizations.

It was natural that the commission, strongly supported by the University of Chicago, should be keenly aware of the university's interests, and equally natural that the conference, which had been created by community residents, should be primarily concerned about them. While these interests were sometimes the same, it was not always so.

Leaders of influential power groups, such as the university and other interests represented by the commission, were accustomed to having staff make decisions for their groups and put them into effect as quickly as possible by immediate and direct action. The conference, on the other hand, was committed to citizen participation in planning. This was regarded as too slow a process by the commission and the university.

In the person of Julian Levi, a dynamic, hard-driving, lawyer-turned-business executive, the commission found a director admirably suited to getting things done. Levi was a man of action as well as of ideas, a brilliant, quick-thinking operator who knew where he wanted to go, was in a hurry to get there, and was not inclined to slow down for advice or directions. He drove ahead with energy and singleness of purpose, often outmaneuvering the opposition with quick, devastating strokes at their most vulnerable spots. He threw himself and the organization he directed into one difficult situation after another as he built up an impressive record of practical successes.

He and the chairman of the Conference Legal Panel worked to get much-needed legislation on the books. His activities put one of the city's most dangerous real estate operators out of business. Improved policing, secured through the constant work of the commission with the police department, resulted in a reduced crime rate. And, most important, Levi helped to swing the power and prestige of the University of Chicago and the South East Commission behind the necessity of a planning operation, to give the university and public agencies the final push into the redevelopment and conservation program the conference had long been pressing for, and then to stay in the center of an increasingly complex picture and keep pushing.

In the process, Levi made enemies as well as admirers. His achievements were often obscured by the waves of antagonism he stirred up. Ideas that seemed to promise concrete results were acted upon without weighing possible community reaction. The methods used by the conference to create understanding and cooperation seemed ponderous and ineffective to a man whose experiences in the legal and business world had persuaded him that powerful pressures strategically applied were much more likely to produce the desired behavior.

Persuaded that the conference was made up of a "bunch of do-gooders trying to talk their way out of a difficult situation" and believing that involvement of large groups of people created unnecessary problems, Levi was disinclined to waste time on such frills as human relations or on talks with any but influential individuals. Why, for example, should he wait for the PTA's to get together through the Conference Public Schools Committee, assemble facts, decide on what should be done about them, get the decision approved by the conference board, and arrange an appointment with the appropriate authorities when he felt he already knew what the community needed and could put the wheels in motion by a direct call to the superintendent of schools? Such unilateral action in various areas was not destined to win him friends among those who believed in the conference approach.

On the other hand, Levi's criticisms of the conference were not altogether baseless. There *was* a good deal of talk before action was taken. For the first few years of its existence conference leadership was woefully lacking in "practical men of affairs" and heavily weighted on the side of "liberal intellectuals" who were interested enough in building a good community to be willing to work at it but were not quite sure exactly how. As one of them recently put it: "We were uncomfortably aware that we were doing a lot of talking and didn't quite know how to begin acting and perhaps were a little uncomfortable about subjecting our beliefs to the test of experience. Under the circumstances, it was strange and wonderful that so many of the things we did turned out to be the right things to do."

While the conference attempt to appeal to the best in people succeeded far more often than its critics knew, it was true that this did not always work. The resistance of conference leadership to the use of coercion when information, reason and legal measures failed, was looked upon as weakness; and the theory of group dynamics on which the block program was based—that since conflict is due to misunderstanding and ignorance it can be largely eliminated by information and discussion—was regarded as naïve oversimplification.

Neither organization, of course, had the complete answer. Events proved the value of a combination of the skills and approaches represented by the two groups, but each was so strongly committed to its own methods that this recognition was a long time coming.

Two areas of frequent difficulty were publicity and financing.

Levi had a flair for publicity and, since he was a dramatic and controversial figure, publicity was easy to come by. The University of Chicago, as a great force in the city, was also big news.

A hardfisted attack on crime, the public exposure of individuals, million-dollar proposals were headline stories. In contrast, the conference had underplayed publicity. It could not very well release stories about cooperation achieved—"Joe Stokes used to violate the law. We worked with him and now he is a good citizen"—nor could it cite improvements in city departments as a result of conference activity without antagonizing officials with whom it was important to work. Thus the community and the city began to hear a great deal about the South East Chicago Commission and the University of Chicago at a time when very little was being printed about the conference. Since in the early days some of the leaders of the commission and the university had a low opinion of the conference's effectiveness, it was not surprising that their publicity should give the impression that nothing had been going on in the community until they had begun to act. People who had intimate knowledge of the conference's work were understandably annoyed when those they considered Johnny-come-latelys to the community improvement effort stepped forward to claim credit for it. While it was encouraging to have suggestions they had long proposed and ideas they had discussed with the commission's director put into action, conference leaders found it difficult to retain perspective when press interviews often failed even to mention the conference in connection with the proposals.

Their concern was closely related to the problem of financing. Both organizations depended for their support on the community. Sometimes the two finance campaigns overlapped in time, and relationships thus strained were not helped by reports that some commission people were advising against contributions to the conference nor by the university administration's practice of enclosing with its salary checks to faculty members and employees an appeal for help to the commission. Confused about the purposes and activities of the two organizations, many people began to question the need to support both groups.

In June 1954 a committee made up of three members of the boards of each organization was appointed to determine what would produce maximum community benefit from whatever money was raised, whether two organizations were needed, and, if so, whether their functions could be defined with sufficient clarity to enable the community to understand what they were doing and why both were necessary.

The committee agreed that the commission and the conference, with clearly defined goals and programs, should be continued as separate organizations—at least for the next few years. The reasons seemed clear. The community was on the verge of a tremendous planning and urban renewal program which would call for all the resources it could muster. An organization as large as the South East Chicago Commission, spread over a wide geographical area, could not conduct a citizens' program in which the people would really feel involved; the commission, for example, had been unable to work effectively in Woodlawn or Oakland because a strong citizens' organization like the conference did not exist there. The use of different methods at different levels had proved effective, was one of the community's great assets, and the strengths of the two groups must therefore be retained. It would be helpful to retain also the allegiances and support that had been built up by each organization.

The evaluating committee did not carry through to the point of clarifying responsibilities and areas of operation. But a beginning was made in mapping out areas for separation of effort and for cooperation, and these were subsequently developed further through private conferences and discussion by other committees. Thereafter both organizations tried to make clear that while both were dedicated to the improvement of the community, they worked on different problems as well as on different aspects of the same problems, and they worked in different ways. Examples were given of the division of labor and of cooperation. The conference, it was pointed out, cared for all block organization, while the commission handled everything relating to crime. In matters of planning, public schools, building and zoning cases, there was interchange and cooperation—and the ways in which this worked were periodically explained.

Even so, the community program continued to suffer from lack of coordination.

A continuing cause of strain was the insistence of the conference on citizen participation. This had begun in October 1953 with the decision of the Chicago Land Clearance Commission to survey part of Hyde Park for blight. In spite of misgivings, Levi, who was impatient to have the survey begin at once, acceded to the conference insistence on a two-week delay so that block leaders could be informed, a public meeting held, and flyers sent to every resident in the area. The result was an enthusiastic and informed citizenry who welcomed and helped the surveyors beyond anything previously experienced by the Land Clearance Commission.

Again, in May 1954, conference leaders insisted that an explanation of the proposals for the site designation of Hyde Park Redevelopment Projects A and B should be made to its Planning Committee, board of directors and block leaders *before* submission to the City Council. Again the commission bowed to the wishes of the conference and again the capitulation paid. Not only the conference as an organization but an informed group of individual citizens directly affected by the proposals supported the general idea of the plan before the City Council, at the same time making intelligent suggestions for improvement.

This, however, was only a partial victory for the conference point of view. True, the disclosure of plans in advance of public action was a large step forward, but the plans themselves did not represent shared thinking between planners and community people.

The first Committee of Six, organized in the spring of 1954 to advise the Planning Unit, had proved ineffective. It was neither a policy-making body—since the conference representatives on it were not policy-makers—nor a coordinating group, since the committee met infrequently and no technique had yet been developed for communicating back and forth within as well as between the cooperating organizations.

When action was taken without advance consultation and agreement, trouble flared up. One instance centered around an internal neighborhood park. The original proposals for the community's first redevelopment project, prepared by the Planning

Unit and approved by the conference, had indicated such a park as a possibility. The site designation plan for the redevelopment project, which would have to be acted on by the Chicago Land Clearance Commission, had not included this proposal since the provision of a park was the province of the Chicago Park District. The people in the proposed park area, however, assumed that the omission of the idea, which they had been told was in any case only a remote possibility, meant that it had since been abandoned.

A short time later, at the request of the commission, a conference officer testified in favor of the internal park at a hearing of the Chicago Park District on the understanding, first, that the park idea had already been approved in principle and, secondly, that the testimony was not support of a concrete proposal but simply a formality necessary to get a Park District investigation under way. Block representatives who had been invited by the conference office to attend the hearing were incensed at what they heard. The commission had prepared a careful document presenting the case for the park, including facts and figures. To block leaders, unaware that the conference staff had had no previous knowledge of the existence of such a document, conference testimony appeared to be a betrayal of the conference commitment to community discussion.

Anger swelled and found outlet in meetings opposing the park. Even under the best conditions, it would not have been easy to win approval, since the creation of the proposed park called for the demolition of sound as well as substandard housing and, with a housing shortage in the city, people found it difficult to believe that recreation space should be given priority. Now antagonism to the conference as well as distrust of the commission made it doubly difficult for people in the affected blocks to weigh the proposal objectively.

To try to regain lost confidence as well as to follow its policy of investigating alternatives, the conference authorized the creation of a joint committee of seven representing its Planning Committee and the affected block groups to explore the whole question of recreation needs, the location of the proposed park, or any other feasible alternatives, in the meantime asking the Park

District to delay decision until the matter could be thoroughly investigated. The commission resented the conference decision to explore and reconsider, and even more the request to the Park District for delay. The conference was angered by the position into which it had been forced by the commission's failure to reveal its thinking during the planning stages and by the belief that there had been no need for such hasty action. The atmosphere was tense with hostility.

In this community setting, the special Committee of Seven met once or twice a week for some weeks, exploring, debating, investigating. In the end the committee was divided. The majority favored a series of alternate proposals less far-reaching than the park. The joint committee was invited to present its evaluation to the board. The board's decision: approval of the minority report favoring the park, since such a park was a vital component in a successful urban renewal program, while at the same time acting to protect the interests of property owners and ensure adequate relocation services.

The result did not make the dissident block groups happy, but the long discussion helped to clear the air. More important, the experience left a deep impression on both commission and conference leaders who realized that a serious mistake had been made. The conference board of directors asked that a working arrangement be initiated under which its Planning Committee would be apprised regularly of the thinking and action of the Planning Unit during the planning process and the effectuation of plans, and be shown drafts of project plans and proposals in advance of public announcement or distribution. And the conference became more thoroughly committed than ever to the principle of full community discussion and shared thinking before firm proposals were made.

Thereafter the conference invariably refused to be pressured into action that might be remotely considered a violation of this principle. When the City Council was preparing to adjourn for six weeks and the commission and university pressed the conference to join them in testifying on the redevelopment plan for Hyde Park A and B before adjournment, conference leaders refused. They would not act before the proposals were considered in the community. The other two organizations were, of course, at liberty to appear without the conference, but they reluctantly postponed action—encouraging evidence of the importance that came to be attached to a united approach and to the support of community residents represented by the conference.

The controversy had pointed up other problems as well. It was not clear what policy was governing the planning. While the two civic organizations and the university were supposedly cooperating in the planning, the conference had no illusions about its share in policy decisions. For that matter, what did the conference itself want?

A special subcommittee was appointed to work this out. In an addendum to its policy statement, the conference decided:

We support sound continuous planning . . . The physical plans should be prepared by professional planners. These plans should be the result of consideration of the various alternatives. Such planning should be sufficiently flexible to adjust to changing conditions, and it should provide for review and revision. It should include planning for community services as well as physical facilities. It should seek the greatest attainable advantages at the least inconvenience to affected interests. While aiming at "must" new construction, it should retain existing serviceable facilities to the fullest extent that balanced development permits. Such planning should include accommodations for families of different income levels.

Among the specific problems outlined for solution were how to maintain the interracial character of the community and how to maintain a reasonable balance between the tendency of property values to increase as the program succeeded and the financial ability of present families to live in the area.

Did the commission and the university share these views? If not, where did the differences lie? How could coordination of effort and reconciliation of conflicting interests be achieved?

On the recommendation of Harold Mayer, then chairman of the Planning Committee, the conference proposed to the chancellor of the university and the director of the South East Chicago

Commission (1) that the advisory Committee of Six, whose role had been somewhat ambiguous, be reactivated and reconstituted as an agency for the formulation of planning policy and coordination of effort in those areas in which the concerns of the commission, university, and conference coincided or overlapped; and (2) that, since the commission and the university were both represented on the Committee of Six by the heads of their organizations, conference representatives be changed to the chairman and the executive director. The conference persisted in the request until this was accomplished.

Thereafter, every week beginning in March 1955, the Committee of Six and Jack Meltzer met for one or more hours. Usually the seven gathered in the chancellor's office—Lawrence A. Kimpton, head of the University of Chicago and chairman of the South East Commission; William B. Harrell, the university's vice-president in charge of business affairs; Julian Levi, executive director of the South East Commission; Newton Farr, a former president of the Chicago Real Estate Board and head of the commission's Real Estate Development Committee; E. W. (Jiggs) Donahue, the new chairman of the conference who, following the precedent established by Sydney Stein, Jr., was also a commission vice-president; Julia Abrahamson, executive director of the conference (followed by her successor, James V. Cunningham, in July 1956), and Jack Meltzer, director of the Planning Unit. For a time the Reverend Irvin Lunger, who had become the new chairman of the Conference Planning Committee, was also invited.

At first the meetings were heavy with strain. Conditioned by the early distrust and suspicion which had not yet disappeared, the members of the Committee of Six tried to conceal their lack of ease by a surface cordiality which was an inadequate cover for their doubts and reservations.

As the meetings went on, however, attitudes changed. Discussions, it was agreed, would be kept confidential by each member until such time as the full committee agreed to release information. This made possible a frank give-and-take in which no subject was barred. While tempers occasionally flared, the meetings brought understanding of the real problems the three organizations and the community faced.

The questions people were asking.

The needs, desires, and reactions of community residents, of large and small business, of real estate and institutional interests.

The conflict in interests and goals.

Planning principles.

Specific planning proposals.

Steps to be taken in the face of economic, social, organizational, and political difficulties.

How to attract developers and outside investors.

Coordination or lack of it among the three organizations and public bodies.

Division of function and areas of effective cooperation—all these and many other questions were analyzed and acted upon.

In the process members of the Committee of Six began to re-evaluate their former judgments. As the reasons back of the actions of each of the three groups became clear, it was seen that many of them made good sense from the particular point of view. But since these points of view were conditioned by different interests, the major problem was to find some basis for agreement among them. Free interchange, the growing respect each member of the Committee of Six developed for the sincerity of purpose of the others, and an increasing disposition to look at proposals from every angle frequently helped the committee to resolve serious disagreements and arrive at a satisfactory basis for action. But the task was always difficult and called for patience and forbearance on the part of all.

There were dozens of problems too complicated for quick resolution. The Committee of Six worried over them, examined and re-examined them and, even when decisions were made and approved by the respective boards, continued to be concerned lest the compromise or synthesis arrived at might either prove too costly in terms of short-range implementation or too inadequate to meet the challenge of the long-range future.

Major planning decisions also involved questions of timing and procedure. Members of the Committee of Six came to see that the conference commitment to shared thinking between planners and people was not simply the desire to conduct a social experiment, but the conviction that cooperation and understanding were essential to the execution of any plan. All agreed that unnecessary delay might prove fatal to the community's future, but it could reasonably be argued that citizen participation was a necessity that would save time in the long run.

Other considerations had to be taken into account, however. Even if there were agreement that it might be a good thing in principle to involve the people of the area, the dangers might outweigh the advantages. At what point was it *safe* to divulge suggestions which, for reasons outside the control of the local community, might never be implemented? Would drawing people in at the beginning, when proposals were simply in the idea stage, lead to exploitation of property by speculators in areas where improvements were suggested and to uncontrollable fear and panic by those who might be displaced? Would early disclosure of the thinking of planners, even if the community were presented with all the possible alternatives, hurt or help morale, keep people in the area or frighten them away, make the effectuation of *any* final plan simpler or more difficult?

The need to arrive at a joint policy on citizen participation came to a focus in connection with the tentative urban renewal plans. At first the Committee of Six, because of the tentative nature of the planning, decided to release general rather than detailed information to a meeting of conference leaders, with the understanding that this information could then be shared with block groups. The presentation, however, proved to be too general to provide a real basis for discussion, and people left the meeting baffled, and with an uneasy feeling that the whole story had not come out. Suspicion was heightened by the accusation of the publisher of the *Hyde Park Herald* that the proposals really were not tentative but had been carefully worked out in detailed drawings which were being concealed from the community.

At its next meeting, the Committee of Six decided to accede to the request of the conference board and present visual as well as verbal material on the planning as far as it had gone, emphasizing its tentative nature. The arguments in favor of such action, all agreed, were convincing: While there was strong support in the community for a good urban renewal plan, there was also a substantial undercurrent of concern and suspicion that the planning was serving certain interests better than others. The fear that early disclosure of plans would give those adversely affected time to marshal effective opposition had no real basis in experience: the most effective opposition to Projects A and B was in fact coming from businessmen who had participated very little in the early discussions or the public hearings. No urban renewal plan was likely to be approved by public authorities unless they could be assured that it had community support. Such support would be unlikely unless the planning was made the subject of community discussion while modifications were still practicable. Possible premature speculation resulting from such early sharing would be less hazardous than the concern of residents about the community's future.

Thereafter, there were frequent meetings to share planning problems and ideas with the people of the community and to get their reactions and suggestions (see next chapter).

Meanwhile, community problems were increasing in intensity as renewal ideas moved from the idea to the action stage.

REDEVELOPMENT BRINGS PROBLEMS

As the first redevelopment project began to take form, one of the major causes of anxiety among conference members was what would happen to the people who would lose their homes.

To explain, reassure, and direct people to the proper sources for information and help, the conference added a second block director to its staff and gave her responsibility for working with the block groups in the affected area. The South East Chicago Commission also offered an information service. The practice of the Chicago Land Clearance Commission already provided for appraisals of property by two independent appraisers and the payment of fair market value, and the law required the relocation of tenants in safe and sanitary quarters.

Phil A. Doyle, then deputy director of the Chicago Land Clearance Commission (now director), devoted himself wholeheartedly to the kind of team operation in cooperation with the community that could well serve as a model for other neighborhoods. He appeared personally at a number of meetings to answer questions and reassure troubled residents, and made himself available to all who wished to see him. One hundred and twenty-seven of the 169 property claims were settled by negotiation (the balance by condemnation), and the settlements were generally considered reasonable. Where tenants themselves could not afford moving costs, these were paid by the Land Clearance Commission.

The relocation office set up in Hyde Park by the Chicago Land Clearance Commission was staffed by unusually able and sympathetic personnel who went out of their way to make the most satisfactory housing arrangements possible for every family seeking help, sometimes even finding jobs for the unemployed. Through block meetings and the *Hyde Park Herald* the community was kept informed of the progress of relocation—how many had been relocated, where the families had gone, the kind of quarters they were in, the relation of new rentals to old. The Hyde Park-Kenwood operation was generally agreed to be the finest undertaken by the Chicago Land Clearance Commission in the city of Chicago.

Of the 892 families to be rehoused, over 700 were relocated in standard housing; another 150 families left the city, were dissolved, or disappeared; only 13 families (in the fall of 1958) were still listed by the Land Clearance Commission as not yet settled into standard housing. There was wide dispersal throughout the city: 34.4 per cent of the relocated families remained in Hyde Park-Kenwood; 34.3 per cent moved into other neighborhoods generally considered uncrowded; 12.4 per cent went into public housing; and the 18.9 per cent balance into areas generally described as crowded. In addition, there were 498 single persons relocated.

Local businessmen in the path of redevelopment did not fare so well. They had become more and more alarmed as the implications of the redevelopment program became clear. They could see that the number of vacant stores and the steady decline in business called for drastic measures. But they had not faced the fact that a renewed community with more concentrated shopping facilities meant some of them would have to go out of business. The larger concerns welcomed the opportunities that upgrading would bring. Even if they could get into the new shopping center, however, there was the problem of carrying on somewhere until the new structures were built.

The owner of business property could count on receiving the fair market value based on a going business concern, but the tenant with a short-term lease would receive nothing. While he could remain on the premises on a month-to-month lease until demolition occurred, business declined as surrounding buildings were torn down. Nor could many of the businessmen who operated on a small margin compete for space in the new shopping center. Relocation would call for heavy moving expenses for which they would not be reimbursed, and the sale of their stock and equipment would bring only a fraction of their worth. And quite aside from the cost of moving and the losses they would sustain, many of them had been in business in Hyde Park for years. Where could they begin again? They could not admit to themselves that the era of the small merchant was passing.

The conference had left to the South East Chicago Commission all contacts with the business group. Now troubled merchants directed angry criticism against the commission and Julian Levi. Some of them charged that they had not been consulted in the planning, that they had been misled, that the whole project was being conducted in a high-handed way. Why, for example, weren't they being invited to be part of the new shopping center? They found it difficult to understand that neither the South East Commission nor the Land Clearance Commission, which was also attacked, had the power to make decisions on tenancy, that this would have to await the choice of a redeveloper.

The businessmen's association took independent action to try to get some compensation for its dislocated members. As the result of their efforts, helped by Alderman Leon M. Despres,

Bruce Sagan of the *Hyde Park Herald,* and Julian Levi who journeyed to Washington to testify, federal legislation was passed.

The new legislation, introduced by Representative Barrett O'Hara and Senator Paul Douglas, Hyde Park-Kenwood's representatives in Congress, provided up to $2,000 (later increased to $3,000) to merchants to cover reasonable and necessary moving expenses and actual direct property losses. This was better than nothing, but it was not nearly enough. No provision was made for the loss of good will it had taken years to build. The small merchant thus became the chief victim in Hyde Park's redevelopment program.

Other problems were created by the inevitable time lapse between the demolition of buildings and the erection of new facilities. As merchants vacated their premises, residents became disturbed over the lack of shopping facilities. Displaced residents who wished to remain in the area, preferably in the new housing that would replace the old, would have to wait several years before it was built and thus would have to move into other quarters in the interim. Whether or not they would be able to afford the new housing was another serious question. In spite of the heroic efforts of Phil Doyle, the process of demolition brought additional worries and irritating inconveniences to community residents: empty buildings which invited vandalism and other undesirable activities; the unsightly appearance of half-demolished structures; the danger to children; the noise and dust as buildings came down; concern over fires as the litter was burned; the condition of lots after demolition.

Under the circumstances, the flow of complaints surprised no one. What was surprising was the large measure of good-natured acceptance of inconvenience, the ability to be amused at their own unreasonableness and fallibility that characterized a large part of the community. This was evidenced again and again. Over a thousand people, for example, chuckled with delight when conference members, in annual meeting skits, poked lighthearted fun at their reaction and those of their neighbors to some of the most annoying of the community's current problems. They sang:

I'm a chap who never grumbled when my own four walls they tumbled
And in fact I helped 'em wreck them, with good grace,
But the thing that's on my mind is the fact that I can't find
All the places that have moved some other place.

There's my car: I couldn't park it at my favorite supermarket
For the lot was always jammed throughout the day
Now there's parking place aplenty; if I had two cars . . . or twenty
But the supermarket's simply moved away.

Lamenting the loss of butcher, barber, cleaner, and tavern to
other locations, they concluded:

Yet we know it's for the best, the confusion and the rest,
And Hyde Park is still the finest place in town.
At the worst, we're slightly harassed and a tiny bit embarrassed
To be caught, you might say, with our buildings down!

Then, taking up a more serious situation, they sang a series of
verses to the tune of "A Little Bit of Luck," beginning:

I know the time has come to tear down buildings,
I'm up on all the plans; I think they're fine
I know the time has come to tear down buildings, but
With a little bit of luck, with a little bit of luck . . . any house they
   tear down won't be mine.

Through the Committee of Six, the conference, commission,
and the university found their way to common ground on various
problems related to the urban renewal struggle and, to the great
benefit of Hyde Park-Kenwood, began to present a united front
to the wider community and the city.

Their leaders appeared together at meetings, prepared joint
testimony for public hearings, combined forces to call on public
officials in behalf of school problems, street lighting, improved
enforcement, larger budgets for city departments, bond issues.

Much thought and joint effort went into a proposed new zoning ordinance. All three organizations had been hopeful that the
new ordinance would help to control conversions and reduce

overcrowding in Hyde Park-Kenwood. Careful study revealed, however, that while its provisions for new construction represented a considerable improvement over the previous ordinance, there were inadequate controls for heavily built up middle-aged neighborhoods like Hyde Park-Kenwood.

Working out a satisfactory solution to this problem brought the conference and commission into the closest daily cooperation they had known. Each made available to the other its full records on buildings in the area and on specific zoning difficulties. Memoranda on errors in classification and on possibly harmful interpretations of the new ordinance, brought to light by block groups and businessmen, circulated regularly between the Planning Unit and the conference office. Jack Meltzer's unit mapped and remapped the data, and representatives from each group worked together on suggested changes, talked with the framers of the ordinance, and made two joint appearances before the City Council. The result was gratifying. Some of the definitions were changed; the errors in classification were corrected; and, much more important, it was officially agreed that zoning for Hyde Park-Kenwood and future renewal areas would be governed by the "special use" section of the ordinance which provided that "large-scale planned development" would be judged in its own right.

Hard-bought harmony and agreement were occasionally interrupted by mistakes made by each of the organizations.

One such case had to do with action by the university to meet its need for married students' housing. The university's real estate agencies sent "termination of tenancy" notices to ninety-nine tenants of university-owned buildings preparatory to taking over the apartments for student use. Legally and morally the university had a perfect right to do this—and its need for student housing was very great. The Chicago City Council had been giving the university permission to use temporary prefabricated housing on a year-to-year basis, but had been asking repeatedly that the "prefabs" be demolished. The university had promised to do so, wished to begin to carry out its promise, and had to provide other housing. From the point of view of the university, this was purely internal business, and it did not occur to its office to consult community representatives about it.

As soon as the notices were received, however, angry tenants began to get in touch with the conference, whose leaders and staff—as well as Chancellor Kimpton and Julian Levi—saw at once that a grave mistake had been made. Some of the affected tenants had lived in the buildings for years and had been actively involved in the community's renewal program. Was this the way stable residents were being encouraged to stay in the community? While there was no question of the need to tear down the pre-fabs, the need had been known for months, and there was no excuse for the abrupt way in which long-time tenants had been notified of termination of occupancy. It was feared that this thoughtless action would undermine confidence, stir up further resentment against the university, and have an adverse effect on the stabilization of the area. The situation was thoroughly ex-plored in talks with Chancellor Kimpton and Julian Levi and in a meeting of the Committee of Six, with the result that the uni-versity wrote to each of the affected tenants stating that their problems would be discussed individually and that community organizations and real estate firms were being asked to help in relocating them. University staff members set about visiting every tenant.

While these arrangements were in process, however, the *Hyde Park Herald* appeared with a strong attack against the university. People in the community began to take sides. Block leaders became so concerned that the conference presented a calming statement to their next meeting, giving the facts, stating that a mistake had been made, and listing the steps being taken by the university to correct it.

This experience taught the three cooperating agencies another valuable lesson, and it was agreed that thereafter the university would inform the Committee of Six before taking action that might affect the wider community. In an institution as large as the university, however, it was not always possible to clear all the communication channels, and occasional failures were bound to occur.

Some of the university policy makers had little contact with the community fears and feelings that conference leaders experienced daily. It was naturally hard for them to foresee the intensity of reaction to the university's plans, or to weigh heavily enough the judgment of conference leaders on this point. When they failed to do both, there was conflict and misunderstanding.

One such failure led to eighteen months of costly delay and litigation.

It had become clear to university authorities that the university's need for housing demanded new construction. Julian Levi saw in the use of the Neighborhood Redevelopment Corporation law an instrument through which several purposes might be accomplished: the university could be helped to acquire land for student housing adjacent to its campus in southwest Hyde Park; additional blighted structures could be eliminated; with the aid of generous federal college housing loans the university could put up new structures which would help in upgrading the community; and finally, standards of maintenance for the surrounding area could be enforced.

Conference leaders felt that the idea had considerable merit but held, as always, that the people of the community—and particularly those in the general area involved—should be invited to think through all the problems and possible alternative solutions *before* the redevelopment corporation plan was even suggested to University of Chicago trustees. It was pointed out that the area suggested was predominantly Negro; and the proposal would be regarded as an effort to clear Negroes out unless the people themselves shared in the thinking that led to a final decision.

Other considerations and other advice prevailed: partly the desire for speed, partly the conviction that people affected by change could not be expected to approve it, and partly the feeling that the university, as a large institution, would be attacked whatever it did.

The conference encouraged local block leaders to study the general proposal, but actual plans were not released to the community in their tentative stage because, Levi stated, "in view of the effect such plans have on the market value of property, it would have been irresponsible to release them before they had any sort of official status."

Conference staff called a meeting of block leaders in southwest Hyde Park (only six representing three blocks came), and subsequently four block meetings were held to discuss the proposed redevelopment corporation. Long before the plans were released to the press in July 1956, a group of area residents, without notifying conference leaders, formed a property owners' association "to protect property owners and residents of the area from unreasonable and discriminatory treatment." By the July announcement date the group had become a formal organization, the Southwest Hyde Park Neighborhood Redevelopment Association.

As soon as the plan was announced, it was violently attacked by the Neighborhood Association, led by St. Clair Drake, sociology professor at Roosevelt University (the first chairman of the Community Survey Committee of the conference), and Michael Hagiwara, a lawyer. In the press and at public hearings, they challenged the corporation's figures on existing dilapidation and blight and asked the city's Neighborhood Redevelopment Commission to reject the development plan on the grounds that the corporation had not proved conclusively that the area was either a slum, blighted, or a conservation area as defined in the Neighborhood Redevelopment Corporation Act, that the proposal did not accomplish the public use required, and that the corporation had not shown that the plan would not result in "undue hardship" to residents of the area. Moreover, "it is our belief," said Hagiwara, "that the basic purpose of this plan and the acquisition of this particular area is to allow the University of Chicago to set up a buffer against the presence of Negro residents in large numbers."

The corporation rejected the charges, bringing in experts from the University of Chicago faculty and from city agencies. Both the Chicago Community Conservation Board and the Chicago Plan Commission approved the plan.

The conference board of directors had supported the general objectives and purposes of the corporation because of the university's real need for student housing, the impetus such a project could give to renewal in all Hyde Park-Kenwood, and signs of approaching blight in the area to be redeveloped. With approval, however, the conference publicly urged that in the execution of the plan special attention be given to safeguarding the interests of residents to be relocated, and to helping to find sources for financing the repair and rehabilitation of buildings in the remainder of the corporation area.

The three members of the city's Neighborhood Redevelopment Commission approved the plan in a two-to-one vote. The Neighborhood Redevelopment Association promptly took the case to court, lost on a technicality, then appealed to the Illinois Supreme Court which dismissed the case.

While this struggle was going on, to the consternation of the conference, the university applied for a zoning variation to permit the construction of a women's dormitory with a lesser number of parking spaces than required under the parking amendment to the zoning ordinance. Both the conference and the South East Commission had pressed for the passage of the parking amendment. They and the Committee of Six had repeatedly urged stricter enforcement of codes, and had opposed zoning variations on the grounds that they contributed to deterioration. It was a blow to public confidence, and poor public relations for the university to ask for special privileges for itself while fighting similar privileges for other property owners. Conference representatives strongly opposed the variation at the public hearing.

Again, a few months later, the conference took a public position in opposition to the university and the commission.

The Planning Unit tentatively proposed that a research park be created along a several-block area in northwest Hyde Park in place of the housing suggested in the Preliminary Project Report, on which there had already been agreement. There were many good reasons to support a research development in close proximity to the university, but the conference had strong reservations against it. The people of the area had been brought to see the need for considerable demolition with the understanding that new housing would replace the units to be torn down. A change in plan at this late date would result in a loss of confidence which might cause strong citizen opposition to the entire urban renewal program. There had long been suspicion that the university had a "secret plan" aimed at reducing the Negro population in Hyde Park. Since the area proposed for the research park was predominantly Negro, this would seem to be one more evidence of it and might serve to unite the Chicago Negro community in political opposition to the renewal program in Hyde Park. The *Chicago Defender* had already printed a front-page editorial and cartoon attacking the proposal on the grounds that it was directed against Negroes. Even though Jack Meltzer might be right in believing that a research park offered the best hope for the encouragement of renewal in northwest Hyde Park, the conference felt impelled to issue a statement opposing the park, tentative as the proposal was, "on the basis of present information."

This action was a reversal of the procedure the conference had been following in its citizen participation program. It had been serving as explainer and clarifier of planning suggestions and had been refraining from making decisions for or against specific proposals until all the facts were in and it was time for the final hearings. In this case, however, reaction against the park idea had become so strong that, without giving Jack Meltzer the time he needed to assemble all the facts, the conference directors felt they had to act at once or suffer a loss of public confidence.

It was not surprising that other members of the Committee of Six should feel affronted. Under the circumstances, they considered it unfair and ill-advised of the conference board to vote in opposition to a suggestion before there had been an opportunity to state the full case for it. Some of the conference leaders agreed. The large research park idea was later abandoned.

Fortunately, the Committee of Six, even when there were the most vigorous differences, recognized that the joint interest of the community and the university in urban renewal demanded a continuing effort to resolve disagreements, and they went right on working together.

This cooperation, while heartening, created almost as many problems as there had been for lack of it.

Not all conference members, for example, were persuaded that association with the University of Chicago and the South East Chicago Commission was a good thing. They questioned the motives and goals of both organizations. Why, they asked, was it impossible to get a forthright statement from either group on planning or racial policy which put them officially on record as the conference was? It was true that Chancellor Kimpton, in a speech in December 1953 had stated that the university's concern was specifically directed toward the creation and maintenance of a community in which its faculty and students would be able to live happily, in fellowship with others of similar tastes and standards. But what did this mean in terms of the planning itself—that only people with incomes above $6,000 would be able to live in the renewed Hyde Park-Kenwood? Julian Levi, it was charged, had said as much at several public meetings and, at others, in response to pressure, had promised that the needs of lower-income people would be provided for as well. At the same time, Chancellor Kimpton was reported to be concerned that planning should not put undue hardship on many university employees whose incomes did not reach that $6,000 figure.

It was also true that Chancellor Kimpton had stated that the university was dedicated to an unsegregated, interracial community since "we view the policy of racial segregation as not only illegal but bankrupt and fruitless." Why then, asked a number of Negroes and whites, was southeast Hyde Park, the immediate university neighborhood, almost 100 per cent white? Could Negroes "of similar standards" rent university-owned apartments? St. Clair Drake, leader of the opposition to the Southwest Hyde Park Neighborhood Redevelopment Corporation, stated categorically that they could not and charged that the university had used its influence to prevent him from renting or buying a house in that area. In connection with the university's plans for acquiring land and building new housing through the Redevelopment Corporation, Drake asked pointedly whether the university would be willing to find accommodations for the displaced Negro residents in presently white southeast Hyde Park. What were people to believe?

Much of the distrust and suspicion centered around the director of the South East Chicago Commission, who was regarded (and regarded himself) as an agent of the university. It seemed impossible for people to be neutral about him. They either regarded his considerable accomplishments with admiration or viewed his every act as a threat to the community.

The uneasiness and suspicion of certain of the block groups and others had repercussions within and outside the community. The reasons behind this uneasiness and suspicion worried conference leaders on several scores. Some of the most articulate espousers of specific causes—such as public housing and adequate provision for minority groups—were suspected of being extreme left-wing radicals who were more interested in sowing confusion and discord than in solving problems. If this were not so, it was asked, why did they call meetings outside conference channels, resist the presentation of facts, and push uninformed people to a vote on issues that demanded clear thinking?

At the same time, a number of others, prompted simply by a humanitarian concern over the effect of urban renewal on the lives of people, declared that the commission and the university were "using" the conference, whose leaders did not know how to cope with what were considered the devious methods of their high-powered associates, and that conference goals would be lost in the struggle.

A few disaffected people insisted that the conference had already capitulated, citing as proof the board's approval of the minority recommendation on the park proposal—which still rankled—the election of a member of the university administration to the conference board ("See, now they're even letting them in!"), failure to "demand" a public declaration of policy.

Inter-organizational relationships were further strained by these pressures. A board member of the commission, for example, refused to allow his committee to work jointly with a conference committee on the grounds that the latter included two suspected Communists. Friendly public officials privately pointed out that certain individuals were doing the conference cause great harm. Individuals in all three community agencies tended on occasion to group all the concerned and dissident together as "agitators" and, because of this, to dismiss too lightly the very real issues that were being raised. It was suggested that the conference ought to "clean house" and remove these troublemakers from its ranks.

The conference decided that it could not look into the motives of those who raised questions or used methods which embarrassed the organization. Its job was community improvement; its responsibility to see that people were informed of the facts as they related to issues of general community concern so that they could make intelligent judgments. The privilege granted block groups and PTA's to choose their own people for committee service would not be rescinded even if their choices sometimes caused difficult problems.

Over and over again conference leaders resisted demands that press statements be issued attacking the university or the commission. Instead, they tried to create understanding in private sessions with the various elements within the community. Every possible occasion was used to stress the difficulty of getting an urban renewal program under way at all, the necessity of uniting all community resources in the effort if this was to be accomplished, the fact that the University of Chicago was the greatest single resource the community had and therefore one of its greatest hopes for success. Instead of dividing the community by attack, the conference insisted, those who were really interested in its future would be well advised to seek common ground among conflicting interests in support of some sound, workable plan.

It is to the very great credit of the people and institutions of the community that, in spite of difficulties and stresses of unimaginable magnitude, in spite of seemingly irreconcilable points of view, sometimes even in spite of great personal sacrifice, they managed to retain the balance and judgment that enabled them to work together for the larger good.

CHAPTER 16

Citizen Participation in Urban Renewal

On a spring evening in May 1957, the members of the city's Conservation Community Council for Hyde Park-Kenwood listened attentively as residents of northwest Hyde Park testified at a public hearing on the Preliminary Project Report for the renewal of their area.

Northwest Hyde Park had some of the toughest planning problems in all of Hyde Park-Kenwood: severe overcrowding; many blighted buildings; an overcrowded school; housing utilizing almost all available land; lack of open space for recreation and off-street parking; too much traffic on residential streets.

The hearing began with a description by Chief Planner Jack Meltzer of the proposals designed to meet these problems: the demolition of a concentrated section of blighted housing and deteriorated commercial area and its replacement with new housing and a small shopping center; clearance of approximately three acres for play space for Kozminski School and the eventual replacement of that school by a modern smaller school to be built on the proposed play site, at which time the demolition of the present building would provide a new site for the play area; the construction of a 600-pupil school at 54th Place and Greenwood; a campus-park development consisting of the Chicago

Osteopathic College and Hospital, George Williams College and Kozminski School; off-street parking and small play areas to be provided through public purchase and clearance of a few selected structures; traffic changes and street closings; privately financed rehabilitation of basically sound structures.

Meltzer was followed by Mrs. Madelyn Stratton, representing the Hyde Park-Kenwood Community Conference. During the past year alone, she reported, the conference had provided literature and speakers for fourteen block meetings and had arranged two large area-wide meetings in northwest Hyde Park to consider the Preliminary Project Report. People attending the meetings had shown a keen awareness of the tremendous problems of the area. There had been considerable support for the improvement program as well as disagreement on specifics of the plan. Attention was called to the principal item of disagreement—the location of a new Kozminski School—and to the alternative proposed by the PTA.

The next speaker testified on behalf of the 5100 Ellis and Greenwood block group. "Prospects of an urban renewal program . . . have brought new hope to the residents of this community," he said. . . . "We request that the following two matters be given serious consideration in this final planning period: that the public school or schools in northwest Hyde Park be adequately programmed for in terms of facilities and play space . . . that the institutions of northwest Hyde Park appraise their space needs and make their programs known in order to alleviate fears about later expansion."

The Kozminski PTA liked the idea of the campus-park development and the closing off of playground space, but suggested that other land immediately east and south of the present school building be cleared for the future school site, since this would both put the play space directly adjacent to the school until the new building could be started, and make possible the saving of the auditorium and gymnasium wing built in 1930.

Other blocks indicated similar concern about the school site.

The 5400 Greenwood block reported that . . . "Our reaction to the urban renewal plan is an enthusiastic one. . . . Opinion was divided as to the desirability of the location of a school at the 54th Place and Greenwood site. . . . Nonetheless everyone agreed that the need for the facilities is overriding and if the site is needed for a school, we do not oppose it."

The 5400 Ellis-Ingleside block groups were in general accord with the over-all concept of urban renewal but "urge spot clearance and enforced rehabilitation rather than the mass demolition now proposed . . . middle-income housing and legislation that will provide it on a nondiscriminatory basis."

"We are favorably impressed," announced the 5300 Woodlawn-University-Greenwood block group and "feel a concern for two aspects . . . the need for park facilities . . . the means to be used in financing the rehabilitation of buildings . . . and that the rental of these buildings be kept within the middle-income bracket."

"The members of the 5400 University Avenue block . . . approve of the community improvement plans . . . qualified only by the admonition that the responsible agencies should exercise all possible care to protect the rights and persons of those residents of the community whose homes and business establishments would be dislocated."

The 5300-5400 Drexel block group agreed with some proposals for demolition to provide for off-street parking, asked that new housing have adequate play space and off-street parking; that urban renewal be integrated and include private and public housing for middle- and low-income families.

The Northwest Hyde Park Neighborhood Redevelopment Corporation, in giving hearty endorsement to the preliminary plan, called attention to a major fear "that the plans may not be ambitious enough. . . . Are the schools we proposed to build as farsighted as was Kozminski when our grandfathers built it in an open prairie in 1890? Are we planning for our thousands of automobiles as well as they provided for their hundreds of horses? Are we adding enough to the almost nonexistent open space in northwest Hyde Park . . . ? Our fear is not that these plans do too much but that they may not be enough. Fifty years from now we want our successors to be able to look back at these

245

pioneering days of urban renewal and say that we did not allow temporary inconvenience or cost or lack of vision to prevent us from laying solidly the foundations of Chicago's first stable inter-racial community of high standards."

As the testimony went on and was followed by questions, Irving Horwitz, one of the block directors of the conference, had listened with growing pride. The people of northwest Hyde Park were acquitting themselves well. The porter, the housewife, the university professor, community representatives of different races and backgrounds were frankly recognizing the severe problems of their area and supporting severe action. In every case of criticism of the plan, an intelligent alternative was being offered. His satisfaction must have showed, for the man seated next to him leaned over and said: "Most constructive meeting I ever attended. I'm visiting here from another city with similar problems and I came tonight expecting the fur to fly. An awful lot of work must have preceded this hearing."

Horwitz nodded. Not only this hearing but all the similar hearings that were taking place in the different sub-areas of Hyde Park-Kenwood. In the less than two years since the tentative ideas on urban renewal planning had first been discussed with block leaders, the conference alone had been responsible for consideration of the various stages of the planning in 12 meetings of block leaders, 101 block meetings, 7 area-wide meetings, 21 meetings of community organizations and institutions. In addition there had been the monthly meetings of the Conference Planning Committee and board of directors, frequent Planning Committee sessions with Jack Meltzer and with representatives of public agencies, weekly conferences of the Committee of Six, and private discussions with affected property owners. And this did not take into account the similar round of meetings devoted solely to Hyde Park Redevelopment Projects A and B, nor the meetings that were still to be held on the final urban renewal plan. Every person in Hyde Park-Kenwood had been given several opportunities to learn about the planning. Horwitz estimated that at least 10,000 of the community's 75,000 population had already been exposed to it, and a sizable number had become exceedingly well informed. How many in northwest Hyde Park he could not say.

But the work showed in tonight's testimony. Horwitz wondered whether the others who had been involved in it shared his pride and satisfaction—those who had talked themselves hoarse in public meetings and private sessions, prepared the flow of printed materials, found the answers to hundreds of questions, repeated explanations again and again and yet again—all those who had helped to evolve from the initial bewilderment, doubt, uncertainty, and angry opposition, this demonstration of understanding and constructive sharing.

No question about it—the people of northwest Hyde Park had come a long way since the first very tentative ideas on urban renewal planning had been presented to all Hyde Park-Kenwood block leaders that hot August night in 1955. In the early block meetings constructive reactions had often been interspersed with emotional outbursts and recriminations.

"Hm," sneered one skeptic, voicing the conviction of many others, "you think anyone's going to listen to our ideas? I get a laugh out of this citizen participation business. The whole idea of sharing in the planning is a trap to keep us quiet. They already know exactly what they plan to do."

Many of those who were not so suspicious had found it difficult to learn the limits beyond which their participation could not go, that they were not being invited to do the detailed planning—which was the job of professional planners—but only to contribute their desires and suggestions and to react to proposals designed to meet them.

They had reacted all right. Horwitz would never forget the first meetings at which rough maps were shown. The initial responses had invariably been the same. Even though specific buildings had not been indicated, everyone had rushed up to try to find his own house and had either relaxed when his general neighborhood appeared to be unmarked or had reacted in shock and indignation if demolition were indicated. Reactions and comments had covered a wide range: anger, indifference, enthusiasm, passivity, confusion, suspicion. Many had begun by opposing the entire renewal program; others by criticizing the proposals affecting their own block while giving only passing attention to neighboring blocks; still others had called attention to new problems, warned of possible consequences, suggested improvements, or pointed out alternative proposals. And a few had been so eager to see something started—*anything*—that they had just given blanket approval.

Horwitz recalled one occasion when several frightened and angry people had kept the block meeting in a turmoil. "The only reason they want our houses torn down is because we are Negroes," shouted one. "They just want to get us out of the community."

"That's right," said another. "We keep getting pushed from one neighborhood to another. There's nothing wrong with my building. They just don't like the color of my skin."

Suspicion had not died easily, but the block leader had kept pointing out that predominantly white areas were also being proposed for major treatment in the total plan.

In other block groups a number of people had insisted that there was no need to demolish so much housing when there was a housing shortage. Instead, they had advised concentrating on stopping conversions and rehabilitating structures.

Hundreds of questions had been raised in these block meetings and as many suggestions had been put forward. After the first exposure to planning and to explanations, the questions and suggestions produced in subsequent meetings had become more and more useful and constructive.

In December 1955, at a public meeting to which all the people in northwest Hyde Park had been invited, they had been told what had happened to their reactions to the tentative urban renewal plans.

"We are here tonight to bring you the answers to the questions you have raised and to share with you the planners' reactions to your suggestions and proposals," said Maynard Krueger, speaking for the Conference Planning Committee.

"The 5300 Maryland block made three major points. The first, also made by the 5300 Ellis block, had to do with the inadequacy of the sewer system and the flooded basements after heavy rains. You will be glad to know that studies leading toward the improvement of all utilities have been provided for in the federal advance that has been requested. Secondly, the block asked that the housing to be built along Cottage Grove Avenue have adequate parking facilities and be constructed in such a way as to give the people on Maryland Avenue a view of Washington Park. Both of these points are being covered in the plan. The third item of concern was buildings at the northeast and northwest corners of 54th and Maryland which need rehabilitation and deconversion. The planners are investigating these buildings and including them in the study to be made of rehabilitation feasibility."

Horwitz had scanned the room swiftly, picking out members of the 5300 Maryland block and watching their reactions. The answers directed at them had brought nods of appreciation and approval. The planners *were* considering what they had to say!

"A number of block groups (they were listed) have asked exactly what plans are being made for recreation space and a school building for Kozminski," Krueger continued. "These have high priority in the planning. Demolition just north of Kozminski is already incorporated and demolition of the school itself is in the long-run planning.

"Several other blocks (listed) urge that more attention be given to a deconversion program and the halting of conversions. The conference and the planners agree. The conference is working with city agencies on this, and the Planning Unit is outlining an architectural study to decide on the economic feasibility of rehabilitation of certain types of buildings, including every type in northwest Hyde Park.

"The 5100 Ellis block felt that the traffic pattern should be looked into again, that Ellis Avenue, for example, should not be the only point of entry on Hyde Park Boulevard, and made other traffic proposals. The Planning Unit feels that changes in the street plan might be advisable and is studying several alternatives. As you know, any traffic or street changes have to fit in with the city's over-all traffic plan.

"The 5400 Ellis-Ingleside block wanted to know about plans

for middle-income housing. The 5400 University block asks about cooperative housing. . . ."

The questions and suggestions of every block had thus received a public reply, and the meeting had then been thrown open to general discussion.

"Why can't we move faster?" All the necessary procedures were explained.

"We urge greatest speed in demolishing buildings north of Kozminski School." The government would have to approve the plan first.

"What happens next?" The Planning Unit was now under contract to the Community Conservation Board, was conducting additional surveys and, on the basis of these studies and community ideas, would prepare the preliminary plan to be submitted to the federal government.

Six months later, with the approval of the Community Conservation Board, the conference and the South East Commission had jointly sponsored a meeting of community leaders, including all block leaders, at which Jack Meltzer had reviewed the Preliminary Project Report, complete with maps. Still other studies would be undertaken before the final plans were drawn up, but the preliminary report delineated boundaries for major action more precisely, clarified some of the earlier proposals, and changed others.

Again the round of meetings, with members of the Planning Committee and the conference staff explaining, answering questions, mediating, carrying ideas back and forth between the planners and the people.

The reaction of community residents to the Preliminary Project Report had again been faithfully reported to all the block leaders and to the Planning Committee which had continued to keep Jack Meltzer and the Planning Unit thoroughly informed.

A list of key questions raised by all the block groups had been prepared, and there had been so many that two area meetings had had to be held to answer them. Public officials from the Chicago Land Clearance Commission, the Community Conservation Board, and the Board of Education had been called in to help the Planning Committee.

"Why is urban renewal needed?"

The main goal of an urban renewal program was to stop neighborhood decline and put aging neighborhoods permanently on the upgrade. It involved some demolition but one of its overriding principles was the conservation of buildings. The success of the program would be highly dependent on private individual efforts in terms of maintenance and rehabilitation.

"Who decides which buildings are to be demolished? If the majority of the residents on a block protest against demolition of their block, will this change the plan?"

The Community Conservation Board was the final authority on which buildings would be torn down. While the opinions of the people in the block would be seriously considered, obviously if only the people in the clearance areas were consulted, nothing would ever be done.

"Why are so many buildings to be torn down? Is so much open space necessary?"

Buildings had to be torn down to provide the necessary facilities and open space. The federal agency which had reviewed the plans had already criticized the skimpy open space. It was thus not possible to reduce the amount shown in the plan.

Again and again there were questions about Kozminski School and about rentals in the new buildings.

By the time the conference had brought the leaders of northwest Hyde Park together to review the reactions of their groups and to encourage them to testify at the public hearing of the Conservation Community Council, most of the block organizations had independently decided to give general support to the urban renewal program and to make their suggestions for change as constructive as possible.

Horwitz turned to the man at his side. "Yes, it *was* a lot of work for a lot of people," he said.

251

"Is this meeting typical?"

Horwitz laughed. "There's no such thing as a 'typical' meeting in this business, but I think this has probably been the most constructive of the public hearings to date."

"There are so many things I need to know about all this. My name is Joe Adams," said the man, "and I head a community organization which is just trying to start a renewal program. Would conference people be willing to answer a lot of questions?"

During the next few days, Joe Adams talked to the staff, members of the Planning Committee, block leaders, anyone he could buttonhole, and made copious notes headed "Citizen Participation in Urban Renewal—Hyde Park-Kenwood."

METHOD

What purposes did the citizen participation program serve? What methods did the conference use to encourage it and make it fruitful? Joe Adams asked.

The system of citizen participation currently being used in planning for the total urban renewal area was designed:

1. To furnish information on the chief problems of the community requiring planning.

2. To create recognition of the need for action.

3. To encourage the formulation of ideas, to be transmitted to the planners, on what people wanted in the community of the future.

4. To provide a method for the review by the community of proposals made by the planners to meet the problems, needs, and desires of the community.

5. To establish avenues by which there could be communication between the planners and the people with a view toward evolving, by a high degree of common consent, a generally acceptable and, hopefully, the best possible urban renewal plan.

The system operated largely through regular contact between the Planning Committee of the conference and the Planning Unit of the South East Commission for the purpose of considering planning proposals and community desires and reactions, and through a series of meetings and conferences with the people of the community.

After discussion by the planners and the Conference Planning Committee and by the Committee of Six, first very tentative ideas and subsequently increasingly firm planning proposals were shared with block leaders at meetings of the Block Steering Committee. Jack Meltzer himself usually appeared at these meetings, and sometimes officials from public agencies.

The block leaders then arranged meetings of their block groups, where members of the Conference Planning Committee, with the help of mimeographed materials and maps, reviewed the ideas and invited questions and reactions.

These questions and reactions were answered at once if possible, in letters after review by the Conference Planning Committee and/or Jack Meltzer when indicated, or in later meetings, and all were reported to the planners to be taken into account in succeeding stages of the planning.

The block leaders of the sub-areas within Hyde Park-Kenwood were then called together to arrange area meetings which served the triple purpose of (1) giving recognition to the thinking and contributions of each of the block groups, (2) providing evidence that residents were actually affecting the planning, and (3) deepening perspective as block groups came into contact with the views and interests of other blocks, sometimes in conflict with their own, and learned the necessity of finding solutions on a wider basis than the self-interest of individual blocks.

Meanwhile, planners also conferred with members of the other conference committees on school and recreation needs, with representatives of the redevelopment corporations, businessmen, institution heads and—continuously—with the public agencies that were and would eventually be involved.

In the meetings which followed the initial round of block sessions, members of the Planning Committee pointed out the differences between the first tentative plan and the one presently being considered, community ideas which had been accepted as well as those rejected and why.

Not all questions and concerns could be handled adequately in public meetings. The conference staff and members of its Planning Committee answered uncounted inquiries from individuals and organizations. In addition, when concern became intense, there were private meetings with individuals, block representatives and others who felt there should be reappraisal of proposals for demolition.

Carefully prepared reports and information sheets covering every phase of the planning and its effectuation were made available to block leaders and other community residents who were urged to attend the meetings on urban renewal.

The *Hyde Park Herald* was an invaluable ally. The paper regularly discussed details of the planning, community reactions, the steps already taken and those still ahead. Special editions devoted solely to Hyde Park A and B and to the wider urban renewal planning were prepared with such clarity that the conference used thousands of copies for community discussion.

Chicago's Community Conservation Board, which had taken official responsibility for the planning soon after its organization, had been sufficiently impressed with the citizen participation program to authorize continuation of the practice of open discussion, and the eleven-member Conservation Community Council, although not required by law to do so, followed the policy of community participation through public hearings.

TOUGH CHOICES

Of the many problems in this kind of citizen participation program, which are the most difficult, Joe Adams wanted to know.

Those stemming from contradictory views which pull different people—sometimes the same people—in opposite directions —the ever-present conflict between various objectives all of which might be desirable in themselves.

Proposals to demolish sound housing were attacked by a great many people because of the housing shortage in the city, the impact of dislocation from Hyde Park-Kenwood on other neighborhoods, the loss of stable families from the area, or the injustice to owners who maintained their properties. While most agreed that space had to be found for schools and parks—for which much of this demolition was proposed—they found it hard to sacrifice good housing for it. A more difficult problem was gaining acceptance of the necessity for occasional clearance of sound buildings for general planning purposes. And in every public hearing there was ample evidence of conflict between the obvious desire for parking space and unwillingness to remove housing to provide it. This appeared to be the most distressing choice of all to have to make, for although very small plots of land were involved and almost everyone clamored for a place to park, most people thought it brutal to tear down buildings in which people lived to make place for automobiles.

How many new housing units should be created in place of the cleared housing? The planners proposed the replacement of only about one-third of the dwelling units that were to be demolished. Community reaction ranged from vigorous opposition on the grounds that the city's housing situation demanded replacement of the demolished units by an identical number of new ones (or an even larger number to care for part of Chicago's increasing population) to the equally firm contention that a still greater amount of clearance was essential if necessary community facilities were to be provided.

The kind of housing to be built was also a major source of controversy. During the early days of the program it was not uncommon to find the same people supporting two incompatible positions: provide the largest number of housing units and provide mostly single-family homes or small apartment buildings. A sizable number of people objected to high-rise buildings in their neighborhoods because they felt such construction would increase population density and destroy the pattern of single-family, owner-occupied homes which contributed to a stable community. They therefore urged that most of the cleared housing be replaced with row and town houses. Others fought for more rental housing but protested the high rentals private construction of high-rise buildings demanded. People asked, "Is it the intent to make Hyde Park-Kenwood an upper-income community, subsidized by public write-down of land values at the expense of its middle- and low-income families?"

The question of public housing aroused some of the bitterest debate and soul-searching. One-third of the families to be displaced were eligible by income for public housing. A few community residents insisted, therefore, that a comparable number of such units should be built for these families in Hyde Park-Kenwood. At the other extreme were those who wanted no public housing on the grounds that it would not fit into the kind of community they wanted and would bring "undesirable" elements into the area (defined as "problem" families, people with no experience of urban living, Negroes). In between were many who supported the general idea of public housing but were torn by uncertainty over the amount that was desirable. How much such housing could be included without discouraging private developers, interfering with the upgrading of the community, concentrating additional Negroes in such a way as to endanger the goal of an interracial community? A group of Negroes who owned fine homes had already protested the proposal in the preliminary plan that public and low-rent projects be located in west Kenwood because, they stated, these would "unbalance population in an already overcrowded section" and "negate the program of adequate school facilities."

The desirability of providing middle-income housing was more generally accepted, although there were conflicting views on the definition of "middle income" and on the methods by which it might be obtained.

The common desire for better standards which demanded reduction of overcrowding and thus elimination of many of the converted and substandard dwelling units was in frequent conflict with an equally common desire that no one should be hurt, that no one who wanted to stay in Hyde Park-Kenwood or to move in should be "priced out."

One resident stated the crucial conflict succinctly: "We want a residential community of the kind Hyde Park-Kenwood has been; we want a lot more green space and other amenities which will attract people back from the suburbs and make the area a desirable one for a long time to come; we all want to stay around; and we don't want to make life hard for our neighbors." Obviously, he pointed out, it was impossible to satisfy all of these; choices had to be made.

Conflicting positions were held on almost every phase of the planning, including the best use for a piece of land when different individuals or groups separately insisted that it should be used for an assortment of different purposes; the necessity of creating one or two major arteries to handle through traffic and thus remove it from residential streets versus opposition to the widening of the streets specifically selected for this purpose; the size of a shopping center, with near-by residents in favor of a small center, local businessmen wanting one large enough to accommodate as many of them as possible, and the planners and redeveloper again caught in the middle.

And, most difficult of all, was the struggle between the individual's abstract, reasoned recognition of the need for urban renewal and his emotional response to a concrete proposal directly affecting his own home and family.

"This whole business," said one of the earliest members of the conference, "is teaching me some grim truths about myself. While I pressed for urban renewal with the same determination as all the rest of you, I can't help feeling the planners don't know what they're doing when they decide that the house I gave so much time and care to needs to come down for some long-range purpose that might benefit people twenty-five years from now."

THE ROAD TOWARD AGREEMENT

Adams opened a second notebook.

"And how are such problems resolved?" he asked.

Not all of them had been as yet. Some might never be. But work was continuing and in a growing number of cases there had been success in achieving sufficient understanding of the issues to produce general agreement on steps to be taken.

"But with so many people tossing in conflicting ideas, how is agreement on any proposal ever reached?"

Primarily eventual agreement is reached through the prolonged explanation and discussion process already described, for which members of the Planning Committee had major responsibility.

A series of guides, dealing with the issues, problems of conflicting goals, and the most difficult questions being raised in the community as well as with the best procedures in conducting discussions, had been developed for the use of Planning Committee members and block leaders to supplement factual information on the planning.

The role of a discussion leader, it was pointed out, "is not to defend or oppose the preliminary plans but to present them clearly, to assist citizens in understanding them, to answer questions when possible, and to obtain as many intelligent criticisms, suggestions, and reactions as possible for transmittal to the planners for their guidance in the final planning."

The first discussion guide, prepared when planning was in its initial stages, stated that "The process of arriving at a finally-agreed-upon and accepted community plan is exceedingly complicated and difficult. Nothing that is done will please everyone. It is natural and human for people to look at every proposal in terms of its effect on them personally. Thus, while *everyone* wants a school or playground or parking lot nearby, *no one* wants it next door or across the street. Obviously these facilities will have to be next door to *someone*. NO URBAN RENEWAL IS POSSIBLE UNLESS THIS IS UNDERSTOOD. THE ALTERNATIVE TO THE URBAN RENEWAL PROGRAM IS TO LET HYDE PARK-KENWOOD BECOME A SLUM."

After pointing out such truths as these, discussion leaders were advised to begin meetings by summarizing the background of the planning and the proposals and then to concentrate on information applying to the particular block and area, discussing every problem in the light of the suggested solutions.

This was to be followed by eliciting information on the other problems concerning the group—"slum buildings? conversions? overcrowding? parking space? *Be specific*—which buildings, what is the parking situation, where do the children have to go to play, to attend school?"

Expressions of opinion were to be sought on different ways of handling specific problems. On off-street parking space, for example, how could the need be met? "By closing off and using portions of existing streets? By angular instead of parallel parking? By using the interior of blocks, combining back yards of a number of buildings? (Would individual property owners be willing? If so, who would be responsible for the lot?) By making parking space out of vacant lots?"

Other sample problems for discussion were listed, dealing with schools, housing, play areas, parks. Then, "assuming that we want all of the above facilities, what price can we afford to pay for them? How do we get them?"

As the planning became more detailed, discussion leaders were again advised to make very clear all of the considerations involved before outlining specific planning proposals.

"Planning proposals are limited by many factors beyond the immediate control of the professional planners and the community . . . Federal, state and city laws . . . the amount of public and private financing available . . . metropolitan area traffic requirements . . . the type of support given by the residents. . . ."

"Planning involves numerous choices among alternatives. . . . Should a particular piece of property be used for a playground or for off-street parking? Should high-rise apartments or single-family housing be constructed in a given area? Should additional land needed for school recreational facilities be provided even if it requires tearing down good housing? . . . Choices must be made and plans prepared accordingly."

One way to organize a meeting on urban renewal so as to eliminate speechmaking and frivolous suggestions, discussion leaders were told, was to pose certain key questions and keep the discussion around them. The pattern for such a meeting.

I. Introduction of proposed plan by discussion leader (20 minutes).

II. Discussion of key policy questions which citizens should resolve (60 minutes). (Such questions, for example, as "Do we want developments that will retain and attract upper middle-income families? measures to facilitate middle-income housing? provisions for lower-income housing, including public housing? Do we approve of reducing the dwelling units by 3,000—about ⅛ of the total—to gain playgrounds, parking space, schools, express streets, and eliminate slums, blight, and overcrowding?)

III. Discussion of effects of proposed plans on blocks of persons present at meeting (60 minutes).

A long list of the questions for which discussion leaders must be prepared was supplemented by briefings on the answers.

"The reduction of dwelling units will result in the reduction of density. Is there justification for this since there is a housing shortage?"

The population of the area had increased about 20 per cent since 1940, four-fifths of this increase occurring through greater density of occupancy of existing buildings. Over 2,100 of the dwelling units to be cleared had resulted from conversion, the cutting up and over-crowding of housing. The average classroom load was over 40. Figures on parking and play space were similarly dismal. In a heavily built up area much of the cleared land had to be used for community facilities and thus could not be available for housing. By building elevator apartments higher and higher into the sky more people could be ac-commodated, but this would be exceedingly expensive housing and there was opposition in the community to the amount of high-rise buildings already proposed. Hyde Park-Kenwood was in difficulty be-cause in recent years it had absorbed too much of Chicago's increasing population. Neighborhoods should not be expected to add population beyond their ability through the use of vacant land or in other ways to provide the necessary facilities for that population.

"Should sound structures be demolished (for this or that pur-pose)?"

The preservation of sound housing was one of the goals of urban re-newal. Like other goals, it could be achieved on a community-wide basis but not always within each block or small area. It was sometimes necessary to take down some good buildings. The law states this is defensible for the over-all good. If there were agreement that good buildings could never be torn down, any urban renewal planning would be defeated. The demolition of sound housing was sometimes necessary in order to fulfill other purposes of urban renewal, such as providing space for additional public facilities like schools and parks, or because of legal or economic factors (in an area where sound housing is surrounded by blighted buildings, for example, the good buildings might also have to be demolished to provide an adequate site for the physical redevelopment of the area, one which would attract potential redevelopers who had to be concerned about the economics of redevelopment and the over-all land use).

"Why put up high-rise buildings when single-family homes are more desirable?"

A minimum number of people could be accommodated if there were only single-family or garden-type homes; yet the concern had been expressed repeatedly that the planning provide for as many people as possible, consistent with desirable standards, and also that diversified housing be made available. The cost of development was involved as well: if a 50 ft. lot cost $7,000, it would be cheaper to put ten units on it than one. While most planners preferred to plan for communities of homes and open space, in an area like Hyde Park-Kenwood the problem was not that there should be no high-rise buildings—an impossible goal to achieve—but how much could be avoided and still deal with community problems.

"What about public housing?"

The conference approved in principle the inclusion of public housing, felt a responsibility that Hyde Park-Kenwood should provide decent housing for some of the low-income families displaced by renewal activity. Whatever people felt about this as individuals, no urban renewal plan would be approved by public agencies without such housing. The question was, how much? An 84-unit project was already planned by the Chicago Housing Authority. A special conference committee, after long study, had recommended that 200 to 250 of the new housing units to be built in the urban renewal area should be developed as public housing. Sites had been suggested on the basis of four general principles: (1) their contribution to the development and maintenance of an interracial community, (2) scattered rather than concentrated housing of low-rise and row-house type that would fit into the architecture of the community (the Chicago Housing Authority had already indicated interest in building such projects on scattered sites to accommodate large families), (3) avoidance of substantial concentration of "problem" or potentially "problem" families in a single neighborhood, and (4) location that would contribute to a blending of different economic levels.

"What will be done about providing middle-income housing?"

The conference saw a great need for middle-income housing (viewed as that available to people with incomes of $4,200 to $7,200 per year) and had been studying the problem. The major source of such housing, it appeared, would have to be the older housing (80 per cent of the total dwelling units in the area). A study of the costs of rehabilitation of older structures, conducted under the direction of the Planning Unit, had revealed that modernization and repair could be done without exorbitant rent increases. There was no way to achieve significant reductions in the cost of new construction and still comply with the building code requirements in a market in which the public demanded increased standards and amenities in new housing. Reduction in the cost to the consumer might be achieved through a combination of special tax reductions or exemptions (which would probably require constitutional amendment in Illinois) and by lower land costs (possibly through write-down procedures). But more likely avenues for getting new housing in the middle-income range were being explored: the Chicago Dwellings Association and cooperatives, which would save the normal profit made by the private developer; union financing; new legislation to lend state credit to limited profit projects which could make money available at lower interest rates and for longer terms. A first step toward the new legislation had already been taken, at the initiative of three South Side aldermen led by Leon M. Despres, when the City Council asked the Illinois legislature to enact the necessary constitutional measures.

Great skill and sensitivity were required to deal with the concerns of citizens in such a way as to reach them on their own level. Members of block groups represented varying backgrounds, degrees of information, understanding, and education, as well as different and frequently conflicting interests, and it was up to the discussion leader to direct his answers to the individual's condition in illustrations and concepts he could understand. Not all members of the Planning Committee were equally successful—they, too, came from different backgrounds and occupations (researchers, public school teachers, university professors, housewives, construction workers, as well as architects and planners) —but experience increased their perception and effectiveness. When discussion leaders operated in a hostile setting, they had to call on all their resources of patience and forbearance as they kept steering the discussion toward dispassionate review and analysis. They found it especially difficult, when tension was high, to explain the planning without giving the impression that they were defending it.

The attitude of block leaders had much to do with the tone and effectiveness of meetings—whether they were primarily interested in an objective approach to difficult problems, in getting support for a pet idea or prejudice, or in opposing a proposal affecting them directly. So block leaders, too, were given briefing sessions.

In situations of unusual difficulty, the conference sometimes found it advisable to arrange special meetings of block or institutional leaders with the chief planner himself. Such conferences were usually helpful. Jack Meltzer's sincerity inspired confidence. People became aware of his understanding and sympathy for their problems and were comforted by being able to talk directly to the man who, they felt, controlled their destiny. Occasionally these sessions resulted in counterproposals of some merit. Conference representatives, however, usually tried to work out conflicts without taking the valuable time of the planners, and in a number of instances mediated between angry residents and the planners and between expanding institutions and the affected population.

Conflicting views were also fully aired in editorials and "Letters to the Editor" of the *Hyde Park Herald*. Bruce Sagan, the publisher, courageously tackled the most controversial issues. Sometimes he or his editor added to the ferment and conflict by lashing out at one or another community organization or institution before all the facts were in or on the basis of a faulty interpretation of them, but for the most part the paper provided a reasonable, constructive approach and a public forum of tremendous usefulness.

"And what has come of all this?" Joe Adams asked the group assembled in the conference office. "What would you say the results have been as of today?"

He looked at each in turn: James Cunningham, executive director; Elsie Krueger and Irving Horwitz, block directors; the members of the Planning Committee who had been free to join the discussion—William Frederick, chairman, Pete Shire, Willard Stout, James Braxton, Maynard Krueger, Eric Friis.

Elsie Krueger felt the development of individuals and groups as they shared in the planning process had been among the most important results.

"Individuals, when first introduced to the idea of change in their blocks," she said, "reacted in shock and opposition. Those living farthest away from sites of proposed clearance found the planning easier to accept, although they sometimes had serious reservations about moral and philosophical implications. An occasional group temporarily gave up the improvement struggle when they learned their block was slated for demolition; others, pleased at being invited in on the planning, knocked themselves out to offer suggestions, many of them unworkable; while still others reacted with bewilderment to the idea of even considering so highly technical and complex a subject. But as meeting followed meeting and information and knowledge grew, so did understanding of the need for urban renewal and the necessity of choosing among various desirable alternatives. This has resulted in a high degree of citizen acceptance of the urban renewal program which could have come in no other way."

Of course, the responses of block groups had differed. In general, those more concerned with city and national issues than with working on concrete local improvements had resisted the planning without offering feasible alternatives, while the groups which worked most actively on their blocks had been most ready to accept and support the urban renewal program.

"Would you say, then, that the block organization program is good training ground for an urban renewal effort?" asked Adams.

"Definitely. The work done by block groups to improve conditions on their blocks *is* urban renewal on a microscopic scale. In a sense, all the work of the conference from the very beginning was preparation for the urban renewal program. Intimate knowledge of block problems and the frustrations people so often felt in dealing with them helped block people to understand and accept the need for the more drastic measures proposed in the urban renewal planning."

Irv Horwitz stressed the importance of changed attitudes. During the earliest discussions, he said, urban renewal was looked on as "pie in the sky," something that wouldn't come about for twenty years or more, if then. As people came to see that it could happen in the foreseeable future, they had become intensely interested. There had also been a broadening of viewpoint and perspective. At first block groups had concerned themselves almost exclusively with the effect of urban renewal on their own small section of the neighborhood. But as perception increased, people had extended their concern beyond their own blocks to take in the whole community.

Bill Frederick supplied illustrations of changed attitudes.

Initially the proposals for extensive clearance in east Kenwood had been severely criticized. After thorough discussion, people had seen the need for it and had accepted the proposals even though they meant inconvenience and sacrifice.

In northwest Hyde Park, residents and the PTA had strongly opposed clearance of a block suggested for school and play development, insisting that only slight clearance was necessary. A series of discussions had convinced them, however, that the school needs of the area required an even larger amount of land than suggested by the planners. The people themselves had then put forward an alternative proposal for the clearance of a different block immediately east and south of the school. In this case, citizen participation had led first to understanding of a need, then to a new and better proposal for meeting it, and a change from strong opposition to support and help.

In other instances, Willard Stout said, block groups had felt the changes proposed by the planners were inadequate to meet the problems and had urged much more far-reaching measures.

"Let's not paint too rosy a picture," cautioned James Cunningham. There were instances of failure as well.

In southeast Hyde Park, for example, many residents continued to be opposed to clearance of their block for school facilities on the grounds that this was unnecessary for the immediately foreseeable future and that fine middle-class homes would have to be destroyed. The difference between this reaction and the one in northwest Hyde Park to similar problems, Cunningham felt, might be caused by the fact that residents in the southeast area were not quite as close personally to the problems which made urban renewal so imperative in other parts of Hyde Park-Kenwood and perhaps believed their immediate neighborhood could remain a satisfactory place to live no matter what might happen in the rest of the community. If so, the sacrifices demanded by urban renewal might have seemed to them too high a price to pay.

In northeast Hyde Park, where the major point of controversy was a proposal to create a park at the expense of standard housing, complete agreement had not been reached after many meetings. Most of the blocks in the area had come to favor the idea, but one block with extremely articulate leadership remained adamantly opposed to it.

It was clear, however, said Eric Friis, that in spite of differences of opinion, the citizen participation effort had brought about general agreement on the need for urban renewal and strong support for the plan. Most block groups, as well as the conference board of directors, had given general approval to the final plan while suggesting specific changes in it.

Maynard Krueger believed the citizen participation program had value also because it gave individuals a means of becoming involved in community affairs. It was difficult to achieve a sense of belonging in an urban community, he said. The work of the conference in involving citizens had had an effect on other activities in Hyde Park-Kenwood, and the sense of unity, of belonging, was becoming more evident daily.

Improvement in morale had also come with knowledge of the planning, James Braxton said. People not only felt involved but now believed that the community's problems would be solved and they wanted to stay around to share in the adventure of helping to solve them.

Joe Adams looked up from his notes. "You've been talking about changes in attitude and the kind of growth and development that helped community people to *accept* the plans, and I've learned a good deal these past few days about the kinds of questions they raised and the suggestions they made. But what effect, if any, did they actually have on the planning itself? Did they change it at all?"

They certainly had, beginning with the first redevelopment project. Bill Frederick listed some of the changes in the redeveloper's plan which had come about as the result of citizen objections and suggestions:

The size of the shopping center had been reduced.

The location of commercial and residential sections had been modified.

More space had been provided for housing, and more emphasis had been placed on low-rise buildings and on family-size units.

Street and traffic changes had been made.

The developer had agreed to sell a fifth (and perhaps more) of the single family houses to a cooperative group.

The Land Clearance Commission had forbidden, in the redevelopment agreement, restrictions relating to race.

In the total urban renewal plan, it was difficult to identify the exact features affected by suggestions coming from block groups. Planning was a complex process, and the program of citizen participation involved continuing interaction between the community and the chief planners. Final changes had obviously not been made solely by the planning group or the citizens but by mutual exchange.

Nevertheless, Pete Shire said, it was possible to identify some features of the plan which incorporated suggestions originally made by block groups. These included:

The provision of middle-income housing. This was to be done through the retention, modernization, and rehabilitation of 80 per cent of the present dwelling units, and the encouragement of cooperative buying of rehabilitated buildings and/or new construction. Other means of providing such housing through the Chicago Dwellings Association were being studied.

The expansion of the Kozminski and Kenwood school sites. The community's alternative proposal for the direction of the Kozminski site expansion had become part of the final plan.

The expansion and improvement of a large play area called Farmer's Field, and the permanent closing of an adjoining street to provide additional green space.

The clearance of Cottage Grove Avenue from 53rd to 55th streets.

The saving of sound structures in the 5000 Blackstone block.

The designation of specific buildings for demolition or rehabilitation.

Joe Adams looked impressed. "I can see that community people might be pleased with that record. But how do planners and public officials react to this citizen participation idea? It must be an awful headache to them."

Bill Frederick was wary of generalizations. He conceded that many planners might believe planning was a technical job which ought to be left entirely to planners. Hyde Park-Kenwood, however, had been fortunate enough to get Jack Meltzer, a planner who, while occasionally impatient of the delays and interferences inherent in citizen participation, fully understood its value. Meltzer had found citizens ready and able to view problems objectively and rationally. Major difficulties, he had pointed out, were "the Balkanization of citizen interest, the inconsistency among equally sought objectives, and the failure, all too often, of citizen leadership to correctly assess the attitudes of the citizens or to, in fact, provide leadership." He believed, however, that Hyde Park-Kenwood had demonstrated that citizen participation in planning could be effective and could enrich the total planning process. In addition, it had personal value for the planner.

"When the planner has to explain his ideas to groups of citizens," Meltzer had said, "he cannot resort to vague generalities or professional jargon. He has to think through his reasons for every proposal—and they have to be good reasons—and he must be able to discuss his proposals in understandable terms. In spelling these out, he is forced to rethink them carefully and, in the process, gains valuable insight."

As for public officials, most of them were now persuaded that citizen participation, in communities with renewal problems similar to Hyde Park-Kenwood's, was not only useful but vital if *any* plan were to be effectuated. Officials had attested to this belief by appearing before local groups to answer questions, by providing information for general distribution, by drawing on the experiences and materials of the conference to help other groups, even by a federal directive pointing out that citizen participation could save both time and money.

Joe Adams turned to the members of the conference staff. "You have no reservations, then, about the value of this program, no changes you would make?"

"On the contrary," James Cunningham answered. "We know what the program has done, but there are any number of things we don't know. While we have reached thousands of people, there are additional thousands with whom we've had no contact —those who don't attend meetings of block groups, PTA's, church and service organizations. How will these unreached thousands affect implementation of the final plan? Will they share the general view that higher standards are necessary?

"In our effort not to sacrifice long-term goals, have we given too little attention to short-term interests and created too much hardship for present residents?

"Which of the many avenues of sharing information were the most effective?

"Did we make the best possible use of the experts—the planners and public officials?

"Would there have been more or less controversy, more or less delay, if citizens had not been given this opportunity? Will the understanding gained through citizen participation speed final approval of the plan?"

These were some of the questions conference leaders were constantly asking themselves. The Community Conservation Board had received a grant from the federal government under Section 314 of the Housing Act for a study that would provide answers to such questions as these so that other communities might profit fully from the experience of the conference.

Some of the answers came in the fall of 1958. In November, the City Council, after prolonged public hearings, voted to approve the urban renewal plan in spite of the opposition of one of the strongest political forces in Chicago. Although there were many complex reasons for City Council approval, one of the plan's chief opponents said to the director of the conference: "I can't get over the way the Hyde Park-Kenwood community has remained united in the face of a plan so drastic and months of controversy."

It was no surprise to the community. The people there understood the plan and the need for it. Citizen participation had proved itself.

The chairman of the City Council Committee on Planning and Housing said the hearings were "the most impressive" he had ever seen and that the (community) witnesses (for or against) were extraordinarily well informed and competent. Another alderman added: "It is amazing that fewer individual property owners voiced objections than in any other public program in my memory, and this is the largest and most ambitious we have ever undertaken."

Opposition to the plan, spearheaded by the Catholic Archdiocese of Chicago and backed from within the community by the Hyde Park Tenants and Homeowners (a newly formed, small but vocal association) had centered around five major points:

1. Failure to provide additional public housing units (the local Conservation Community Council had recommended against it).

2. Failure to make definite commitments for new middle-income housing.

3. The destruction of sound buildings.

4. The large number of people to be relocated, and the fear that they would be rehoused in already crowded neighborhoods.

5. Ambiguities relating to rehabilitation standards.

In the effort to compromise, the Community Conservation Board, before the plan reached the City Council, had secured a commitment from the Chicago Dwellings Association for the inclusion of two million dollars' worth of new middle-income housing, reduced the amount of clearance in the northwest corner of the community, clarified rehabilitation standards, and re-affirmed its intention of doing a careful and humane relocation job.

The conference, eager to have the work of renewal begin, was willing to approve the plan as amended while continuing to press for later inclusion of the scattered public housing program it advocated and for the development of a better relocation plan. Other critics seconded these two points (insisting also that there be further reduction in clearance) but took the position that the plan should not be passed until these changes were made. The University of Chicago, the South East Chicago Commission, and others who threw their weight against a scattered public housing program expressed fear that such housing would freeze real estate values and discourage mortgage financing.

During five days of debate before the City Council's Planning and Housing Committee—one of the longest public hearings in the history of the council—150 witnesses testified (90 from within the community). The overwhelming majority favored the plan, and the mayor remained firm in his support of it. On October 22, 1958, the committee unanimously voted to recommend that the City Council give its approval, adding a strong recommendation that 120 public housing units be included.

CHAPTER 17

The Challenge of an Interracial Community

"Let's not have any illusions about the size of the job we are taking on," said a member of the first Steering Committee in 1949. "Neighborhoods are either white, Negro, or in process of changing from white to Negro. No northern urban community has ever stabilized itself on an interracial basis. History, tradition, economics, social patterns, and population pressures are all against us."

"The fact that it has never been done doesn't mean it can't be," said a Negro member. "Besides, what's the alternative? If we sit back and do nothing, Hyde Park-Kenwood will become an extension of the Negro ghetto. Whether people like it or not, an interracial community is the only solution. We've got to make them see that."

"We ought to make it very clear," said another, "that we're not for or against the coming of Negroes. We simply recognize that the shift in population is a fact and we want to handle it creatively. The question is 'how and where do we begin?'"

"It might clarify our thinking," the chairman said, "if we reviewed the facts and the problems once again."

The two world wars with their demand for workers in war industries had brought large numbers of Negroes to Chicago.

Postwar industrial expansion was continuing to encourage a rapid increase in the Negro population as migrants poured into the city from the South. Because there had been little building during the war years, housing was in extremely short supply, particularly for lower-income groups. The war had also brought new economic opportunities to Negroes and created a much larger Negro middle-class who wanted and could pay for better housing. A number had found homes in areas formerly closed to them by the now unenforceable restrictive covenants, but racial intolerance kept them from competing freely with white citizens of similar standards for the limited housing that was available. Many real estate brokers refused to show them property in white neighborhoods. Builders would not sell them housing in new developments, and property owners in white sections would not rent to them. Lending institutions had fewer loans available for Negroes than for whites, the interest rates were higher, and the repayment time shorter.

The additional thousands who came to Chicago therefore had little choice. They crowded into the already overcrowded Negro sections until pressure forced the population to spill over into adjacent white areas. Those who could afford to leave the Negro slums went first, buying property in aging neighborhoods adjoining the Negro areas. Others followed rapidly, their departure sometimes forced by slum clearance.

Everywhere this movement had been aided by speculators. The acute need for housing promised tremendous profits. As a Negro family moved into an all-white block, it was not too difficult for speculators to persuade neighboring white property owners, who not infrequently suffered from irrational fear of Negroes, that they ought to sell their buildings. The sale of one or two buildings created panic among other property owners who rushed to put their buildings up for sale. White tenants in adjoining buildings hurried to find apartments elsewhere.

In addition to all the pressures of attitude and fear which caused people to leave areas of changing population, white residents sought escape from the very real problems of overcrowding in housing, schools, and recreation facilities, from the further deterioration of buildings, from parking problems, from neighbors of different economic and social standards, from increasing transiency and the threat of crime. And so they moved from block after block, community after community, to homes farther and farther out from the center of the city in the remaining all-white sections of Chicago or the suburbs. Thus one Chicago block after another had become all-Negro.

History seemed about to repeat itself in Hyde Park-Kenwood. The community bordered on the rapidly expanding section referred to by both Negroes and whites as the Black Belt. It was already experiencing increasing in-migration of Negroes and out-migration of whites.

"The general direction we should take seems clear enough," decided the Steering Committee.

"We must persuade whites not to move away, that they do not need to leave their homes when their neighbors are Negro.

"We must make Negroes feel welcome and convince them that they do not need exclusively Negro neighbors.

"We must see that occupancy standards are established and maintained and city codes enforced and improved, with the cooperation of both groups.

"We must work for open occupancy throughout the city so that the tremendous pressure on a few communities may be relieved."

Everything the conference did in the months and years that followed was tied to the ultimate goal of creating and maintaining an interracial community of high standards. It was toward this end that the work described in other chapters was undertaken.

In addition to the programs already described, conference people constantly sought new ways of dealing with the tangled complex of race relations. Each small success was greeted with elation, but over and over again minor advances proved inadequate against the tremendous pressure of ancient prejudices, tradition, economics, and fear.

How could the attitudes of white people be changed? How could they be persuaded to stay?

Should the block groups be subjected to education on race

relations in the hope that they would then react constructively when and if Negroes moved into their blocks?

Should there be a more comprehensive program of citizen education through church and civic meetings, personal visits, correspondence, publications?

Or should chief reliance be placed on the programs already directed toward stopping practices that drove people away?

It soon became clear that block groups were not interested in abstract discussions. They were willing to work only on problems of central concern to them. When the coming of Negroes was felt to be a problem, they would face it, not before. That time was to come with increasing frequency, and when it did, conference leaders were recruited to guide one troubled group after another. The attempt was always made to hold these meetings in the home of a respected neighbor, and the educational process began not with a general treatise on sociological trends and historical developments, but with facts on the particular cases causing concern and a review of the alternatives for action. Often participants in the meetings were agitated and irrational. Leaders learned to help them by listening to their fears and predictions of doom, pointing up facts that justified other conclusions, directing attention to ways the group could keep the fears from being realized, reporting on measures the conference was taking to prevent the threatening developments they foresaw. Often the fearful ones, reassured, became active workers.

Speeches and publications about the history and purposes of the conference provided opportunities for citizen education about population shifts, what had happened in other communities as the result of fear and precipitate action, how these fears could be and were being handled, the future of Hyde Park-Kenwood if people kept their heads and stayed to work together.

Members of block groups were warned against the panic-creating tactics of speculators and asked to obtain and report information on any who approached them. They sometimes cooperated with such zest as to make a lasting impression on the hapless caller.

In one case, a harassed, bewildered man made his way to the

conference office. He had called on a community resident, had asked her if she wanted to sell her home since Negroes were moving into the neighborhood, and "all hell broke loose," he said.

"At first I couldn't understand what she was getting at, she was so mad. But she finally calmed down enough to tell me what you are trying to do. She said people like me were killing your chances and we ought to be horsewhipped. She even made me promise to come here and talk to you."

He paused and wiped his forehead with a limp handkerchief. "Honest lady, I didn't mean to do anything wrong. I'm only trying to make a living."

A long talk followed, at the end of which he seemed eager to make up for adding to the community's problems. "Just tell me what I can do—go on, just tell me," he urged. "I don't like slums either. I got a couple of hours right now I can work for you for nothing."

He was put to work.

Unfortunately, other operators did not react in the same way.

Block groups in the large single-family home area of Kenwood undertook to deal only with the most reputable real estate firms and made this clear to every operator in the community. They would cooperate fully with those who acted in the community's interests, they said, even to the point of working without commission to find purchasers of all races who would maintain properties adequately.

Most of the Negroes who moved into Hyde Park-Kenwood in the late 1940's were well-educated, middle- and upper-income people in the professional and white-collar class. An early statement to the conference mailing list pointed out that "the majority of these new residents come here eager to cooperate, are maintaining and improving their property, and want to share in community responsibilities as well as benefits. They will be even more cooperative if they are made to feel a part of the community."

The conference worked diligently to promote integration of the newcomers in every phase of community life. Block groups were urged to call on all new residents, welcome them to the block, offer information about the community, invite them to share with their neighbors in the improvement program. For some time, committees concerned with public and private schools, recreation, restaurants, hotels, employment, and real estate gave their entire attention to problems of race relations and the elimination of discrimination in the use of all the community's facilities and services.

Conference leaders were so eager to have their own house in order in matters of race relations that they bent over backwards to insure Negro representation. It was not uncommon in the early days to have an earnest member speak up whenever a new committee or delegation was being proposed. "Are there any Negroes in that list? We must make sure that our Negro friends are represented." And there would be a dismayed silence as sensitive whites and Negroes inwardly cringed with embarrassment.

People unaccustomed to friendly contacts across racial lines sometimes came to the new experience with an almost frightening fanaticism. They were going to be democratic and there were no two ways about it. Negroes could not take exception to the clumsy efforts in their behalf because they were so well intentioned. It was not easy to make the newly "converted" see that patronizing Negroes was also a form of discrimination, that Negroes did not want to be given status because they were Negroes but because they were responsible and qualified men and women.

Private self-consciousness on racial matters, carried over into contacts with the public outside the inner circle of the conference, was sometimes accompanied by the same lack of sensitivity. If the attitudes of whites seemed to need changing, some of the more zealous missionaries made the mistake of telling offenders against democracy exactly what was wrong with their behavior and what they ought to do to set it right. A few who adopted race relations as a cause for personal or political reasons and were belligerent in its service added to the suspicion and hostility already being directed at the conference. Although only a small number of conference people were guilty of this approach, it was a cause of sufficient concern to others to produce in February

1952 a statement that "Several board members feel strongly that we would do well to concentrate our major efforts on preventing an exodus en masse of the white population and a rapid deterioration of the neighborhood, refrain from militant agitation of the race question, and do what will be in the long run more helpful to the cause of race relations, *demonstrate* that people of different races and creeds will not only work well together in a common cause but can live happily together in a fine community they have shared in building."

Thereafter this is what the conference tried to do. And as people of different races worked together within the conference and grew in wisdom and maturity, racial self-consciousness was gradually replaced by a joint search for solutions. "What Negro should we put in that spot?" changed to "Who is best qualified to do the job?" The result was qualified people in all important posts—some Negro, some white.

Later, conference leaders could recognize without embarrassment that sometimes a man's race made him particularly well qualified for a specific assignment or, conversely, in spite of other qualifications, unfit for it. Thus, even the ablest and most tactful Negro would be an obviously unwise choice for the first call on a fearful property owner in an all-white area. The fears of Negroes had to be reckoned with as well. White conference workers were frequently not admitted to Negro homes unless accompanied by Negroes. The attitudes of certain public officials dictated the choice of white representatives in contacts with them, while Negro witnesses were invaluable in court cases against other Negroes, particularly when judges feared they might be accused of "persecution" by members of the Negro community.

Outside the ever-widening conference circle, changes in attitude came much more slowly. Most of the white people in Hyde Park-Kenwood were frankly opposed to the coming of Negroes and, although violence was never a real danger, some sought ways to keep them out. Others characterized the whole race with a few ill-chosen words and spread their fears to friends and neighbors. Still others, who had come to believe prejudice shameful, felt guilty and said nothing, but quietly prepared to move. A limited number reluctantly accepted the idea of an interracial community because, population trends being what they were, they saw no alternative. "No use moving to another community," they said. "The same thing will happen there before long. We'll just have to get used to the idea." To a small minority the goal of an interracial community seemed "Christian" or "democratic" or just plain right, and they pursued it, some with humorless determination, with self-righteous officiousness, or with clumsy good will, and others by quiet example.

A wide range of attitudes found expression in actions and reactions with which the conference somehow had to deal.

One was the tendency to seek someone or something to blame, and the conference proved a handy scapegoat. "The conference is responsible for the coming of Negroes. By making them feel welcome, it is really inviting them in." "Mixing races is a Communist principle; therefore the conference must be a Communist-front organization."

"Negroes are coming into Hyde Park-Kenwood, and no other organization has any program which even tries to deal constructively with this fact," said Oscar Brown. "All efforts to keep them out of areas in the past have failed, including bombing and shooting. All we have to do is show the people who are suspicious of us that the situation would be much worse if the conference were not in existence."

Easier said than done.

Conference reports emphasized that its efforts to curb rumors, dispel fear, and create understanding among neighbors were directed toward decreasing tension about newcomers. "With less tension there is less likelihood that old residents will sell their homes or move out in panic, and there is less chance of creating conditions that lead to the development of segregated neighborhoods here or in other sections of the city."

Nevertheless, certain community leaders clung to their conviction that the conference was a major cause of the community's troubles. They could not see that the real causes were deterioration and the fears that were driving white people away.

What exactly were people afraid of? Conference leaders tried to identify the major fears and to dispel them in public and private sessions by a careful marshaling of facts, and always by an attack on the problems that gave rise to them.

Fear of losing money on property investments? Property was actually dearer on the Negro market. "The temporary decline when Negroes first move in is caused by the panic of whites who glut the market by putting their homes up for sale. The whites who stay do not lose money," public speakers said again and again, and they referred their audiences to authoritative sources available in print.

Fear of crime? The crime rate in the nation had been increasing, outstripping the United States population rate of growth by four to one. The rate of increase was proportionately less in Hyde Park-Kenwood. As for the coming of Negroes: "They have no more natural tendency toward crime than whites have. The social conditions forced upon them are responsible for the higher incidence of crime among them. We propose not only to control crime in this community by stricter enforcement of the law but to try to eliminate the conditions which cause it."

Fear of neighborhood decline? "Neighborhoods do not deteriorate *because* Negroes move in; they have often deteriorated before property is sold to them. The real enemy is not the coming of any minority but overcrowding which leads to deterioration and the development of slums. Even if all overcrowding among Negroes were eliminated, in certain sections of our area there would still be deterioration caused by overcrowding among the white population." Deterioration could be arrested and reversed if residents united in pressing for vigorous enforcement of building codes and improvements in all facilities and services.

Fear of being in the minority? Negroes were not so different from whites. Some were actually closer to the present residents of Hyde Park-Kenwood in culture and in social, professional, and economic background than many whites would be. However, since any area which *suddenly* became predominantly Negro was likely to become entirely Negro, the maintenance of an interracial community demanded that Negro in-migration follow a scattered rather than a concentrated pattern.

Fear of overcrowded schools? The increasing school population was not limited to Hyde Park-Kenwood; it was creating a national problem. No community, therefore, offered escape from it. People would have to solve the problem where they lived, not run from it.

Fear of intermarriage? Many Negroes were as opposed to the idea of mixed marriages as whites. Because of the general attitude toward such marriages and the burden placed upon them by society's disapproval, intermarriage was rare even when there was normal association between young people of different races. Statistics showed that in metropolitan Chicago marriages across racial lines were far less than 1 per cent of all marriages ("Population Characteristics of Metropolitan Chicago," the *Chicago Tribune*, 1955, Table H-9, page 46). This being so in a city where many Negroes and whites shared high school and college classrooms and membership in various organizations, it was unlikely that living in the same block would make an appreciable difference.

Fear of losing prestige? This was rarely mentioned but it was a motivating force all the same. In spite of the high social and economic status achieved by a number of Negroes, neighborhoods into which any Negroes began to move were no longer considered fashionable. People who worried about such things quickly arranged to find an address more in keeping with their "untainted" station. The solution here was to restore pride and prestige by working to recreate Hyde Park-Kenwood as one of Chicago's finest communities.

These fears were expressed in many ways.

They gave rise to countless rumors about Negroes which grew and were magnified, as rumors have a way of doing, with each retelling.

If a Negro family was seen looking at an apartment, by the time the story reached the conference the building was reported sold to Negroes who were allegedly evicting the white tenants. Rumors of attempted rape or an outbreak of robberies grew from a single case of purse snatching. It was not uncommon to be told in all seriousness that "Negroes have formed a secret alliance for the purpose of moving at least one Negro family into every block." Some credence was given to this by an occasional boast by a Negro that he "knew how to crack a block." School incidents which were casually dismissed as everyday happenings among white youngsters were looked upon by uneasy parents as serious problems when school attendance was mixed. As more Negro children went to the single high school, rumors and distortion added to the fears of parents. A white girl, according to her own story, slipped and fell down a few stairs. Soon a different version was being spread through the community—she had been pushed by Negro boys.

A steady flow of complaints about Negro families who had taken in roomers or Negro couples who shared apartments reached the conference office. Similar complaints had seldom been made of whites. Occasionally thoughtful whites were caught in a difficult dilemma. They had first become aware of violations of the housing and zoning laws because of their suspicions of Negroes who were guilty of them. They rightly feared that a continuation of these practices would cause neighborhood deterioration. At the same time, they realized that certain white neighbors whom they liked had been guilty of the same practices for years. They did not want to make trouble for these white neighbors, yet they knew that the same standards should be applied to all residents. Sometimes this conflict resulted in concealing from the conference violations which were known to everyone in the block.

In the early days the conference office received groundless complaints whenever a Negro family moved into a block. It seemed to be taken for granted that the new residents intended to break the law. After initiating a number of fruitless inspections on the basis of such reports, the conference learned the technique of separating justified complaints from suspicions, pinning complainants down to what they actually saw or heard ("Would you be willing to testify to that in court?"), sending someone to visit the newcomers, and seeing that the facts reached the neighbors almost as quickly as the original rumors had.

Fear was sometimes so deep that it made intelligent behavior impossible, even for otherwise intelligent human beings. One woman came into the conference office so upset as to be almost incoherent. Negroes had moved into her block and she wanted to know what the conference was going to do about it.

"Do you mean to sit there and tell me that you aren't going to put those people out?" she demanded angrily, "that you aren't going to take any action against them?"

"If they are doing anything against the law, of course we'll take action," she was assured. "We want the same thing you do —a good community. But we need the facts before we can decide whether any family is a threat to that goal. So won't you tell us the whole story?"

The woman—a school teacher—began to talk and as she talked she began to calm her own fears, even to be a little apologetic about them. She had never seen the Negro family, had only heard they were moving in, knew nothing about them. As a matter of fact, she had never known any Negroes, though she had attended a teachers' workshop once and thought a Negro sociologist had delivered the best lecture. She would have no objection to a Negro family of his caliber living in her block.

She was told of people in another block who had also been worried until they met the Negro lawyer who had bought one of the homes in the area. Her new neighbors might be equally desirable. Certainly the thing to do was get the facts, she agreed. Since other neighbors were equally upset, maybe a block meeting would be a good idea. The result: friendly communication was established, another block group was formed, and the school teacher became a conference volunteer.

Even when there was cause for suspicion, it frequently turned out to be unfounded. In one case members of a block group, already uneasy about a building's change of ownership, were gravely disturbed to learn that at 2 A.M. a Negro family had been seen moving into one of the four-room apartments, with a "whole host of adults," a refrigerator among their possessions. This confirmed the worst suspicions of the neighbors. The apartment was to be put to multiple family use and overcrowded—witness the many adults and the refrigerator. The Negroes were violating the law, probably criminal types, otherwise why move in the middle of the night?

It took calls on the new tenant, the real estate agent, and the janitor, followed by a block meeting, to get the facts and pass them on. Only one couple had moved in—the other adults were friends who were helping them. They had not known the apartment was equipped with a refrigerator and so had brought their own, which was now stored in the basement. They had moved in the middle of the night because they were the first Negroes in the block and were afraid of violence. Far from being a criminal, the soft-spoken head of the family had been a post office employee for years.

Tension relaxed. The newcomers were invited to future block meetings and gladly accepted.

Negroes as well as whites were ridden by fear, distrust, and suspicion. Years of discrimination had left their mark. They sometimes saw rebuffs where none were intended, and felt threatened even at actions not directed by racial bias.

In one case a Negro family, newly moved into a white building, reported a fire which they were convinced had been set deliberately to frighten them away. Investigation proved that not arson but a childish prank had been involved. In trying out a device for the fourth of July, a neighboring child had dropped some lighted matches into a paint pail which happened to be near the Negro apartment and, frightened by the fire, had run away.

The house-to-house inspections conducted by the Building Department at the request of the conference were looked upon by some Negroes as persecution, since they did not really believe that the homes of white neighbors were also being inspected. The knowledge that their actions were carefully watched, that they were reported for practices overlooked when whites were guilty of them, that neighbors made frequent unjustified complaints to the Building Department and to the police added to their resentment.

The well-intentioned efforts of the conference were also subjected to scrutiny. A Negro bought a large apartment building, and the usual rumors began at once. He would convert the building and evict all white tenants. The tenants were upset, neighboring property owners spoke of putting their buildings up for sale. A call to a Negro member of the conference board revealed that the new owner intended to improve the building, would definitely not convert it, and wanted only one of the apartments for himself. The rumors, however, had reached crisis proportions. To allay them, the conference asked the owner whether he would attend a block meeting and share with his neighbors and tenants his plans for the future of the building. He agreed, and spoke convincingly. But the conference learned later that he had been deeply offended by the request.

"If I had been white they wouldn't have suspected my intentions," he confided to a Negro friend, "and they wouldn't have dared ask me to tell everybody what I proposed to do."

Securing the participation of Negroes in directing and operating the conference was a constant problem. Leaders among them accepted office on the board and committees, others worked diligently as volunteers, and some became valued members, but many failed to attend meetings or to share in the discussion when they did.

In the attempt to understand the reasons for this failure and to remedy it if possible, the question was thoroughly explored with active Negro members. For the most part they attributed the lack of participation to the many demands Negro leaders were subjected to, both for help with Negro agencies which had a harder time than their white counterparts in securing financing as well as leadership and, increasingly, for cooperation in the affairs of interracial groups.

Others felt that because Negroes through the years had been having such a bitter struggle to get food and clothing and an education, there had been no opportunity to develop a tradition of social service and voluntary participation in public affairs. Now, with the rise in their educational, economic, and social status, they were at the beginning of this long new road. Increasingly, potential new leaders began to travel it through their introduction to the conference.

Suspicion may have kept Negroes from full participation. Were they really wanted in the conference organization, they asked, or were they simply there for "window dressing"?

Negroes were also subjected to criticism from their own people when they left their segregated neighborhoods. Said one: "I don't know why it should hurt when other Negroes say 'You just want to associate with white people,' but it does. I want to associate with all kinds of people. A person misses something important if he mixes only with his own kind. For that reason I would hate to see all-Negro institutions begin to transplant themselves here. But you can see that this wouldn't be a popular position for a Negro to take."

People of both races who desperately wanted to do the right thing frequently were handicapped by not knowing exactly what to do or how to do it. They would not have had these uncertainties if they had been able to approach one another simply as human beings. But they were not yet mature enough in race relations to identify themselves with one another and found it hard to apply to neighbors across racial barriers the same standards and feelings they assumed for their own group. Real acceptance and understanding came only with experience.

A case in point involved the southern-born wife of a block leader. She telephoned the conference office one day, concerned because a Negro family had moved into her block, rumors were spreading, panic growing, and the neighbors seemed afraid of the new family. What should she and her husband do?

"What would you do if *white* neighbors moved into your block?" she was asked.

"Why, I'd call on them and invite them to the next block meeting." She paused. "Oh," she said, and hung up.

In a few minutes she called back. "Do you think it would be a good idea to bake a pie and go over there with John tonight?" A splendid idea, she was assured.

The next day Ann came in to report. She and John had gone to visit the new family, pie in hand, rung the bell, and waited for a long while. Finally a child's timid voice asked who was there. They tried to explain through the closed door.

"Mommy and Daddy aren't home," said the child, and kept the door locked.

The visitors asked if they could leave the pie. After a long silence, they heard one lock turn, then a second, a third, and a fourth before the door opened and a child with great frightened eyes appeared, took the pie, said "Thank you. Mommy will be here tomorrow," and hastily shut the door.

The couple were walking away when the frightened little face reappeared. "The light went out," the child called, "can you fix it?"

John discovered that the parents were away at work, that they had had four locks put on the door and had warned their two children to keep it securely locked "and not let anyone in, *not anyone*," that the fuse had blown and the terrified children had been sitting in the dark for two hours trying to obey their parents.

When Ann told the story, there were tears in her eyes. "*They* are afraid of *us!*" she said.

Slowly, as neighbors of different races became acquainted and began to work together, their attitudes changed. In many cases, acceptance then active partisanship replaced fear and hostility. Negroes began to be looked upon as individuals, not as representatives of a race.

In the Kenwood area of lovely single-family homes, residents took unusual steps to see that the properties were well maintained by all races. Beginning in 1951, area committees and block groups of the conference became actively engaged in securing desirable buyers for homes that were on the market. This effort developed into an outstandingly effective real estate committee which later became part of the Kenwood Redevelopment Corporation. The committee gives wide publicity to the advantages of Kenwood, proudly including the fact that "people of all races and creeds live here in harmony." In the spring of each year the group sponsors an "Open House" during which visitors are guided through the beautiful homes and grounds of selected white and Negro residents. Their determined program, in which most of the Kenwood people participate, resulted in stabilizing their "suburb in the city" on an interracial basis. By 1957, of the forty "Open

House" guests who had returned to make their homes in Kenwood, nearly all were white.

In some instances the ideal of an interracial community was sufficiently powerful to over-ride economic considerations.

Under the courageous leadership of Rabbi Jacob Weinstein, K.A.M. Temple, which suffered most from the Negro inmigration, had taken its stand when the in-migration began and, in spite of loss of membership, had steadfastly refused to sell out. The First Baptist Church, finding its plant too large and expensive, considered selling and relocating on vacant land elsewhere in the area but abandoned the idea, with the approval of its Negro members, when it was found that only a Negro church was interested in buying. This, the congregation felt, would not contribute to the maintenance of an interracial community.

A growing number of people began to take pride in the fact that they were sharing in an exciting venture, and they were determined that it should succeed. This spirit was dramatized at the conference annual meeting of December 1954. Someone onstage asked the executive director whether she thought an interracial community would work.

"A lot of people are determined to make it work," she began, when a Negro woman rose from the audience and said with dignity:

"I am one of them. My husband and I bought a home here because we wanted a decent home. We have had the experience of living in a ghetto and are even more concerned than our white neighbors about community deterioration. We are sorry when white neighbors move away . . . My husband and I are teachers . . . We want the children we teach to learn to work with people of all groups, to have respect for human dignity. We want them to accept the full responsibilities of citizenship in a democracy. We'll do everything we can to make an interracial community work."

The audience, moved by the honesty and courage of the statement, had just begun to applaud when a white woman spoke.

"We'll do everything we can, too," she said. "We moved here because we liked the neighborhood and we liked especially that

it is a community where differences can be respected and simi-
larities discovered. I think our entire family is benefiting by being
part of an interracial neighborhood. Raising children makes you
think about such things . . . My husband and I want our children to learn as much as possible about living with people. We
think their own neighborhood is the ideal place for them to
learn."

The city's housing coordinator rose.

"I never dreamed I'd hear such things said before an audience
of a thousand people *and* applauded," he said. "This is a truly
remarkable community. If what you are trying to do can succeed
anywhere, it must succeed here."

The director of the Chicago Urban League faced the audience.

"I had to say something too. I wish the people of every city in
the United States could have the experience we've had tonight.
You ought to take this show on the road."

The audience cheered.

Some of the people who had moved out of the Hyde Park-
Kenwood area came back. A woman whose husband worked a
considerable distance from Hyde Park wrote: "We chose this
community because it's a neighborhood that has come alive, the
most exciting place in the country to live!"

One of the major concerns of white and Negro neighbors
affected by Hyde Park Projects A and B was that the interracial
character of the area should be preserved after rebuilding. Speaking for them and other conference members, and with the full
backing of the block groups, the conference testified before the
City Council that "One of the important reasons for the conference's approval of the land-use plan is our understanding that
nondiscrimination is implicit in it. . . . The conference wishes
the future developer to know that this representative organization of residents of this community not only does not resent or
resist the principle of nondiscrimination but on the contrary has
been fighting for it for years and urgently desires that no compromise shall be made in Hyde Park A and B with segregation or
other traditional forms of discrimination."

A new experience for the City Council, this—to listen to such a statement in the same hall where alderman after alderman, acting for their constituencies, had defeated proposals for badly needed public housing on vacant sites because it would bring Negroes into their wards!

Nondiscrimination in itself, however, was no guarantee of an interracial community, as the conference was finding out. Where the population was of similar social and economic status, as in the Kenwood single-family home area, interracial stabilization had proved possible. But even here the demonstration was threatened by what was happening to the apartment house buildings surrounding central Kenwood. The attitudes of many residents had changed, it was true, but they still represented a minority. In spite of the unprecedented efforts to create and maintain an interracial community, many pressures which had their source outside Hyde Park-Kenwood were inexorably pushing block after block into all-Negro occupancy.

In the fall of 1957, conference leaders estimated that, of the five elementary schools within Hyde Park-Kenwood itself, two—Murray and Kenwood—were about 50 per cent Negro; Ray, 45 per cent; Kozminski, 95 per cent (and badly overcrowded); and Bret Harte less than 5 per cent; while the schools outside the Hyde Park-Kenwood area which were affiliated with the Conference Schools Committee were all predominantly Negro.

Primarily because of the Kozminski school situation, the market for houses and apartments in northwest Hyde Park became largely limited to Negroes or to white people who either had no school-age children or who could afford to send them to private schools. Various proposals were put forward to improve the situation at Kozminski. As a temporary solution to overcrowding, the Board of Education was persuaded to rent space at a nearby temple pending completion of the new Reavis School. Community pressure directed toward equalizing facilities for all youngsters in the community also resulted in the transfer of some 150 children, in the fall of 1957, from overcrowded Kozminski to Ray School which was operating at less than capacity.

Some of the people who had always fought gerrymandering of school districts as a device to keep Negro children segregated, now advocated the kind of redistricting that would artificially force integration. Others privately suggested a redistricting that would remove the remaining white children from predominantly Negro schools in the attempt to induce their families to stay in the general community, an idea vociferously opposed by those who considered this a "writing off" of northwest Hyde Park. The University of Chicago made additional private facilities available by expanding its laboratory school. Some white families kept their children in Kozminski School as a matter of principle, while working at the same time to improve conditions and bring the goal of an interracial community to realization. The Board of Education agreed—at the urgence of the community, led by the conference and the high school PTA—to move one of the boundaries for attendance at the high school further south. This made possible a more racially balanced school population.

In 1957, of the residential blocks in Hyde Park-Kenwood (exclusive of those demolished in the redevelopment program), approximately 34 were predominantly Negro—those closest to the adjacent all-Negro communities; 39 were predominantly white— the sections around the University of Chicago and east Hyde Park— and 33 were interracial. The latter, however, with the exception of the stabilized blocks in central Kenwood, might simply be in transition from white to Negro as they followed the pattern of others before them.

The fact that the community should still be more than 50 per cent white after eight years was in itself considered a remarkable achievement. Areas on the south and west sides of Chicago, into which Negroes had begun to move long after their advent into Hyde Park-Kenwood, were already 90 to 95 per cent nonwhite. Nevertheless, the trend was unmistakable.

A number of factors were responsible.

The city's Negro population had been continuing to grow. It was estimated by the Chicago Community Inventory (University of Chicago) that Chicago's Negro population, which had been 509,000 in 1950, was 749,000 in July 1957—20 per cent of the city's total population. The tremendous pressure for housing was causing block after block in every section bordering Negro neighborhoods to change from white to Negro.

While panic selling had virtually stopped in Hyde Park-Kenwood and the process of change was much slower there than in other communities, white people continued to move.

The Negroes who had first come to Hyde Park-Kenwood had been largely of the same general status as their white neighbors. They had been followed by skilled factory workers and then by the unskilled, white as well as Negro, who had just arrived from the South. Many of the newcomers had no experience of urban living, little education, and no knowledge of the customs of their new neighbors. Like other immigrant groups before them, they saw nothing wrong with crowded living, and they doubled up with friends and relatives or took in roomers and boarders to help them pay the rents they could not afford alone. In the homes from which they had come there was no grass, and their children were permitted to run about freely, careless of the lawns. Adults were unaccustomed to using care in the disposition of trash and litter. They were fearful of city folks and did not respond to the approaches of block groups.

"We've got to get the new Negroes who are moving in to see that they have some responsibility," said a Negro board member vehemently. "Too many landlords already have the attitude that Negroes won't take care of property. When these landlords rent to just anyone, without proper screening, they soon have their worst fears confirmed and then use the experience as an excuse for not keeping the property up. Furthermore," he continued, "some of the lower-class Negroes throw bottles around, litter up the neighborhood, are noisy, honk their horns. That gives white people a chance to say 'You see what happens when Negroes move in!' and they start apartment hunting elsewhere."

A liberal white leader in Hyde Park-Kenwood, long known as an advocate of Negro rights, was equally concerned.

"I think the time has come," he said, "when we ought to be able to sublimate our guilt feelings about the past oppression and exploitation of the Negro (my father, God knows, was not a plantation owner) and ask the Negro to take a more active part in the rehabilitation of his people. The harsh fact is that Negroes who are financially and professionally successful have not properly concerned themselves with the Negro's problems, and altogether too many of the Negroes themselves act as though they have a mission to make the white man pay for past sins. I have been disappointed in the failure of Negro leaders to take a responsible part through contributions of time, thought, and money in the redemptive work of this neighborhood and the larger community. But this, of course, is something their own leaders have to tell them."

As deterioration and overcrowding intensified, some of the liberals who believed in the Hyde Park-Kenwood demonstration and would have been glad to live in an integrated community with Negroes of similar income and education found the price of interracial living too high. They left, and other whites with them, a movement accelerated by speculators who took advantage of the uncertainty of property owners over the future of their buildings under the urban renewal program.

There were enormous profits in "turning" buildings from white to Negro. The simplest way to get whites out was to raise rents, and these increases ranged from 30 per cent to 110 per cent. Other speculators moved Negroes in at high rents, reduced maintenance, and relied on the decline in service to drive the white tenants out.

One speculator shamelessly advertised: "Presently white, this property should be changed and rentals increased, $7,000 on stores and $7,000 on apartments." Within a year multiple Negro families had moved into each apartment, and an inspection revealed a seven-page record of deterioration.

Local real estate men blamed individual owners and outside real estate operators for excessive "turning" practices. Most of those who reluctantly decided to rent to Negroes did so only after trying unsuccessfully for months to rent vacant apartments to whites. Since housing was higher on the Negro market, it was regarded simply as good business to charge Negroes higher rents.

Real estate people had serious problems. Sales were now infrequent, and most of their income came from managing properties. It became more and more difficult, however, to fill vacancies, particularly large apartments, with single families—Negro or white. Some of the new laws made it impossible to convert to smaller units. Building owners expected their properties to show a profit. Reputable real estate men who tried to maintain standards and refused to overcrowd and lease to undesirable tenants were often replaced by less scrupulous managing firms.

Without exception, every one of the white real estate men and most of the owners of rental property in the community genuinely believed that Hyde Park-Kenwood would inevitably become all-Negro. Their experience had convinced them that whites would not live in buildings occupied by Negroes, and many held rigidly to a policy of excluding nonwhites as long as they could. When inability to rent vacant apartments to whites forced them to rent to Negroes, they thought it only honest to tell white tenants of their plans so that they could prepare to leave. Since such an approach never encouraged people to remain, and other whites who came seeking apartments were usually told thereafter that "this is a Negro building," both white and Negro real estate men and property owners unconsciously contributed to a result which many of them did not want.

The personal prejudices of white janitors were another factor in discouraging the interracial occupancy of buildings. Janitors of buildings with a few Negro tenants refused to show apartments to white prospects who were more concerned about the character than the race of their neighbors. They were convinced that it was wrong for the two races to occupy the same building and believed that whites who did not share this view were "crackpots," "troublemakers," or "Communists."

In the attempt to find solutions to these problems, the conference, in addition to its regular programs, began in 1949 and continued over the years to try a number of different approaches at various levels.

The spread of overcrowded Negro ghettos and the deterioration of the entire central city were inevitable *unless* housing was made available to Negroes in communities throughout the metropolitan area. "We must seek open occupancy," said conference leaders in February 1950. Working in cooperation with the Chicago Commission on Human Relations and other agencies, they began to try (1) to influence the Chicago Real Estate Board and real estate owners and builders to create fair practices in renting and selling housing to minority group members; (2) to persuade mortgage bankers and banks to make loans in transition areas, and to allow interest rates and repayment periods similar to those in other communities; (3) to "educate" people of other communities; and (4) to push for public housing on vacant land sites.

The Committee on Maintaining an Interracial Community, formed in 1953 and headed successively by Hubert Will, Bernard Meltzer, Richard Meyer and William Bradbury, kept reiterating the need for open occupancy. Somehow leaders who could influence change had to be convinced of the disastrous cost to the city and to businessmen of the continued flight of white residents to the suburbs. Talks with civic leaders continued.

In November 1955, in response to an invitation from the Commission on Human Relations, conference representatives appeared before a subcommittee of the mayor's Committee on Community Welfare. They presented a summary of the problems facing Hyde Park-Kenwood and the city, together with seven recommendations which were later endorsed by the Commission on Human Relations, sent by that organization to six hundred leaders in public office and in civic groups, and sponsored by a number of community agencies. The recommendations called for

1. The development of a broad city policy of open occupancy and an effective program to promote and enforce it.

2. The provision of the necessary additions to Chicago's housing supply through cooperation between local government, community agencies, private real estate and building interests, this housing to be available without discrimination because of race, religion, or national origin.

3. The provision of easier and more adequate financing of housing for middle-income groups as incentives to builders and to prospective property owners through low interest, long-term, government-insured mortgages and loans.

4. The enactment of state and city ordinances to prevent discrimination in the rental or purchase of housing anywhere in the city.

5. The prevention of further deterioration of neighborhoods by government and local community effort through a combination of measures dealing with rehabilitation of buildings, enforcement of codes, occupancy and maintenance standards.

6. Expansion of present redevelopment and conservation plans and their integration into a city-wide master plan.

7. Encouragement to community organizations to become active in support of a sound city plan.

The final recommendations sent to the mayor by his committee drew heavily on the conference report. They called for the public declaration and development of a broad city policy of creating a free housing market supported by legislation, the development of a program to bring about the availability of mortgage funds in transition areas, and the prevention of further deterioration of neighborhoods by government and local community effort through enforcement of building and zoning laws and public education.

In the meantime, legislation prohibiting discrimination in any housing financed or insured with federal money, introduced by state representatives from the Hyde Park-Kenwood community in the Illinois General Assembly in 1957, passed the House but failed in the Senate. To develop the kind of public climate necessary for future success, the conference began to work with the Chicago Commission on Human Relations on a city-wide conference on open occupancy.

In the attempt to get federal action, the conference testified before the Subcommittee on Housing of the Federal Banking and Currency Committee, stressing the relationship between success in the government's urban renewal program and the ability to stabilize neighborhoods on an interracial basis.

To deal with the problems within Hyde Park-Kenwood itself, a number of other measures were tried.

"At present much of the community work is aimed at encouraging residents to stay in the area," reported the Committee on

Maintaining an Interracial Community in 1953. "This must be supplemented by a program designed to attract new white residents while at the same time making it possible for all groups who will observe the legal and community standards to live here."

Such a program, inaugurated with phenomenal success by the people of central Kenwood, has already been described. The Public Relations Committee of the conference was asked to apply similar methods to "selling" other sections of the community.

Experiments intended to benefit both the community and real estate interests were attempted.

Two board members of the conference, one white and one Negro, brought together a majority of the owners and managers of properties along a four-block stretch and got their informal agreement "to rent dwelling units only to those who will aid in making and keeping this a good neighborhood." The experience here pointed up two conditions which had to be met to make such a plan effective: (1) some way of policing or enforcing the agreement; (2) a central clearinghouse for the securing and screening of tenants.

The South East Chicago Commission got the agreement of a number of real estate agencies to tell prospective buyers about legal restrictions on the use of property and to insert "occupancy clauses" in leases, indicating by name the occupants permitted to use the premises. This would have been a much more useful tool than it turned out to be had all operators of property been parties to the agreement.

The Kenwood Redevelopment Corporation and later the Northwest Hyde Park Redevelopment Corporation set up services through which members secured real estate listings and acted as a clearinghouse for home and apartment hunters. Though limited to two sections of the community, this service did succeed in getting desirable tenants and homeowners of all races.

The conference invited as many real estate people and property owners as possible on an individual basis to share in talks on the urban renewal plans, the future of Hyde Park-Kenwood, and ways in which there might be mutual cooperation to protect both their interests and the community. During these discussions the problems of real estate interests were thoroughly explored. Their major difficulties seemed to be filling vacancies and the expense of redecorating and repairs caused by the transiency and habits of the new renters. These problems could be met by (1) encouraging present tenants to remain by charging reasonable rents and maintaining adequate upkeep and services, (2) replacing curt notices of impending change, which served only to frighten tenants out of buildings, with friendly constructive information designed to keep them there, (3) screening all prospective tenants carefully and accepting them only on the basis of yearly leases. If such a program were followed, the voluntary real estate committees in Kenwood and Northwest Hyde Park and members of the block groups would refer prospective tenants to them. Where rent increases were justified, block people would explain to tenants the necessity for them and urge them to stay. "If high standards are maintained," the conference repeated again and again, "many whites will live in buildings with Negro neighbors. Try it."

These measures persuaded some of the real estate men and property owners to improve maintenance, revise rent schedules downward and, where necessary, send tenants reassuring letters framed by the conference. The letters usually began: "The management hopes to have you remain in the building for many years to come. With this in mind . . ." Plans for the improvement and stabilization of the building were then outlined. A few real estate men made personal calls on their tenants to discover their requirements and meet them if they could.

The response of tenants was gratifying. The contacts with property interests were promising enough to persuade the board of directors that a full-time real estate operation must be undertaken. A new real estate committee was formed and in June 1956, with the help of foundation funds, a professional worker, Pierre DeVisé, was employed to direct the program.

DeVisé spent his first nine months conferring with all the real estate firms active in Hyde Park-Kenwood. His experience emphasized the pressing need for a central referral service, a clearinghouse for property listings and prospective tenants, first proposed in 1953. Such a service, DeVisé and his committee suggested, would not only promote stability and occupancy standards but could be used to encourage white occupancy in blocks that were tending to become all-Negro.

If a stable interracial community was to be achieved, immediate steps had to be taken to restore some balance between Negro and white residents. A referral service could try to do this by encouraging whites to rent apartments that became vacant in predominantly Negro sections while working to maintain the interracial character of those blocks with some racial balance.

Many members of the conference were deeply troubled by the choice they had to face. They had fought for years to demonstrate to the city and the nation that an interracial community of high standards was possible. With equal vigor they had urged open occupancy throughout the city, the freedom of all citizens to live anywhere their means allowed. Now the two ideals were in conflict. Continued open occupancy in Hyde Park-Kenwood meant destruction of the hope of an interracial community. On the other hand, deliberate efforts to secure a balanced turnover in tenancy would appear to be abandoning the open occupancy ideal for Hyde Park-Kenwood while advocating it for other communities.

Negroes who believed in the conference goals faced an even greater moral dilemma than whites. Many professional men among them made their living from a Negro clientele. It had been difficult enough to advocate an interracial community publicly. They had already faced criticism for demanding the observance of occupancy standards and the enforcement of codes which would, in effect, bar the majority of the Negro population from the area. Could they now be expected to support a proposal frankly designed to limit the number of Negroes who might live in Hyde Park-Kenwood? It was all very well to stress the long-term gains, but Negroes could point out with equal justice that they had only a certain number of years to live and needed housing now.

The urban renewal program—vitally necessary if the area was to be saved from blight—was already being attacked as a scheme of the University of Chicago and the South East Chicago Commission to eliminate Negroes from the community. Without question, lower-income people could not afford to live in Hyde Park-Kenwood except under conditions of occupancy that equaled slums. Unless there were publicly subsidized housing, only middle- and upper-income people would be able to pay the rentals in an upgraded community where there was rigid enforcement of occupancy standards. The conference had pressed for some public housing in the area but recognized that Hyde Park-Kenwood could accommodate only a fraction of the total need. Drs. Philip M. Hauser and Harvey S. Perloff had both pointed out that to achieve an interracial community in Hyde Park-Kenwood "the middle-class character of the area has to be maintained with only a small low-income mix." True, but unpalatable to lower-income people.

It was clear that Negro politicians, whose personal ambitions could more easily be realized through predominantly Negro constituencies, would react with vigor to a policy of controlled occupancy. At the same time, it was also clear that many Negroes were as concerned as whites about having neighbors of similar standards. The problems and the proposal were explored with individual Negro leaders.

The soul-searching with regard to a tenant referral service went on for several months before conference leadership decided that it should be undertaken. A Negro board member presented the joint recommendations of three conference committees and moved their adoption. On September 18, 1956 the board of directors approved the establishment of a referral office with the proviso that it be sponsored jointly by the conference and the South East Chicago Commission and seek the support of responsible realty management firms and the University of Chicago.

To clarify the conference position, the executive director wrote to the press:

For seven years residents of this community have worked through the conference . . . to achieve a stable interracial community. We are now in danger of losing this battle in many parts of Hyde Park-

Kenwood. Therefore the conference feels it is reasonable and necessary in the pursuit of its goals to support a referral service which, while serving all people, will seek to encourage more white families to move into Kenwood and central and northwest Hyde Park.

Conference leadership, which is representative of all races in the community, feels that the establishment of one successful interracial neighborhood will do more in the long run to solve the housing problem of Chicago's minority groups than any other single factor.

The conference is hopeful that many good things for the community can be achieved through an efficient community-wide referral service. . . ."

The goals for the service included a single rent standard for all people, leases to be offered to all new tenants, and careful screening by building owners and managers to insure good tenants for all vacancies. It included an expanded program of code and zoning enforcement and public exposure of landlords who overcharged and failed to maintain their properties. Meanwhile, the work of the conference toward open occupancy throughout the metropolitan area would be intensified.

The proposed new service aroused surprisingly little criticism. It was approved by the Hyde Park Unit of the NAACP as well as by St. Clair Drake who had been leading the fight against the Southwest Hyde Park Redevelopment Corporation partly on the grounds that it was a plan to drive Negroes out of southwest Hyde Park.

Three years before, the board of directors had approved a proposal that the cooperation of the South East Chicago Commission should be sought in the establishment of a corporation which would offer a clearinghouse service, do the necessary public relations job for the community, and find more adequate financing to encourage the purchase and repair of properties. The commission had felt that such a venture was impractical, and the idea had had to be abandoned since the conference had not been in a position to carry it forward alone. The director of the conference had also discussed with the director of the commission the possibility of forming a corporation which would use a revolving fund to buy property and arrange for its management on an interracial basis, as well as to encourage rehabilitation and new construction, but this idea, too, had been considered impractical. Subsequent efforts to secure the cooperation of the commission in finding solutions to the problems of maintaining an interracial community had resulted, for a brief period in 1955, in joint meetings between representatives of the two organizations, but the suggestions which emerged from these meetings had not been implemented.

Now the conference went again to leaders of the commission and the University of Chicago. Would they help to establish and finance a tenant referral office? After giving the matter careful consideration, they decided against it. Already distrusted by the Negro community, they feared that public alignment with an effort designed to limit Negro occupancy, even from the best motives, would be misunderstood and would create additional hostility. They believed also that it would be more fruitful to try to attract white residents by working with the redeveloper of Hyde Park Projects A and B on publicizing Hyde Park-Kenwood as a desirable place to live.

The conference decided to proceed alone and at once.

On March 17, 1957, the tenant referral office opened in the headquarters of the conference. Elsie Kruger, block director for three years, was named coordinator for the new service. She and DeVisé, with the guidance of the Conference Real Estate Committee, headed by Mrs. Bernard Meltzer, concentrated their efforts to maintain an interracial community primarily on helping landlords find responsible tenants, helping tenants find apartments, and encouraging good maintenance of rental units. Under their leadership the referral office involved the block groups in a building-by-building canvass to develop a basic file: names of owners or managers, types of apartments, rentals, occupancy policy, and maintenance standards. It secured the cooperation of real estate men in establishing a list of available apartments and investigated the needs of the various institutions in the area for housing for staff, employees, and students. Applications for apartments were received and referred to real estate agencies and property owners. Properties for sale were listed. Prospective residents were given information on schools, community services, and urban renewal plans.

From the beginning of the service the conference recognized that it was impossible to get white tenants for all-Negro apartment buildings, and that pressure for the inclusion of Negro tenants in all-white buildings in areas of rapid transition might jeopardize the interracial goal. Efforts therefore had to be directed toward encouraging interracial *blocks* rather than individual interracial buildings, even if this meant that some properties would have to be kept all white. In order to do this, prospective tenants were referred to vacant apartments on the basis of lists of buildings classified by their owners as "white" or "interracial." The racial classification was undertaken reluctantly, it was explained in public releases, "only because of the problems which property owners feel in this interim period of instability."

The early experiences of the conference had shown little progress in maintaining interracial buildings, and successes on interracial blocks, it was found, occurred primarily in areas of single-family homes. Stability would not be achieved in predominantly Negro areas, conference leaders agreed, until vacancies could be filled with either white or Negro applicants.

After one month of operation, the tenant referral office reported to the community through the *Herald:*

The vacancy picture is remarkably stable . . . the majority of the 240 vacancies referred to the office for listing were surprisingly in the areas of Hyde Park-Kenwood that are predominantly white. Vacancies in interracial areas are few in comparison. . . . The rate of nonrenewals of May leases . . . is lower than the city average and considerably lower than those of other South Side communities. . . . Most local realtors attribute what vacancies there are to rent increases of more than 10 per cent. . . . In buildings in a typical north central Hyde Park block where no increases were applied not a single tenant was lost.

By October 1958 the tenant referral office was servicing about 140 applicants a month, twice as many whites as Negroes, with 45 per cent of the applications coming from outside the Hyde

Park-Kenwood area. All of the community's twenty-five real estate firms were cooperating with the conference office. It had not proved too difficult to find tenants for well-maintained buildings with reasonable rents.

In one case, an interracial block had been moving toward deterioration and all-Negro occupancy because one apartment building with high rents had eight vacancies, and a second building was so badly in need of repairs that tenants were moving out. After persuading the owners of the first building to reduce rents and the managers of the second to make extensive repairs, the conference office filled the vacant apartments. The block today (late 1958) continues to be stable.

A local realtor reported that he had no difficulty finding buyers for homes in interracial blocks—in one such block four white families competed for the same house. Another white real estate agent showed his confidence in the community by buying a cooperative apartment in a nine-apartment building in an interracial block.

A local businessman living in northwest Hyde Park gave enthusiastic endorsement to the tenant referral program in a speech to a group of his business associates. The trend toward all-Negro occupancy of his section had been slowed down, he said, largely because of the work of the conference in encouraging white families to stay and new ones to move in. "In my own block," he said, "four houses have been sold in the last six months, all of them to white families, families who were found by the conference. We also have Negroes living in our block, fine people who are good neighbors and whom I would like to have for customers."

On the basis of this record, a special grant was received from the Division Fund which made possible the full-time operation of the tenant referral office for the following year.

What did all the efforts of the conference and other groups add up to in terms of an interracial community in Hyde Park-Kenwood and open occupancy in Chicago? What was the outlook for the future? The questions were put to Dr. Philip Hauser.

"Open occupancy for the Chicago area will probably take

several generations," he answered thoughtfully. "We can only work to accelerate the process and reduce friction. Chicago will continue to have slum areas until (1) private industry finds a way to create good housing for low-income families; (2) there is sufficient public housing for low-income families, or (3) the income level of the lowest quarter of the population is raised sufficiently for them to afford decent housing in the regular market.

"In spite of this," he continued, "and even though no community in Chicago has ever stabilized itself interracially, there is hope in Hyde Park-Kenwood for several reasons: we have here a substantial nucleus of white people who are determined to stay; a number of Negroes with fairly high economic and social standards; unprecedented participation by the major organizations and institutions of the community; and various government programs designed to improve the area. In the face of historical forces running in the opposite direction, these factors can prevent the area from becoming a slum and make it possible to maintain an interracial neighborhood."

Prognosis: hopeful.

The Community Within the City

The conference was well aware that the problems of Hyde Park-Kenwood could not be dealt with in isolation from those of the city of which it was a part.

If the city of Chicago did not provide enough housing to serve its total population, neighborhoods like Hyde Park-Kenwood would inevitably be overcrowded. Without strong city ordinances and codes and an effective system of enforcing them, Hyde Park-Kenwood would be powerless to prevent slum conditions growing out of the abuse and exploitation of property. Unless Chicago faced up to its responsibility for helping to create a housing market open on the same terms to all its citizens, efforts to maintain selected areas like Hyde Park-Kenwood on an interracial basis would have little chance of success.

Chicago's inadequate housing supply—a problem of every large urban center—was a constant source of concern. Early in 1950, and on every possible occasion thereafter, the conference pressed the mayor and members of the City Council to approve public housing sites on vacant land so that slum clearance in one community would not create overcrowding in other areas. The development of middle-income housing by the Chicago Dwellings Association was given public support, beginning in 1951. The

conference joined other citizens' groups in urging the appointment of a citizen action committee to expedite a housing program
for Chicago designed to "increase the housing supply for low-
and middle-income people most in need of it, on a nondiscriminatory basis." As slums continued to develop with frightening speed,
the conference continued to plead before city, state, and federal
bodies that the provision of low- and middle-income housing was
imperative if Chicago's pioneer urban renewal program in Hyde
Park-Kenwood was to succeed. Conference committees were
formed to suggest ways of obtaining such housing, and interested
representatives of other community groups were brought together
to consider possible procedures. By 1957 city and state representatives were at work on the necessary legislation, and a movement to enlist the support of citizens in other sections of Chicago
had begun.

To improve community facilities and services, the conference
worked to secure reforms and developments of benefit to the city
as a whole. It initiated or supported recommendations designed
to strengthen city departments, helped to create new laws,
worked to secure citizen support throughout the city for adequate
budgets and bond issues for public purposes. Earlier chapters
tell the story of these efforts.

Almost every city problem, almost every proposed city development, had some bearing on local communities, and the conference was repeatedly being asked to take action in behalf of
one cause or another. Limitations of time, staff, and money and
the many local problems which had to have first call on a community organization's resources made it impossible to share
constructively in all of them. The conference therefore had to
choose carefully the causes to which it should give attention.

In general, these had an immediate and direct relationship to
the Hyde Park-Kenwood community. But even here it was not
always possible to draw a clear line. For example, the conference
joined other organizations in opposing the building of a convention hall on the lake front, even though the proposed site was two
miles north of Hyde Park-Kenwood. Sharp criticism was leveled
at the conference for becoming involved in an issue which, it was

said, was far removed from the original purposes of the conference. It did not seem so to conference leaders. The lake front was one of the major assets of both Hyde Park-Kenwood and the city. The development of beach space for recreation along the very area proposed for the convention hall was badly needed for the use of thousands of residents who were now crowding the limited beach area available to the South Side of Chicago. The increased flow of traffic the convention hall would bring to the South Side would seriously inconvenience residents who were already troubled by traffic congestion between the center of Chicago and their community during rush hours, congestion which would increase many times over with the completion of Calumet Harbor as the terminal of the St. Lawrence Seaway. Already too much park land was being used for nonpark purposes. And, finally, according to the city's own planning experts, the selection of a site so far from the center of Chicago did not represent sound planning. (In spite of all the arguments against the site, its supporters were strong enough to get the necessary approvals.)

Activities of the conference in behalf of improvement for Hyde Park-Kenwood also had city-wide implications which raised difficult questions in the minds of some of its own members as well as among city officials and community organizations in other parts of Chicago.

Hyde Park-Kenwood knew what it wanted and had strong organizations with effective leadership. It was thus able to get a disproportionate share of the facilities and services for which all Chicago communities were in competition. In spite of the insistence of public officials that the city had equal responsibility to every neighborhood, it was a well-known fact that they responded most quickly to the areas where pressure was greatest. Did the conference have a moral right to exert such pressure at the expense of other communities?

How could Hyde Park-Kenwood justify its demands for more and more school facilities when other communities had buildings at least as old and overcrowded if not in worse condition; for more building inspectors and police officers when these men would have to be obtained by transfer from areas equally in need of inspection and police service; for land clearance and the demolition of housing in a city already overburdened with housing and relocation problems?

The conference had given evidence of its willingness to work on the larger responsibilities of the total city; it had no desire to settle the problems of Hyde Park-Kenwood by aggravating those of other areas, and it believed its direct activities in behalf of Hyde Park-Kenwood were justified for several reasons.

First, the only alternative was to let the community become a slum. Its decay could not possibly help other communities and could only add to their burden and the city's the cost of the eventual slum clearance that would be necessary.

Second, it was obviously impossible for the city in any of its capital improvement programs (street lighting, schools, sewers, etc.) to provide facilities for all Chicago communities simultaneously. Choices were always necessary and there had to be a start somewhere. It made good sense to select for concentration a community united behind an improvement program. A coordinated effort to provide adequate services and facilities in such a community would maximize the benefits obtained from them and create the climate necessary to encourage additional private investment.

Third, improvements in Hyde Park-Kenwood, by increasing tax revenues, would make additional funds available for improved facilities and services in the city.

Fourth, the Chicago communities most inadequately serviced would continue to suffer whether or not the organizations in Hyde Park-Kenwood demanded improvement for their area precisely because those communities were not sufficiently well organized or well informed to bring their problems and needs forcefully to public attention. By effective and responsible citizen action, Hyde Park-Kenwood could set an example of inestimable value to every other community in Chicago.

Fifth, an increase in the number of strong community organizations throughout the city would have a beneficial effect on Chicago's government, the conservation of its neighborhoods, and its ability to raise the sums necessary to serve its population adequately.

And lastly, hope for the future of other Chicago communities and of the city itself was tied to the outcome of the urban renewal experiment in Hyde Park-Kenwood. If renewal could not work there—in an area with assets few other communities could boast —it would not work anywhere. Success would be difficult enough to attain in any case. Neither the organizations within Hyde Park-Kenwood nor the people of other communities could afford to handicap the demonstration by failure to seek or provide the essentials of a good community which alone could help to make success possible.

At the same time, conference experience underlined the fact that a responsible organization, committed to serving a particular community, also has certain obligations to the city administration.

Such an organization has an obligation to learn everything possible about the functioning and work procedures of city departments, to create understanding of their responsibilities, powers, and limitations, and to channel citizen action realistically in the light of them. This does not mean that community groups should allow the limitations under which city departments work to stand permanently in the way of necessary improvement programs, but rather that they should work with officials to lift such limitations. Striving for change and reform is always more difficult than maintaining the status quo. City officials, like other human beings, often find it simpler to defend failure to act on the grounds of inadequacy of funds, personnel, equipment, or laws than to think through ways of overcoming obstacles. Citizen groups can encourage them to broaden their vision of public responsibility, enlarge the scope of public efforts, and enrich the quality of public service.

This involves recognition of another obligation—to give public servants the support they need to carry out an effective program. It is not enough to ask for improved services, however well-documented the need may be, to call attention to the responsibilities or inadequacies of city departments, or even to recommend challenging solutions. An organization must also be willing to give time and effort to ensuring that the various city departments have the tools and resources with which to work. Here citizens' groups are frequently at fault. They find it easier to make demands than to work on means of satisfying them. They have an obligation to understand and act on several truths: facilities and services cost money; city departments cannot provide them without adequate resources; these can be obtained only through taxes, license, and other service fees, and bond issues; citizens therefore have to be educated to the importance not only of making their acceptance of these facts known to the city administration but of standing up to be counted when it matters most— at the City Hall in budget hearings and at the polls on bond issues.

Ensuring the wisest use of any funds that are made available to the city is a corollary obligation. Larger and larger budgets do not guarantee effectiveness, and blind support to demands for more money is not synonymous with responsible citizen action. In some instances good government might point instead to a reduced budget for certain departments and the elimination of unnecessary positions and operations. It is not suggested that most leaders of community organizations should be political scientists or should devote any considerable block of time to studying methods of administering the affairs of cities. But elected representatives and private experts should be encouraged and supported in continuing efforts to eliminate duplication and waste, coordinate the work of the many departments, and transform the government into the most efficient possible instrument of service to the city's people.

PART 4

A Look at Results

CHAPTER 19

The Community Today

Visitors returning to Hyde Park-Kenwood in the fall of 1958 after an absence of nine years find the community greatly changed.

Where decaying buildings once crowded together in a stretch of blocks centered around the 55th Street business area, there is now a wide expanse of open land, some of it still covered with the rubble of recent demolition. In this 47-acre tract, an occasional building stands alone, boarded up, awaiting destruction, or, neighborless, carries on as usual until its time is up. Misery Mansion—the huge firetrap of a tenement with the ugly façade —is gone, and so are the adjoining slum buildings. The stores east of Kimbark Avenue to the Illinois Central tracks have vanished —the small vacant ones with dirty windows and rotting floors; the marginal stores of shoddy merchandise which over the years had taken the place of once-fine shops; the taverns from whose murky interiors drunks had stumbled in the early morning hours; the familiar places run by pleasant people who had served Hyde Park well—the corner drugstore, the hardware store, the cleaning establishment, the repair shop, the 55th Street post office. And gone, too, are some of the places of taste and distinction which had helped to give the community its special flair: Bordelon's modern furnishings shop, the Continental Gourmet featuring foods of many lands, the Buddhist Church.

Some of the missing places can now be found in different locations in the community: Morton's swank new restaurant near the lake front; Mitzie's well-known flower shop, the Hyde Park Art Center, Wolff's Toy Shop, the Domino with its clever and sophisticated specialties. Others still plan to find a place in the renewed community. Alone in the center of Harper Avenue, but also slated for eventual demolition, is the Hyde Park Cooperative Store, its management looking forward to relocating in the shopping center to be built a block away.

Construction has already begun on the redevelopment project. Meanwhile, published maps and materials on display at several centers help the community to visualize what the temporarily desolate-looking section will be like in a few years when all of the new buildings will have risen from the cleared land.

Not far from the demolition site, the Windermere West Hotel is vacant. Too old and worn-out to be renovated, the building will be destroyed by its owners.

Cleared land, where the used-car lot at Cottage Grove Avenue and 50th Street used to be, awaits the construction of an 84-unit public housing project.

Near the lake front at 50th Street are seven skyscrapers which make up the residential area called the Indian Village; and another elevator structure—Twin Towers—has been built close by. Two small synagogues are no longer in the community, but almost all the other temples boast handsome new central buildings or community houses: K.A.M. Temple, Temple Isaiah Israel, Sinai, Congregation Rodfei Zedek. Construction is under way on the new St. Paul's Church in Kenwood to replace the edifice twice destroyed by fire.

Billings Hospital has a new wing, and additional buildings are being constructed on the University of Chicago campus as part of a $21 million development program. A new science building represents the first step in the projected $8 million construction and expansion program of the Chicago College of Osteopathy and its hospital. The Chicago Theological Seminary is expanding.

Near the lake front in Hyde Park a motel now prospers, and another is under construction in Kenwood.

The University National Bank is larger and handsomer than it was, and the National Bank of Hyde Park has added an ultra-modern drive-in bank and new parking area. Walker Sandbach, general manager of the cooperative store, reports that the Co-op is doing five times its 1950 business, has tripled its physical size and membership, and is planning greater expansion in its new location. The façades and interiors of some of the other stores are more modern than they were.

Three large new apartment buildings now stand in Hyde Park, two of them cooperatively owned and managed, and two attractive single family homes have been built in Kenwood and Hyde Park.

A number of the homes and apartment buildings show signs of work and investment. Deconverted rooming houses and kitchenettes have been transformed from liabilities to neighborhood assets. Yard, garden, and parking space, replacing rundown structures privately purchased and demolished, add to the attractiveness of several cooperative apartment buildings.

Two privately owned parking lots and one municipal lot are in operation, and another is under construction. Two new playlots are being developed by the city.

Central Kenwood looks very much the same. The beautiful homes and grounds are as well kept as ever, and there is the same feeling of space and gracious living. Many of the blocks in Hyde Park similarly retain their quiet, clean, tree-shaded attraction, and the high-rise apartment area near the lake still seems impressively expensive.

In marked contrast are the streets on the eastern, western, and northern peripheries of Hyde Park-Kenwood and certain of the adjoining blocks. Most of the buildings here are dirtier, shabbier, and more overcrowded than they were, worn and dilapidated with neglect and abuse: unwashed, littered stores, with airless cubbyhole apartments above; decaying houses whose rickety stairs lead to the "Rooms for Rent—Transients" advertised on the cracked windows; run-down apartment buildings, their hallways marred with penciled notations testifying to overcrowding—"Ring once for Smith, twice for Jones, three times for Thomas"; the smells of grease and stale cooking and overflowing garbage pails.

"A few years hence," people of Hyde Park-Kenwood say, "these areas of blight will be gone." They are to be removed under the urban renewal plan, together with isolated slum buildings that threaten the stability of otherwise sound blocks.

Scores of sturdier buildings in other sections give evidence of sloppy maintenance or inadequate conversion or cry out for attention to drab, sooty exteriors and old-fashioned apartments. These are the buildings suggested for rehabilitation and modernization.

At night the once-dark streets of Hyde Park-Kenwood are dark no more. New street lights cast an impartial glow over the new buildings and the old, the cleared land and the overbuilt, the worn-looking, slovenly structures and the well-preserved ones. A few cracked and broken sidewalks remain, but most of the community has the solid underfooting of new or repaired walks.

More building is devoted to school use today in the school area served by the conference. There are the new Murray, Reavis, and Carnegie schools; the Bousfield and Doniat schools established in older buildings purchased by the Board of Education; and additions to the Shakespeare, Bret Harte, Ray, Wadsworth, and Oakenwald schools. Yet in spite of these additional facilities, classrooms are more crowded than they should be; facilities do not yet match the swelling school population.

The wide parkway strips along Drexel Boulevard are scraggly and partly grassless with overuse and neglect, but beach and recreation facilities in Jackson Park are profiting from much-needed care. The Wooded Island is beginning to regain some of its lost charm, and bicyclists once again pedal leisurely along the park's bicycle paths. Children can be found playing in newly created recreation areas in Washington Park and along the Outer Drive, and in small play-lots within the community. But some still play in the streets, which have more cars parked along their sides, crowded together more tightly than they used to be, and traffic—in spite of the one-way streets—is heavier.

Mechanical sweepers can now be seen cleaning the streets on specified days, and garbage collection is as good as conscientious city workers in an overcrowded area can make it.

The housing market is tight, the vacancy rate for apartments in good condition extremely low. "For Sale" signs on the large Kenwood homes have disappeared; instead Kenwood residents proudly boast a waiting list. The conference tenant referral office has many more applicants for rental and sale housing than there are recorded vacancies. Some of the families who left the community in the early years of panic have come back.

Finance and realty companies are showing interest in investing in Hyde Park-Kenwood after years of having written it off. Said one realtor: "Maintenance money spent in the area is not being thrown down the drain. Similarly, we feel assured that investment dollar equities are safe . . ." Another said: "Many real estate firms have chosen to remain in the area because working in the urban renewal program has been an exciting experiment and a good investment. The neighborhood is on the upgrade. Our firm is selling to many outsiders."

Slum operators are less numerous in Hyde Park-Kenwood and more frightened than they were. New building, zoning and housing laws, improved inspection and enforcement methods, an alert citizenry, quicker and more decisive action, unwelcome publicity, and larger penalties combine to keep them in partial check. But they have not yet been put out of business, and violations of building and zoning codes continue to threaten the community.

So does crime. There are more and better police officers in the district, redevelopment has removed many of the taverns and tenements where trouble was bred, and the crime rate in Hyde Park-Kenwood has been reduced since 1950. Residents, however, are still concerned about the incidence of crime.

The greatest change is in the people.

There are several thousand more than there were, even after the displacement of several hundred families by the redevelopment project.

Many of the same faces are still around, but a number of the older, middle- and upper-income business and professional families are gone. So are most of the Japanese Americans. In their place are newcomers of varying origins, backgrounds, income levels, and occupations; younger white-collar workers with small children; laborers from the rural South and Puerto Rico; new faculty and staff members of educational institutions and hospitals, transients in search of a temporary stopping place, stable families drawn to the area by its atmosphere and spirit.

The complexion as well as the character of the population is different. There are many more dark-skinned people—almost as many as white—living in the now solidly Negro blocks along the western and northern boundaries of Hyde Park-Kenwood or among white neighbors in the interracial heart of the community. Most of the church congregations are now interracial. Negroes and whites work together to improve their neighborhood, and their children share classrooms, playgrounds, and the facilities of recreation agencies.

A returning visitor would probably be struck most of all by the change in attitude.

It is evident in the reaction to an interracial community. Where once the possibility was viewed with horror and opposition, it is now generally accepted as a matter of fact. One member of the businessmen's group said thoughtfully, "We who believe in an interracial community are no longer on the defensive. We have become so prominent that even those who still do not like it keep quiet and are at least willing to live with it." But there is still a great deal of worry about forces which may prevent the community from stabilizing on an interracial basis.

The change in attitude is evident, too, in the changed approach to problems. A basic realism, a willingness to try to understand and solve community problems has replaced the vague forebodings, the head in the sand, and the scapegoating approach of earlier years.

An increasing number of citizens now see deterioration, rather than the Negro, as the chief enemy. This realization came as they discovered, with the in-migration of southern rural whites, that lack of urbanization created the same problems regardless of color and that the real difficulty was one of class.

Physical planning to control and reverse the process of decay, dismissed as an unpopular, ivory-tower idea in 1949, is accepted in 1958 as an essential factor in the community's progress.

Unlike other urban areas, Hyde Park-Kenwood has long had a special small-town atmosphere, traceable perhaps to its university setting. This is even more pronounced today. People still use the huge tree in front of Woodward's Bookstore and the bulletin board in the Co-op to advertise possessions and services for sale or lease; and others frequently gather round these centers to keep posted on who has, needs, or wants what, or just to pass the time of day. Professional colleagues and their families still have a flourishing social life within the community, visiting back and forth, reading plays, attending lectures and concerts and the local movie houses together.

But something new has been added. Neighborliness has spread to take in people who never shared social pleasures—people formerly unknown to one another even though they lived in adjoining apartment buildings, who now stop to exchange greetings and chat in the street, over back fences or in neighbors' homes. Common interest in the community, first discovered at block meetings, draws them together.

A warm new spirit of kinship is abroad, the feeling that "we are all in this together." It finds outlet in neighborhood improvement projects, in eagerness to share with the Land Clearance Commission responsibility for the satisfactory relocation of families displaced by redevelopment, in lending friendly help to neighbors.

In this always articulate community, people are more articulate than ever. They know what is going on and have opinions about it, and whether they approve or disapprove, they speak up in a continuing round of talk and argument that adds to the liveliness and vitality of the neighborhood if not to its serenity.

The community of 1949, immobilized by fear and anxiety, lethargy and pessimism, is immobilized no longer. Fears and anxieties exist now as then, but today's are the kind that go with action. Confidence and optimism are evident in conversations among friends and acquaintances, in public meetings, in the fact that present residents have decided to remain, and in money invested in the area. Where nine years ago people talked nostalgically of the never-to-be-regained glories of Hyde Park-Kenwood's past, and social scientists prophesied inevitable decay and doom, everywhere today there is talk of the future and how to achieve the finest possible community with the least injury to individuals and institutions. Differing concepts of a fine community and how to attain it sometimes cause sharp conflict; there is sometimes bitter controversy over details of urban renewal proposals; but those who are making their voices heard are unmistakably united in the desire to see their neighborhood revitalized.

Working toward this end as well as talking about it, their efforts are channeled through community agencies and institutions. Some of the old organizations, with their one-man or part-time operations, are dead: the Hyde Park Planning Association, the Oakland-Kenwood Planning Association, the Hyde Park Community Council. But other stronger groups with more comprehensive programs are flourishing. The Hyde Park-Kenwood Community Conference, now generally accepted as a potent force by all community interests, uses its annual budget of over $60,000, its eleven-member staff, and its network of block organizations to channel the energies of as many people as it can reach (over 10,000 to date, 3,800 of them members) in the service of the community. The South East Chicago Commission, with a budget of $50,000, a staff of six, and an influential constituency adds urgently needed strength to the citizen program through the confidence its membership and operations inspire among financial and investment groups and public bodies.

In addition, every other responsible community organization and institution is actively supporting the urban renewal effort. Most powerful ally is the University of Chicago with its great prestige and assets, now fully committed to community improvement and a leading factor in it. The churches and temples, the PTA's, the businessmen's associations, the *Hyde Park Herald*, the educational institutions and hospitals, the recreation agencies, the local Independent Voters of Illinois and the League of Women Voters, the Hyde Park Cooperative Society, the redevelopment corporations, the Cooperative Homes of Hyde Park—are also involved in greater or lesser degree. So are Chicago's mayor, the community's two aldermen, every department of the city government, state and federal bodies—all putting tremendous resources into Hyde Park-Kenwood as Chicago's first urban renewal area.

And perhaps this is the greatest change—the powerful array of forces committed to saving a community where once a few people struggled alone.

CHAPTER 20

Appraisal

The outcome of the Hyde Park-Kenwood story is still unknown. It is not yet certain that public urban renewal aid will spark the private investment in rehabilitation and new building needed to upgrade the community and set in motion the process of continuing self-renewal. There has not yet been sufficiently strong action to stop the further spread of blight as the renewal program is initiated. Stabilization of the community on an interracial basis is not yet assured.

Whether or not the goal for Hyde Park-Kenwood is reached—and held—depends on many factors.

It depends on the community's ability to bring about maximum cooperation in the maintenance of high standards and the improvement of property. It depends on success in retaining and attracting desirable residents of different races, backgrounds, and economic levels. And such success depends in turn on whether the plans for the future will prove imaginative enough to make living in the central city as interesting and esthetically desirable as it must be to compete with the advantages middle-class families find in the suburbs—not on the same terms but in terms of comparable satisfactions.

It depends on the willingness and ability of the city, state, and nation to develop a better coordinated, more determined, and more adequately financed attack on the whole problem of blight than has yet been undertaken. Such a program needs to concern itself with the reorganization and tightening up of public departments to eliminate the overlapping, costly delays and inefficiencies caused by the multiplicity of agencies now involved in housing, redevelopment, and conservation. There is need for the creation of a sound, comprehensive plan for the city of Chicago as well as for the metropolitan area, within which the development of communities may be charted; rigid enforcement of building, housing, and zoning codes, the provision of an adequate supply of middle- and lower-income housing, encouraged by whatever public subsidy or financial incentives are necessary. Aid must be extended to declining neighborhoods adjacent to Hyde Park-Kenwood. Additional communities must be stimulated to work on conservation programs of their own, and community organizations throughout the city must be strengthened to make this possible. There must be a city policy and program that will put an end to public and private discriminatory practices which encourage the extension of all-Negro areas.

And finally, effective action by the city and the nation depends upon the creation of an informed public opinion vigorous enough to insist on the kind of program the problems demand and determined enough to be willing to pay for it.

In Hyde Park-Kenwood the problems are regarded as staggering but not insurmountable. It is believed that they, like some of the seemingly insoluble problems before them, can and will be resolved. The community finds hope for the future in the record of the past.

The changes brought about since 1949 add up to an impressive list: new schools, new street lights, new recreation areas, improved municipal services, new laws, private investment in new building, institutional expansion, the elimination of pockets of slum, the beginning of an urban renewal program, high morale, changed attitudes, the involvement of an unprecedented number of citizens and of city, state, and federal agencies in a concerted attack on the problems of a single community.

Many forces contributed to these results, but it is generally agreed that the conference created the atmosphere which made them possible.

In the interest of objectivity, dozens of people in and out of Hyde Park-Kenwood—public officials, the heads of religious, educational, and business institutions, and other leaders, including some of the former critics of the conference—were asked to appraise the conference effort as honestly as they could in terms of its value, if any, to the community, public officials, and the city. Their comments were highly laudatory.

The conference was credited with having prevented the entire area from becoming a slum; restoring confidence; encouraging individuals and institutions to remain in the area and to invest in it; "establishing a working format for citizen organization and action" in redevelopment and conservation; helping individuals to become politically effective within the city; "creating the public climate which made possible public unity on the desire for an interracial community"; "providing a prod on the city to do a better job," and "supporting, guiding, correcting, and supplementing its work"; creating the citizen understanding necessary for the success of urban renewal.

Officials in public and private agencies placed special stress on the contributions of the conference to the city of Chicago and their value to public officials. They commented on

The leadership it provided in city affairs;

Its work in helping to raise city standards, create new legislation, improve the quality of public service; secure more adequate funds for public facilities and services.

Its role in changing the attitudes and practices of a number of city officials.

Its value in changing the attitudes toward community organizations on the part of officials as well as in the city at large.

Its significance as a demonstration of new ways of dealing with problems of conservation and race relations and of citizen cooperation with government in a common task.

Many communities found in the conference experience patterns for dealing with some of their own problems. From 1950 through

1956 approximately 600 requests for information and advice came from 76 cities in 24 states and from 12 foreign countries, exclusive of the additional hundreds of unrecorded inquiries by telephone and in meetings and conferences. Over half of the 34 new neighborhood conservation organizations formed in Chicago since 1952 have turned to the conference for counsel and help. Urban renewal officials continually refer leaders of other communities to the conference for guidance in securing citizen participation in renewal programs. Potential leaders of other organizations have been trained in the community clinics and workshops of the conference, and neighborhoods in many cities have sent representatives to Hyde Park-Kenwood for investigation and consultation.

Nevertheless, there are limitations on the value of the conference demonstration to other areas. It cannot be successfully duplicated in its entirety by communities lacking some of the distinctive features of Hyde Park-Kenwood. The conference grew out of a setting unique in many respects: a neighborhood full of trained minds, expert knowledge, and a wide variety of skills, with a tradition of liberalism and civic leadership; a university of great power and prestige; and sufficient community interest and monetary resources to create and support two strong organizations. William L. Bacon of the Welfare Council of Metropolitan Chicago feels, therefore, that the conference "is not, as some people have felt, a new social invention" but a "unique instrumentality of a specific community."

The structure and program of the conference *were* peculiarly suited to Hyde Park-Kenwood. But all communities can profit from the demonstration by applying the experience of the conference, and tailoring its basic principles and methods to their own condition, needs, and resources. While their efforts must necessarily be limited by their assets, it is possible for most areas to support an improvement program by enlisting the cooperation of real estate firms, stores, banks, churches, and other institutions whose interests depend upon community conservation. They can work on community problems without the large funds and the extensive activities employed in Hyde Park-Kenwood by starting on maintenance and improvement at the first sign of decline, not after it is well advanced, carrying on even small projects to make the neighborhood better each year; by combining all community groups in one organization rather than two; and by taking advantage of lessons learned by the conference only after costly expenditures in time, effort, and money.

It is clear from conference experience with block organization and the attempt of other communities to duplicate it that this widely copied tool for citizen direct action does not work successfully everywhere, that its effectiveness depends on the character of the population, general community conditions, and a strong central organization with competent leadership. A new community organization would do well, therefore, to study the conditions and methods necessary for successful block organization before investing in it. (These are discussed in "Block Groups and Community Change," by Bettie Sarchet, "Neighbors in Action," by Herbert A. Thelen and Bettie Sarchet, and Chapters 7 and 8 in this book.) Even though another kind of organizational structure might be preferable, the methods tested in the block program and other conference activities provide insight into ways of leading citizens from apathy to participation.

Much can also be learned from conference mistakes and accomplishments about factors making for success or failure. Community groups attach special value to lessons derived from conference experience which stress the importance of the following in developing a successful program:

Knowledge of community problems and their causes.

Involving the major interests in the area in efforts to solve them; (obviously, a large institution with substantial investment in a community offers the best hope for a continuing and successful conservation program because of its sustained interest).

Setting up an office with professional staff at the earliest possible moment.

Creating understanding of the community's role in conservation, and enlisting as many individuals as possible in actual work.

Developing and making maximum use of volunteer leadership.

Knowledge of step-by-step procedures in the handling of factors contributing to community deterioration and of methods for dealing with panic, fear, and tension involving different racial, cultural, and economic groups.

Understanding the laws applicable to the community effort and the function of public departments, their powers, responsibilities, and limitations.

Marshaling the facts about community conditions and complaints, presenting them convincingly to authorities, and following through until action is taken.

Establishing relationships with public agencies in ways designed to produce maximum cooperation and mutual respect.

Giving active leadership in creating the necessary instruments if they are not available, bringing about reforms, and providing public support for them.

My own evaluation of the history and activities of the Hyde Park-Kenwood Community Conference confirms a number of the values stressed by the many people I consulted. But it also points up the failures of the conference, the things I would change if it were all to be done again, a few of the additional lessons we learned that might be of special help to other communities.

Our most serious mistake was making ideological demands on people and institutions, asking them to share our beliefs, to take part in the conference program *for our reasons*. Instead, we should have helped them to analyze their own problems as they bore on the community, to approach their problems with more community realism, and thus to do a better job in their own interests for their own reasons. Such an approach could have helped them to see the urgency of acting constructively to meet the challenge of an aging community and a changing population. After all, a church, in its effort to create and hold a strong congregation, must be concerned with its environment, just as a university must be if it is to build a fine community of scholars and students. Through this very self-interest, all of the local institutions and forces could have been helped to make their most vital contribution to the community.

It does not seem to me now that it was either necessary or desirable to engage in *formal* programs for the integration of

Negroes in community life, such as the early work of the Employment, Hotels, Private Schools, and Restaurant subcommittees. Although these efforts did win us friends among Negroes, they were not really productive and created many more problems than they solved. We found that preaching and crusading are never as persuasive as example or awakened self-interest. The policy statement of the conference made our position on the race question very clear. Thereafter, it seems to me, we should have concentrated on involving *all* community people in a common improvement program. The very process of involvement, the experience of working together, would have improved race relations more naturally than all the self-conscious programs we undertook in this area.

If we had acted on these beliefs from the beginning, I think a stronger and more effective conservation program could have been initiated at an earlier date, and much antagonism and misunderstanding would have been avoided.

Equally damaging was the failure to try to involve all community interests at the outset, the deliberate decision "at least for the time being, to work with people who believe as we do," steering clear of "power groups." If the approach to these groups had been made earlier and differently, there might not have been so much distrust and suspicion to overcome. In any event, experience taught a valuable lesson: that an organization for community betterment needs more to achieve its purposes than the loyalty and interest of such "people of good will" as churchmen, teachers, PTA members, and social workers; that the banker also has a vital role to play, and the real estate man, shopkeeper, hotel owner, university trustee.

Another error in the early days was the tendency of some block groups to think of good leadership in terms of verbal proficiency. Gatherings of residents were thus sometimes subjected to hours of interminable theorizing and talk which alienated busy people, when a few concrete actions like getting garbage containers, lighting up alleys, or cleaning dirty lots would have raised morale and encouraged people to go on to more difficult conservation tasks.

Such mistakes as these made inevitable the creation of a second community organization, described as having a "practical" rather than an "idealistic" or "naïve" approach to community problems, to work in the interests of power groups and individuals who had no confidence in the motivation or effectiveness of the conference.

Undoubtedly the existence of two agencies devoted to conservation—one an organization of the neighborhood power structure and the other representing the "grass roots"—has had special value for Hyde Park-Kenwood. The different methods used by each and the different strengths they provided produced results which neither could have achieved alone. The facts of history made two organizations necessary in Hyde Park-Kenwood (and probably will in many other communities). I believe, however, that a single strong organization *supported by all community forces and keeping their interests in proper balance* could have combined the strengths and methods of the conference and commission and might have achieved more with less conflict, less cost, and greater speed. Chancellor Kimpton also thinks now that it was "a fundamental mistake not to have one organization from the start. In retrospect it would have been better if the University of Chicago had jumped in and supported the conference. At the time, however, I certainly would not have done it and for pretty good reasons." There are community residents who feel strongly that two organizations were inevitable because of the need of a major institution like the University of Chicago to be dominant in any community group with which it is associated.

Since we cannot begin over again, it is impossible to know what would have happened if. . . . It seems reasonable to believe, however, that if the University of Chicago had been given reason for confidence in the conference and had backed it, other large interests would also have swung to its support. An adequate budget would have enabled the conference to employ personnel with the planning skills and the drive needed to carry forward a renewal program. A renewal plan developed by a single organization representing all community interests might not have been an improvement on the one created by the Planning Unit of the University of Chicago and the South East Commission. But it would have been less vulnerable to attack on the grounds that it gave priority to university needs at the expense of other interests. As it is, in spite of the very real effort of the commission, the conference, the university, and the Community Conservation Board to work cooperatively in the planning process, in spite of the fact that the conference did in many instances affect the planning, there is still some feeling in the community that the final product is a "university plan."

A backward look reveals another failure and another reason in favor of a single organization including all groups. The conference concentrated on involving individual residents in community action and made no serious attempt to mobilize community organizations and coordinate their efforts around the program. There seemed to be good reasons at the time. In the beginning it was thought that the Hyde Park Community Council, the official "organization of organizations," was the proper coordinating agency, and later the South East Chicago Commission was expected to discharge this function. In fact neither did the job adequately, both the conference and commission now work with community organizations in different ways, and occasionally it is still not clear where responsibility lies. As a result, a source of potential strength has not yet been fully tapped. The fact is that thousands of people are not reached either by the conference or the commission.

We learned that whether there is one conservation agency or two, community organization alone is not enough—no matter how fine the structure, how brilliant the methods and program nor how great the involvement. No conservation program can succeed unless the community and the city work as a team, each assuming obligations and carrying them out. And the renewal of declining areas like Hyde Park-Kenwood demands a great deal of outside help as well, in public funds and private investment. The creation of a better urban environment is terribly expensive. Our experience convinced us that citizens have to involve themselves seriously in the effort to get government aid if declining neighborhoods are to be restored and given new life.

Conversely, we learned that a renewal program cannot succeed, however handsomely it is financed, unless the people of the community understand it, are kept informed, and are given a channel through which they can make their voices heard and their actions count. If this is done, the program gains greatly by intelligent citizen participation and support. If it is not done, the entire project may be destroyed by opposition. The power of the veto is no small power, and many good causes have been lost because people used it in ignorance, in resentment, in fear that their rights were being invaded, or for political reasons. Jack Meltzer of the Planning Unit and Bruce Sagan of the *Herald* are convinced that had there been no conference to represent "the people" a protest movement without responsible leadership would have developed and, said Meltzer, "we would have folded up two or three years ago. There would have been no renewal program."

We learned from experience the necessity of educating people not only on community issues and their responsibilities but on their limitations as participants in a citizens' organization. In the early days the work of the conference sometimes suffered from the mistaken belief that "democratic participation" meant everyone had a right to decide everything. The effectiveness of the conference as an organization increased as people learned that, while their informed opinion was an important factor in guiding decisions, final decision making in the conference had to be left to its elected leadership.

At first we failed to recognize the very great power of a strongly knit citizens' group and thought in terms of "the people" on the one hand and "the power groups" on the other. Slowly we came to see that the people of a community united in a common cause could be a force as potent as any in the moneyed or political power structure, and that such a force, used wisely, could affect—if not reform—existing power groups, lead them in new directions, and serve as a check on action not in the public interest.

The awakening of the individual to the realization of this power gave new meaning to the democratic process, new dimensions to the role of citizen. "Government" was no longer the abstraction it had been. It had become real to hundreds of people who found through personal experience that what they said and did could make a difference. They came to see that responsible citizenship meant a great deal more than voting for "the right people" or "throwing the rascals out" if they failed to do their job. It meant active and informed participation, and shared responsibility for the conduct of government and the future of their community.

In the people of every community everywhere there is a vast, untapped potential, almost limitless energy and resources which can be released for community betterment. Freeing that potential and channeling it into constructive citizen action can provide a powerful source of strength in the saving of our cities and the regeneration of the nation.

ORGANIZATIONAL CHART
Hyde Park-Kenwood Community Conference

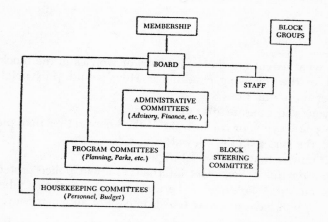

Materials concerned with the organization and structure of the Hyde Park-Kenwood Community Conference—policy statement, bylaws, the functions of all committees—may be obtained at a nominal cost from the conference office, 1305 E. 53rd St., Chicago 15, Illinois.

The following are samples of information and instruction sheets that have been widely distributed to block groups. Similar instruction materials dealing with other problems are listed on the "Information Sheet for Block Leaders," page 349, and may also be obtained from the conference.

Block Problem Finder

To what extent are there problems or worries in the block as a result of the following conditions? How would your neighbors answer these questions?

Is your street unsafe after dark?

Do you leave your car in front of the house rather than putting it in the garage in the alley after dark?

Is it unwise to walk alone at night?

Suggestions for action Get information about police protection; check on street lighting; make arrangements with neighbors so that you will have someone to call in case of an emergency.

Are small children adequately supervised at play, or do they "run wild" all over the block?

Do teen-agers form as noisy gangs outside, or does the block provide other satisfying recreational opportunities?

Suggestions for action Several groups of neighbors in this area have gotten together and found a vacant lot where they can put up play equipment and take turns playing with the children; assess resources for working with children and youth: scouts, church groups, and Y's, Campfire Girls, etc.; provide parties, dances, discussion groups in homes if space is available (one neighborhood has rented a store and organized a youth club);

discuss the possibilities for youth-adult cooperation on neighborhood problems; investigate possibilities of using school facilities for leisure-time groups, working through PTA's, if possible; create opportunities for teen-agers and adults to work together on recreation problems and on the question of youth's role in the community.

Has the cutting up of large apartments into too-small units, with resulting overcrowding, gotten under way in your block?
Suggestions for action   If violations are suspected, get accurate information and take action as a group; join with neighbors in putting pressure on the City Council to expand housing facilities.

Can you find a place to park your car?
Do trucks rumble up and down your street and park in your block?
Suggestions for action   In some streets, removal of old cars which have been abandoned will release additional parking space; a city ordinance requires that adequate parking facilities be provided where new construction is contemplated; cooperate with the conference to see that this ordinance is enforced; work with the Planning Committee on the possibility of neighborhood parking lots in already overcrowded areas; see that the ordinance forbidding overnight parking of trucks in residential areas is enforced.

Does the manager or janitor of your building take it upon himself to comment about people you entertain?
Suggestions for action   Work with neighbors to formulate policies for dealing with the situation, for making your position clear, for having individual rights respected; think through with other people the kind of approach which will make an impression on this kind of prejudiced person; avoid intimidation, and be clear about the circumstances under which eviction is possible.

Have you and your neighbors ever really talked together about conditions which determine how many roomers may be taken in?

Suggestions for action Talk over the situation and come to an agreement about occupancy standards.

Are you bothered by trash or refuse in the street or alley, or by soot?

Suggestions for action Put pressure on building owners to obey smoke abatement law; if there are repeated violations, report to Smoke Violations Dept., RA 6-8000; contact your alderman about trash disposal; suggest provision of more public trash cans; if the problem is one of local carelessness, make agreement with neighbors about "clean-up squads."

Is the block periodically swept by wild rumors about the sale of property?

Do real estate agents come into your neighborhood to entice or threaten you into selling your property?

Suggestions for action One block where neighbors were worrying about possible sales of property got together and agreed to let each other know if they were thinking of offering their homes for sale; they also agreed to take the names of real estate salesmen who try to force sales and to boycott these firms if they could not reach an understanding with them; a list of such firms should be referred to the Steering Committee for action in the name of the whole organization.

Are certain buildings eyesores or fire hazards, or really not fit for human habitation?

Suggestions for action Take action with neighbors to report such conditions to the building inspectors; report to the conference for action by the total group.

Are you satisfied with the standards of education in your school?

Suggestions for action Share with neighbors your information about the methods, attitudes of teachers, and facilities of your neighborhood school; work through PTA's to improve these where necessary.

What To Do About Tracking Down Rumors and Stopping Panic

Rumors of sales of property, illegal conversions, and petty crime can be most destructive to neighborhood morale. If not properly handled they may easily set up hostilities between groups of people, or touch off panic and flight from an area.

The time to stop rumors is when they first come to your attention. The following steps will be helpful in doing this:

1. Try to find out from the person who repeats the rumor the source of his information.
2. Find out the facts by making personal contact with whoever is most likely to know them: e.g., the owner of a building, the building commissioner's office, etc.
3. Tell your informant of the true facts, quoting the source of your information.
4. If the rumor has spread to other residents of the block, call a block meeting to inform everyone of the facts. If any additional steps are needed, these should be worked out by the block group.

The following brief examples illustrate the way in which a number of rumors have been handled.

Conversion and Eviction Rumors

In one instance where a conversion permit had been issued, rumors about the extent of the conversion were greatly exaggerated. A block meeting was called and a committee appointed to examine the suspect building. The committee reported back at a subsequent meeting that good conversions had been carried out. Neighborhood fears were thus allayed. Had an illegal conversion been in progress, appropriate action could immediately have been taken by the group (for instructions, see work sheet on how to handle building and zoning violations).

In another case, one resident of an apartment building investigated a rumor that the building was up for sale and that all the present tenants were about to be evicted. She talked to the janitor and agent, and, learning that the rumor was false, invited the other women in the building to coffee and reported the facts to them.

Rumors and Panic about the Future Intentions of Negro Newcomers

In one such case a committee of women called on Negro newcomers to the neighborhood, who, it was rumored, planned to turn their new home into a boarding house, contrary to the neighborhood standards. It soon became clear to the callers who were served refreshments by a butler, that their hosts had no intention of running a boarding house. In another case, where a Negro newcomer was suspected of undesirable conversion plans, the block organization leader sent her a letter inviting her to join the group and to share in its program of neighborhood improvement. He mentioned especially the need to prevent overcrowding by stopping conversions. The reply he received stated that the newcomer would be happy to cooperate with the block organization, and that she had no intention of cutting up the building.

On another block, when it was heard that Negroes were about to move in, a meeting was held to discuss the matter. At first the atmosphere of the meeting was tense, and some anti-Negro opinions were expressed. Then it was discovered that most of the people in the block wanted to stay, and wanted reassurance that their neighbors wanted to stay, too. Three positive measures were taken to encourage a desirable buyer: some of the men cut the grass in front of the house; they succeeded in having a decrepit car removed from the premises; and a committee called on the agent handling the property to urge him to find a buyer who would maintain the single-family standards of the block. When the new owners arrived, they were invited to a block party and were soon well accepted in the group.

Cases Where Real Estate Agents Have Tried To Spread Panic

In one case, in an area where Negroes had been seen looking at properties, a real estate agent called on people to advise them to sell out "before it was too late" (and incidentally at a low price). In the process, he saw a property owner who happened to belong to the Hyde Park-Kenwood Community Conference. There was no block organization in the area, so this owner got in touch with conference people, who helped to form and to organize a large area meeting a week later. The area meeting was attended by about 250 people, who were informed of the move made by the speculator. The landlord who had been approached announced that he did not intend to be scared into selling out. The other property owners present then informally agreed to keep one another informed if other speculators tried similar tactics; and to tell people that they did not intend to sell out. The speculators soon gave up their efforts in the neighborhood.

Another conference member who lived on an organized block was approached in the same way by a real estate agent. She reported this at a block meeting to forewarn other property owners of what was afoot and to prevent panic on the block from any false rumors that real estate operators might spread.

What To Do About Building and Zoning Violations

Illegal Conversions

1. The first step in preventing illegal conversions and over-crowding is to have alert block members who note the first signs of possible conversion: moving in of lumber and other building materials.

2. Try to involve the owners of a suspect building in the block group—send a committee to call on the person responsible for the conversion, and tell him about the block's program for maintenance of standards. If the owner will not cooperate, and the block group is convinced that a bad or an illegal conversion is going in—

3. Report to conference office the following information.

Address and type of building (e.g., frame house; six-flat, etc.).

Location in building of suspected conversion or other problem (e.g., 3rd floor, rear).

Reasons for suspicion.

Name of owner of building—if known.

How long the violation existed? (If a conversion is just beginning it is very important to call at once, to "nip it in the bud".)

4. The conference will check to see if there is a conversion permit. If there is no permit, the Building Department issues a "stop" order at once, which is served on the owner by the police. If there is a permit, an inspection will be made to see if the work conforms with the blueprints. If not, work is again stopped. The conference will report back to you concerning its actions and findings.

5. If the conversion is stopped, the block group must keep alert to see that it does not start again. If the owner (who was converting without a permit) secures a permit, the block should check to be certain the work is conforming to the permit, and keep conference informed.

6. If the case goes to court, block people will be asked to appear in court. The presence of interested neighbors demonstrates to the court that the citizens are concerned. If some neighbors have been inside the building, they may be called as witnesses.

7. Throughout the whole process, keep trying to involve and get the cooperation of the building owner. Also be sure to keep all the block people informed right along.

Other Types of Violations

1. Other violations which should be corrected are: defective porches and stairs; inadequate fire escapes where required by law; defective wiring or plumbing; improper garbage and trash disposal; need for rat extermination.

2. As in the case of conversions, the best practice in dealing with these violations is to call on the offender, tell him about the block group, and invite him to attend meetings. If the block has any agreed-upon standards, these should be explained.

It is important to be friendly and enlist the cooperation of the violator. Present the block program as something that everyone is working in, rather than suggesting that the neighbors are up in arms against him.

3. In the event that friendly efforts do not get the desired results, the conference has prepared a complaint form which

should be in the file of every block leader for use in reporting such violations.

Other Materials Available

The following materials may be obtained from the conference office:

1. Case studies of how conversions have been handled.
2. Overcrowding and conversion: a report of what the conference has done.
3. Detailed information on minimum standards and on residential conversions permitted by law.

APPENDIX **5**

Brief Guide for Determining Housing Violations

General Comment

When noting complaints list the following:

1. Exact and complete address of building.
2. Name of owner or agent.
3. Exact location of every violation—*apartment number, which floor, which address.*

Overcrowding

What is the size of each dwelling unit? How many rooms? How many occupants—adults and children? Count them.

Bathroom

Does each dwelling unit have its own bath? How many units share each bath?

Does plumbing work? Toilets flush? Faucets leak? Drains stop up?

Does bathroom have a window or a mechanical ventilator? Can window be opened?

Sash cords broken? Windowpane cracked or broken?

Does electric fixture work properly? Shock hazard? Enough electric outlets?

Is flooring in good condition? Cracks? Holes?

Are ceilings and walls in good condition? Cracks? Holes?

Kitchen

Does each unit have its own kitchen? If not, how many families share it?

Does room have a window or mechanical ventilator? Is window in good working condition? (see above).

Is it rodent and vermin free? If not, does it have regular exterminator service?

Are stoves and refrigerators in good condition? Do they leak gas?

Does kitchen plumbing work properly? Adequate water pressure? Leaky faucets? Stopped drain?

Is garbage disposal provided for every unit?

Do electrical fixtures work properly and without shock or fire hazard? Is there extensive use of extension wires?

Are ceilings, walls, and floors in sound condition? Holes? Cracks?

Bedrooms

Is the size adequate for its occupants? 70 sq. ft. minimum for one occupant? 50 sq. ft. for each additional occupant?

Does room have a window? Is it in good working condition?

Does bedroom have access to toilet without having to go through another bedroom?

Are walls, ceilings, and floors in good condition?

Are electrical fixtures in good condition? Is there extensive use of extension wires?

Other rooms

Are ceilings, walls, and floors in good condition?

Are electrical fixtures in good working condition? Is there extensive use of extension wires?

Are living rooms, halls, closets, or others used for sleeping? Which ones? How large? What ventilation?

Exits

Does every dwelling unit have *two* accessible ways of getting out of building in case of fire? Without having to go through another dwelling unit? If so, how many rooms to go through to reach exit? Is there a glass panel door?

Are all exits well lighted and marked? Are all exits unobstructed?

Public Hallways

Are they safe, clean and well lit? Steps in good repair? Missing railings? Torn carpeting on stairs and halls? Litter? Obstruction? Are they clean?

Are outside doors kept locked?

Garbage disposal

Do all garbage cans have tight-fitting covers? Does every unit have its own garbage can?

Are premises, including basement, porches, and yards, kept free of rubbish, litter, and debris—from the standpoint of health, fire, and rodent control?

Help Keep Our Block Clean!

*This is your check list
to help us all take pride in the
appearance of our block.*

——Do you sweep litter, leaves, grass clippings, or any other waste into the street or alley?

> If you do, you are liable for a fine of $2 to $200 for each offense. Incidentally, you are also responsible for clogged sewer nuisances.

——Do you have enough garbage containers to store all the litter between collections?

> The law requires that refuse containers have tight-fitting covers, two handles, 20–32 gallon capacity, and be of strong material.
> There must be at least one garbage can per apartment or home.

——Do you leave your garbage cans uncovered while awaiting collection on the street or alley?

> It causes the scattering and blowing of litter down your street or alley, and is punishable by fines of $2 to $200.

——Do you allow waste or rubbish to be dumped or spilled on your premises?

> It is unlawful to dump or throw rubbish anywhere, which might be blown or scattered by wind or rain onto streets, sidewalks, or alleys. There is a fine of $5 to $200 for each offense.

——Do you throw handbills, newspapers, sharp objects of any kind on streets, lawn, sidewalks, or alleys?

> Before you throw that candy wrapper—THINK! What would your block look like if all your neighbors did the same thing? Don't pay a fine of $2 to $200 for such careless action.

——Do you burn garbage on your premises?

> This is a nuisance to your neighbors, and makes you liable to a fine of $2 to $200.

The block where you live can be as clean as you make it. Your cooperation is needed and appreciated.

YOUR BLOCK GROUP

——————

Information Sheet for Block Leaders

I. Conference Services to Block Groups
  A. Program suggestions for block meetings
     Slide sequence, "It Can Happen Here" (conference office has projector and screen).
     Film strips pertinent to city planning and better human relations.
     Speakers on urban renewal program, neighborhood redevelopment corporations.
  B. Leaflets and reprints on the program of redevelopment corporations, the program of the Hyde Park-Kenwood Community Conference, etc.
  C. "How To Do It"—mimeographed information:
     Removing abandoned cars.
     Getting sidewalks and curbs repaired.
     Developing tot-lots.
     Street cleaning and garbage collection.
     Rat control.
     Securing traffic lights and signs.
     Alley and street parking regulations.
     Minimum housing code.
     How to determine housing violations.

D. Information on how other blocks have handled problems: Tenant-real estate management relations for improving maintenance, etc.

Improving street and alley lighting, etc.

E. Membership information

List of conference membership in block area.

Names of block residents who have inquired about block organization and want to be active.

F. Reporting building and zoning violations, complaints.

Notice of housing and zoning complaints in the block.

G. Referral service on apartment vacancies and homes for sale.

H. Block Steering Committee meetings for all block leaders (monthly).

I. Block leadership training workshops.

II. How block groups cooperate with conference program

A. *Providing Conference office with notice of block meetings,* so that:

Block director can visit.

Conference can provide advance publicity in *Hyde Park Herald.*

Observers from other block groups, or other organizations can visit.

B. *Sending reports on block meetings to conference office, together with attendance list, in order to:*

1. Inform conference office of services and information required by block groups.

2. Facilitate conference membership drive.

3. Provide names of volunteers for conference office work, and committee assignments.

4. Give all block groups the benefit of each other's experience.

C. *Participation in special conference events.*

D. *Providing volunteers and leadership to help organize and to visit new block organizations.*

E. *Provide regular representation to monthly Block Steering Committee meetings,* in order to:

1. Report on own block activities.
2. Become fully informed of conference program and policies, and the work of other community organizations.
3. Report back to own block on the activities of the conference, and other block groups.

APPENDIX

Time Schedule For Urban Renewal Program

Hyde Park Redevelopment Projects A and B

July 28, 1954	Site designation resolution of the Chicago Land Clearance Commission adopted by City Council, after approval by the Chicago Plan Commission.
August 6, 1954	Site designation resolution passed by the Illinois State Housing Board.
December 22, 1954	Redevelopment plan passed by City Council, after approval by Chicago Plan Commission.
January 17, 1955	Redevelopment plan approved by State Housing Board.

February 15 and 17, 1955 Federal approval and authorization of over $6,500,000 in federal funds, automatically producing more than $600,000 in city and state aid.

May 10, 1955 Beginning of demolition.

October 9, 1957 Chicago Land Clearance Commission plan, based on the redevelopment proposal submitted by Webb and Knapp, Inc., approved by City Council.

March, 1958 Relocation and demolition substantially completed.

August, 1958 The beginning of reconstruction.

Total Urban Renewal Area

March 28, 1955 The city of Chicago submitted an application for urban renewal planning funds to the federal Housing and Home Finance Agency.

September 14, 1955 The city of Chicago, through the Community Conservation Board, entered into a contract with the Housing and Home Finance Agency, for an advance of $198,680 to pay the costs of survey and planning work in connection with Hyde Park-Kenwood's urban renewal plan.

April 19 and May 10, 1956 Community Conservation Board of city of Chicago held public hearing and designated Hyde Park-Kenwood as "Conservation Area," as provided in the state Urban Community Conservation Act.

August 31, 1956 Preliminary Project Report submitted to Housing and Home Finance Agency by Community Conservation Board.

September 19, 1956	Mayor appointed an eleven-member Hyde Park-Kenwood Conservation Community Council.
December 20, 1956	Housing and Home Finance Agency approved Preliminary Project Report and authorized final planning. The urban renewal commissioner thereupon established a revised reservation of capital grant funds in the amount of $25,835,000.
January 28–May 28, 1957	Hyde Park-Kenwood Conservation Community Council held seven public hearings on Preliminary Project Report.
February 13, 1958	Community Conservation Board transmitted the final plan to the Hyde Park-Kenwood Conservation Community Council.
March 12, 1958	Public hearing by Conservation Community Council.
September 2, 1958	Final plan approved by federal Housing and Home Finance Agency.
November, 1958	Final plan approved by Chicago City Council.

Materials on Planning and Urban Renewal

The documents listed below are for and about the Hyde Park-Kenwood urban renewal program, or contain general information which proved helpful to it. Most of the materials produced by the conference may be obtained from its office at a nominal cost; the other documents may be consulted at the conference headquarters or at the offices which prepared them.

Hyde Park Redevelopment Projects A and B

CHICAGO LAND CLEARANCE COMMISSION
> Site Designation Report, Slum and Blighted Areas Redevelopment Projects Hyde Park A and Hyde Park B, June 28, 1954.
> Redevelopment Plan Documents, Slum and Blighted Areas Redevelopment Projects Hyde Park A and Hyde Park B, October 25, 1954.
> Redevelopment Plans, Revision of Plan dated October 25, 1954, Redevelopment Projects Hyde Park A and Hyde Park B (January 8, 1957).

Hyde Park Herald. Special issue on redevelopment project, June 30, 1954.

HYDE PARK-KENWOOD COMMUNITY CONFERENCE
> Memorandum to block leaders, June 9, 1954.

Reactions of block groups to original tentative plans for Projects A and B, 1955.

Land acquisition, relocation, and demolition procedures, Hyde Park Projects A and B, August 31, 1955.

Series of progress reports to block leaders on redevelopment projects.

NATIONAL OPINION RESEARCH CENTER

Survey on housing requirements for families to be displaced by Hyde Park Projects A and B.

SOUTH EAST CHICAGO COMMISSION

South East Chicago Renewal Project No. 1, 1954.

Report of Citizens' Committee on Law Enforcement, adopted at mass meeting on May 19, 1952.

Annual reports.

Urban Renewal for Hyde Park-Kenwood

CITY OF CHICAGO, Survey and Planning Application, Hyde Park-Kenwood Urban Renewal Area, March 28, 1955.

COMMUNITY CONSERVATION BOARD, Chicago

Preliminary Project Report, Hyde Park-Kenwood Urban Renewal Area, June 1956.

Urban Renewal Plan, Final Project Report: Hyde Park-Kenwood Urban Renewal Project, Illinois R-1.

(Prepared for the Community Conservation Board by the University of Chicago Planning Unit.)

Hyde Park Herald

Special issue devoted to urban renewal, August 22, 1956.

Special issue devoted to final urban renewal plan, February 19, 1958.

HYDE PARK-KENWOOD COMMUNITY CONFERENCE

"A Report to the Community," a preliminary review of area problems and possibilities. June, 1951.

Community Appraisal Study: Report on Housing and Social Survey. Published in behalf of the collaborating organizations by the conference and South Side Planning Board. Autumn 1952.

Planning for the urban renewal program in Hyde Park-Kenwood

Report No. 2 to block leaders, September 8, 1954.

Report No. 3 to block leaders, August 31, 1955.

Memorandum for discussion leaders on block group discussions of urban renewal planning, September 14, 1955.

Discussion guide on urban renewal planning, August 1, 1956.

Questions on urban renewal (a guide to discussion leaders), September 11, 1956.

Planning reports on "Problems and Proposals" for Northwest Hyde Park, Southeast Hyde Park, East Kenwood, West Kenwood, East Hyde Park, North Central Hyde Park.

Reports of block and area meetings on urban renewal.

Testimony at Conservation Community Council hearings on Preliminary Project Report, February 25, April 2, April 25, and May 28, 1957.

NATIONAL OPINION RESEARCH CENTER, representing Chicago Community Inventory

The Hyde Park-Kenwood Urban Renewal Survey, conducted for the Community Conservation Board and the University of Chicago, September 1956.

PERLOFF, HARVEY S.

"The University of Chicago and the Surrounding Community," Program of Education and Research in Planning. The University of Chicago, July 1953.

Urban Renewal in a Chicago Neighborhood, An Appraisal of the Hyde Park-Kenwood Renewal Program. Chicago, Illinois: *Hyde Park Herald, Inc.,* August 31, 1955.

Proposals by six organizations, February 1952, for joint action on community problems (Hyde Park-Kenwood Community Conference, University of Chicago, Hyde Park Planning Association, Oakland-Kenwood Planning Association, Woodlawn, Inc., Hyde Park Community Council).

General—City, State, National

A.C.T.I.O.N. (American Council To Improve Our Neighborhoods). Series of studies on conservation and renewal. Box 462, New York City.

BRUSSAT, WILLIAM K., "Citizen Organization for Neighborhood Conservation." Special Publication No. 12, April 1957. Renewal information Service, National Association of Housing and Redevelopment Officials, 1313 E. 60th St., Chicago 37, Illinois.

CITY OF CHICAGO

Housing Code.

Office of the Housing and Redevelopment Coordinator.

Neighborhood Conservation.

The Neighborhood Redevelopment Corporation Law as Amended (as applicable to the city of Chicago).

Zoning Ordinance.

Conservation, a 3-volume study published by the Metropolitan Housing and Planning Council, Chicago, January 31, 1953.

HOUSING AND HOME FINANCE AGENCY, Washington, D.C.

FHA-Insured Financing and Rehabilitation (Sections 207 and 220).

Replacing Blight with Good Homes, FHA Section 220 Mortgage Insurance.

The Workable Program, What It Is.

Urban Renewal, What It Is.

NEIGHBORHOOD REDEVELOPMENT COMMISSION. What You Should Know about Neighborhood Redevelopment Corporations.

STATE OF ILLINOIS. Urban Community Conservation Act.

Source Material

Most of the reference material I consulted is not generally available, although serious students will find it in the records of the Hyde Park-Kenwood Community Conference: the files on building and zoning cases; the minutes of meetings, memoranda, correspondence, press releases, and testimony at public hearings of the board of directors, committees and subcommittees, individual block organizations, the block directors, and the executive director.

Materials on planning and urban renewal which have specific application to the Hyde Park-Kenwood community are listed in Appendix 9.

The reader interested in other publications about the conference will find them listed below.

PUBLICATIONS ABOUT THE CONFERENCE

Press

"A Colour Barrier Broken: Chicago's Housing," *The Manchester Guardian,* October 8, 1953.

Article in *Harian Umum,* Surabaja, India, October 1955. Not translated.

Articles in *Wiesbadener Kurier,* Berlin, Spring 1957. Not translated.

"Block Leader Hero of Drive on Blight," *Chicago Daily News,* March 13, 1954.

"Chicago Blocks Hit Vital Problems," *Christian Science Monitor,* February 2, 1952.

"Chicago Is Reviving Its Decaying Areas," *St. Louis Post Dispatch,* November 29, 1953.

"Citizen Organizations Fight Chicago Blight," *Milwaukee Journal,* December 7, 1954.

"Hyde Park Shows How To Win War on Slums," *Chicago Daily News,* September 25, 1954.

"U. S. Style Block Captains Save Chicago Community," *The Citizen,* April 5, 1954.

Magazines

Abrahamson, Julia. "Citizens to the Rescue of an Old City," *Group Work and Community Organization* 1955. (Papers presented at the 82nd annual forum of the National Conference of Social Work.)

Abrahamson, Julia. "Who Volunteers and Why," *Adult Leadership,* November 1954.

"A Mind To Build," *The University of Chicago Magazine,* October 1954.

"An Encroaching Menace," *Life Magazine,* April 11, 1955.

"An Urban Community Meets Its Needs," *Community News,* December 1953.

Chase, Stuart. "We Can Do Something About It!" *Reader's Digest,* May 1953.

"Chicago Fights Slums Before They Develop," *Commerce Magazine,* April 1953.

"Chicago Fights Slum Growth . . ." *National Municipal Review,* February 1955.

Cunningham, James V., Jr., "Citizens' Role in Planning for Urban Renewal Related," *Journal of Housing,* November 1957.

"Democracy Works on the Block Level," *The Progressive*, January 1953.

Hudson, Robert V. "The Community That Refused to Die," *Together*, the mid-month magazine for Methodist families, January 1958.

"Is Your Neighborhood Going to Seed?" *This Week*, October 7, 1955.

Sarchet, Bettie Belk. "Slides Tell Our Story," *Adult Leadership*, February 1955.

Star, Jack. "All-America Cities," *Look Magazine*, February 8, 1955.

"The Chicago Story," *Journal of Housing*, November 1955. Résumé of paper presented by Elsie Krueger, conference block director, at National Association of Housing and Redevelopment Officials' annual meeting, October 1955.

Thelen, Herbert A. "Communication among Neighbors Combats Urban Blight," *Etc.*, A Review of General Semantics, Autumn 1953.

Thelen, Herbert A. "Social Processes versus Community Deterioration." *Group Psychotherapy*, a journal of sociopsychopathology and sociatry, Vol. LV, No. 3, December 1951.

"To Dispel Fear," *Together*. The Reporter of the Chicago Urban League, January 1951.

Books and Manuals

Report from Action. "Organization of Block Groups for Neighborhood Improvement: The Hyde Park-Kenwood Community Conference." New York: American Council To Improve Our Neighborhoods, Inc. 1956.

Sarchet, Bettie Belk. *Block Groups and Community Change: An Evaluation of the Block Program of the Hyde Park-Kenwood Community Conference.* Human Dynamics Laboratory, University of Chicago, July 1955.

Thelen, Herbert A. *Dynamics of Groups at Work,* Chicago: University of Chicago Press 1954.

Thelen, Herbert A. and Sarchet, Bettie Belk. *Neighbors in Action,* Human Dynamics Laboratory, University of Chicago 1954.

Index

Abandoned cars, 68, 76
Absentee landlords, 18, 72
Acquisition. *See* Land
Advisory Committee, 100, 140
Alleys, 18, 55, 66, 201; cleaning of, 68
American Veterans Committee, 11
Andrews, Marjorie, 53, 130
Andrews, William J., 54
Anxiety, 84, 142, 199, 229, 321; relief of, 35, 36, 68, 77, 89, 92
Articles of incorporation, 52
Association of Community Councils, 121, 170
Attitudes, 10, 35, 277, 281; change in, 55, 135, 287–289, 290, 320–322. *See* Fear and Morale

Babcock, Russell, 14, 20, 29, 32, 52, 130
Bacon, William L., 327
Badal, Ozzie, 152
Bailey, Roland, 131
Bain, Herbert, 141
Ballard, John, 131
Beaches, 178, 179, 180, 308, 318
Beasley, Mrs. E. W., 14
Beaudry, William, 13
Bentley, Frances, 86
Berman, Rabbi Morton M., 13, 18, 43
Blight, 6, 9, 61, 62–63, 194, 197, 198, 199, 200, 207, 222, 236, 237, 238, 260, 325; effort to stop, 144–166, 243. *See* Slums

Block, Jean, 132
Block groups, 87, 215–216, 275–276, 302; relation to conference, 102–103, 104–108, 136, 138, 223, 224, 236–237, 242. *See* Block organization
Block leaders, 182, 202, 222, 235, 236, 237, 263; information for, 351–353; training of, 50, 87–94. *See* Block organization
Block meetings, 90–91, 230, 237, 274, 283, 284, 285. *See* Block organization and Citizen participation in urban renewal
Block organization, 26, 29, 31, 32, 33, 34–36, 52, 53, 66–86, 89, 91, 92–94, 123, 137, 143, 145–146, 221, 322, 328, 338–340
Block Steering Committee, 29, 96, 97, 100, 102, 103, 105–106, 138, 139, 236, 253. *See* Block organization
Board of directors, 52, 81, 100, 124, 129, 139, 142, 200, 222, 224, 237, 239, 241, 266, 300, 301; relationship to block groups and committees, 102–108
Board of Education, 104, 119, 203, 251, 290, 291. *See* Schools
Bond issues, 167, 169, 170, 172, 177, 182, 307
Bradbury, William, 14, 19, 30, 295
Braxton, James, 131, 264, 267
Bret Harte School, 169, 170, 290, 318

INDEX

Brody, Babette, 95
Brown, Beverly, 83
Brown, Oscar C., Sr., 14, 16, 17, 53
Brown, Mrs. Oscar C., Sr., 14, 43
Brown, Mrs. Sydney P., 14
Browne, William Y., 14
Buddhist Church, 7, 316
Budget, 51, 54, 100, 135, 136, 137, 141, 142, 322
Building Code, 85, 153–154, 197. *See* Municipal Code
Building Department, 36, 37, 38, 39, 40, 61, 81, 115–118, 199, 208, 216, 284. *See* Blight, effort to stop
Burnham Park, 180, 210
Business, 30, 231; associations, 63, 123, 124, 231, 322
Businessmen, 171, 183, 204, 253; and conference, 45, 48, 101, 122–124, 190; and redevelopment, 229, 230–232; cooperation with, 123, 133, 140
Bylaws, 52, 99

Calumet Expressway, 209
Carner, Lucy P., 30, 52
Catholic Archdiocese of Chicago, 270
Chicago, city of, 28, 98, 165; Bureau of Small Parks and Playgrounds, 178; City Council, 72, 160, 165, 166, 194, 195, 196, 201, 203, 204, 208, 212, 222, 224, 234, 262, 270, 271, 289; Commission on Human Relations, 11, 12, 15, 40, 97, 119, 295, 296; Community Conservation Board, 165, 182, 195, 196, 199, 208, 210, 237, 250, 254, 270, 271; Department of Law, 37, 119, 157, 158, 162, 165; Department of Streets and Sanitation, 72, 177, 182, 184; Dwellings Association, 57, 262, 268, 271, 306; Housing Authority, 119, 165, 199, 203, 261; Land Clearance Commission, 57, 97, 119, 163, 165, 193, 194, 199, 200, 201, 202, 222, 223, 229, 230, 231, 250, 267; Neighborhood Redevelopment Commission, 196, 205, 237, 238; Park District, 57,
119, 175, 176, 177, 179, 180, 182, 184, 223, 224; Plan Commission, 57, 119, 199, 201, 207, 237. *See* Public agencies
Chicago College of Osteopathy, 211, 244
Chicago Community Inventory, 59, 291
Chicago Community Trust, 136, 143
Chicago Council Against Racial and Religious Discrimination, 14
Chicago Real Estate Board, 226, 295
Chicago Theological Seminary, 316
Chicago Urban League, 14, 289
Children's activities, 67, 70, 72, 131–132. *See* Tot-lots and Playgrounds
Churches, 7, 23, 43–44, 51, 121, 140, 178, 320, 322
Citizen participation, 207, 236. *See* Involving people and Volunteers
Citizen participation in urban renewal, 142, 197, 212, 217, 221, 222, 224–225, 228–229, 239, 243–271; methods used, 252–254, 258–264; problems of, 254–257; purpose of, 252; results of, 264–271
Citizens' Committee to Fight Slums, 152
Citizens Schools Committee, 168, 170
Clark, Florence, 132
Clean-up, 70, 133; campaigns, 123; instructions, 349–350
Clearance, 210, 243, 244, 245, 250, 255, 265, 266, 268, 271; slum, 28, 194, 197, 273, 306. *See* Redevelopment
Cohen, Alderman Abraham, 36
Cohen, Martin, 86, 131
Cohen, Mrs. Martin M., 41, 51
Cole, Reverend David H., 14
Committee of Six, 213, 217, 222, 226, 227, 228, 233, 235, 238, 239, 246, 253
Committees, 99–100, 138, 139, 143; coordination of work of, 105–108, 110; relationship to board, 100–108
Communication, 84, 125; channels of, 50, 235; methods of, 126–129, 283; problems of, 83, 101, 106–108, 139. *See* Involving people

362